THE BERMUDA TRIANGLE MYSTERY—SOLVED

THE BERMUDA

TRIANGLE MYSTERY
–SOLVED

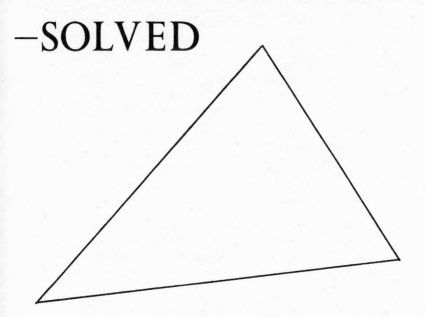

Lawrence David Kusche

HARPER & ROW, PUBLISHERS

NEW YORK, EVANSTON, SAN FRANCISCO, LONDON

Grateful acknowledgment is made for permission to reprint excerpts from the following:

The New York Times. Copyright © 1921, 1925, 1926, 1935, 1944, 1951, 1952, 1953, 1954, 1955, 1956, 1958, 1969 by The New York Times Company. Reprinted by permission.

The Miami Herald; The Virginian-Pilot; The Galveston Daily News; The San Juan Star; The Times-Picayune; The Arizona Republic and *The Washington Post Service; The Times* (London); *The Yomiuri Shimbun* (Tokyo). All reprinted by permission.

The United States Naval Institute. *Proceedings,* January 1920, April 1920, September 1923, July 1969.

Dictionary of Disasters at Sea During the Age of Steam by Charles Hocking. London: Lloyd's Register of Shipping, 1969.

Lloyd's Register. Wreck Returns. 1900–1904; 1925–1926. Lloyd's Register of Shipping.

Lloyd's Weekly Casualty Reports. December 18, 1925; October to December, 1955; July 9, 1963. Lloyd's.

Lloyd's List. September 25, 1840; October 17, 1840; April 24, 1950; May 2, 1950; June 3, 1950. Lloyd's.

Designed by Sidney Feinberg
Maps drawn by Lawrence David Kusche

Library of Congress Cataloging in Publication Data
Kusche, Lawrence David.
    The Bermuda Triangle mystery—solved.
    Bibliography: p.
    Includes index.
    1. Bermuda Triangle. I. Title.
G525.K87   909'.09'634   74–1828
ISBN 0–06–012475–X

To the members of the Interlibrary Loan department at Arizona State University and their unseen partners in other libraries

Contents

Illustrations following page 156

Preface

Strange events seem to be taking place in the Atlantic Ocean off the coast of the United States. In and around an area formed by an imaginary line connecting Bermuda, Florida, and Puerto Rico, a significant number of ships and planes have disappeared under mysterious circumstances. Known popularly as the Bermuda Triangle, the Devil's Triangle, and Limbo of the Lost, the area has also been called the Hoodoo Sea, the Twilight Zone, and the Port of Missing Ships. Mysterious occurrences continue to be reported there, and the sequence of events has grown into a modern-day sea mystery.

The Bermuda Triangle has received much attention in the last decade. It has been the subject of books, magazine articles, and radio and television talk shows. A television special was devoted to it, and it also figures in the UFO and ancient astronaut mysteries. According to all accounts, there is something very strange going on out there.

My interest in the Triangle began in 1972 when, as a reference librarian at Arizona State University, I was frequently asked to help someone find information on the subject. Nothing seemed to exist. A new reference librarian at ASU,

Deborah Blouin, had previously experienced the same frustration of being unable to locate anything, so we combined forces and spent several months advertising in journals and writing letters to various government agencies, research organizations, and libraries along the east coast to see if anyone could suggest any sources. Some of those we contacted sent a citation or two and we eventually compiled a fairly lengthy bibliography which we made available to anyone who needed it. The demand was overwhelming. Nobody, it seemed, had been able to find much on the Bermuda Triangle. The problem was that although several dozen articles and book chapters existed they were not the type of material that could be found when they were needed by consulting card catalogs or periodical indexes.

After reading all the chapters and articles I realized that the Bermuda Triangle mystery was much more than just an account of the strange disappearance of a large number of vessels. Proclamations of the Navy, the Coast Guard, the Air Force, and Lloyd's (London) had been repeated, interpreted, and assimilated into the story. Many writers who had made the earlier attempts to solve the mystery later found themselves and their theories an integral part of it. New incidents were continually being incorporated into the tale.

These writings, then, taken together, constitute what might be called the story, or the legend, of the Bermuda Triangle as it is usually told. The most important of these are listed in Section I of the bibliography. I decided to investigate the mystery further; to collect all the information that could be found on each incident, to see if there might not be an answer here and there. The sources I discovered are listed by incident in Section II of the bibliography.

I have adopted a somewhat unusual format to present the results of my research. First I retell the entire legend of the Bermuda Triangle (in italic typeface), to give the facts and flavor of the story as it has developed over the years. Then I examine individual incidents in chronological order. For each I give a detailed account of the episode as it usually has been told. Next come pertinent extracts from the various sources that I found during my research. My own comments, assumptions, opinions, and deductions either follow or are interspersed with the quoted material. The purpose of this arrangement is to let the reader know the origin of the information he is given and thus permit him to draw his own conclusions about whether a particular incident is mysterious or whether it appears to have a logical solution. In a few cases the information is inconclusive and a decision cannot be made.

The word Legend, capitalized, has been used throughout as an abbreviated way of saying "This is how this incident has usually been told as a part of the story of the Bermuda Triangle." It was almost always possible to do this because most versions of any particular incident were similar. There are a few cases, however, for which it is not possible to say "This is how it has usually been told," because there is considerable difference between versions. For these incidents I have told what appeared to be the best-known account.

Because the Legend is a composite of many sources, no individual is cited for his particular contribution except where a part indisputably "belongs" to a given writer. To have attempted to show who contributed each part of the story would have required a different kind of book. My concern here is with the incidents themselves, not with those who have publicized them.

Repetitious and extraneous material has been omitted from quoted matter to spare the reader tiresome duplication of facts in news accounts and details in reports such as the thickness of bulkheads and the serial numbers of planes and servicemen. In a few official reports the time of day has been converted from the military twenty-four-hour clock to Eastern Standard Time, and directions and positions have been simplified or explained.

In many cases the facts given in the quoted material differ from those in the Legend. It is left to the reader to decide for himself which version is more likely to be true.

L. D. K.

May 1974
Tempe, Arizona

Acknowledgments

The research for this book was done in widely scattered locations around the world—Tokyo, Oslo, Paris, London, St. John's, Nassau, San Juan, Santo Domingo, Washington, D.C., Norfolk, New York, Chicago, Miami, New Orleans, and Galveston. I traveled to all these faraway places by airmail, teletype, or telephone. Thanks to the cooperation of many librarians, newspapermen, and members of the military I was able to obtain the many sources of information that I requested.

I especially want to thank Lyn Ashley, Virginia Brown, Joyce Casagrande, Jewel Hayden, and Lois Schneberger of the Interlibrary Loan Department, Arizona State University, Tempe, for their efforts in fulfilling my many requests for microfilm, books, and photocopies of sources held by other libraries.

Many others at ASU were also helpful: Deborah Blouin, my partner on the *Bermuda Triangle Bibliography;* Debbie Engelmann, whose honest evaluation of my first attempts sent me back to the writing desk; Shirley Cooper, Doohe Chang, Barbara Cox, Kay Gilman, George Ilinsky, Donna Larson, Jim Lestikow, Greg Middleton, and Gene Price, who all lent their special skills. Larry Young of Sawyer School of Aviation, and Ron Dobbins and Don Bruce also provided a great deal of help.

I am indebted to the following people for taking the time to answer my questions and to search for the material I requested:

Commander F. A. Rice, Lt. Arthur Whiting, and Lt. Richard Tate of the Casualty Review Branch, U.S. Coast Guard, Washington, D.C., Lt. G. F. Johnson, Public Information Office, Seventh District, U.S. Coast Guard, Miami.

D. Gail Saunders, Archivist of the Ministry of Education and Culture, Nassau, Bahamas. T. M. Dinan, Head of Casualty Records and Historical Research, Lloyd's. Shigeru Kimura of the *Asahi Shimbun,* Tokyo. "Action Line" of the *Mainichi Daily News,* Tokyo. Yasuchika Ohno, Maritime Safety Agency, Tokyo. Dean D. Hawes, Norfolk. Barbara Case and Helen Porter, Newfoundland Arts and Culture Center, St. John's. William Felker, Free Library of Philadelphia. Else Marie Thorstvedt, Librarian, Norwegian Maritime Museum. H. Vinje, Office of the Director General of Shipping and Navigation, Oslo.

John A. Shelton, National Climatic Center, Ashville, North Carolina. James N. Eastman, Jr., Maxwell Air Force Base, Alabama. Richard F. Gerwig, Norton Air Force Base, California. Federico A. Mella Villanueva, *El Caribe,* Santo Domingo, Dominican Republic. Joel Kirkpatrick, *Galveston Daily News.* Lt. A. Solano, Sheriff's Department, Galveston. D. A. F. Ingraham, Department of Civil Aviation, Bahamas. Samuel L. Morison, Washington, D.C.

Special thanks go to my wife Sally, and the kids, Rebecca and Andrew; and most of all, to Jeanne Flagg, editor, Harper & Row.

"The fact is, we have all been a good deal puzzled because the affair *is* so simple, and yet baffles us altogether."

"Perhaps it is the very simplicity of the thing that puts you at fault," said my friend. "What nonsense you *do* talk!" replied the Prefect, laughing heartily.

"Perhaps the mystery is a little *too* plain," said Dupin.

"Oh, good heavens! whoever heard of such an idea?"

"A little *too* self evident."

"Ha! ha! ha!—ha! ha! ha!—ho! ho! ho!"—roared our visitor, profoundly amused, "oh, Dupin, you will be the death of me yet!"

—"The Purloined Letter"
Edgar Allan Poe

THE BERMUDA TRIANGLE MYSTERY—SOLVED

The Legend of the Bermuda Triangle As It Is Usually Told

The night was ablaze with stars as the DC-3, pushed along by a friendly tailwind, began a gentle descent toward Miami. A slight lowering of the nose increased the airspeed a few knots, and the altimeter slowly began to unwind. In the cabin the passengers, on their way home after a Christmas vacation in their native Puerto Rico, sang "We Three Kings" as the stewardess served cookies and punch. In the cockpit the captain reached for his microphone.

"Miami Tower, this is Airborne Transport N16002, over."

"Airborne Transport N16002, this is Miami Tower, go ahead."

"N16002 is approaching Miami from San Juan, Puerto Rico. Am now fifty miles south, all's well, have the city in sight. Landing instructions, please. Over."

"Zero zero two, continue your approach, advise when you have the airport in sight.

"Zero zero two, this is Miami Tower. Please acknowledge. Over.

"Zero zero two, do you read? Over.

"*Airborne Transport N16002, this is Miami Tower. Do you read? Do you read? Please acknowledge. Over.*"

But N16002 never acknowledged the call from Miami Tower on that early morning of December 30, 1948, nor did it answer repeated calls from New Orleans and San Juan Overseas Radio, and from the Coast Guard. A massive search began almost immediately. Hundreds of ships combed the sea, while planes scanned the area from above. The weather was ideal, the water clear and calm and so shallow in the area that large objects on the bottom could easily be seen. But the sea guards her secrets well; no trace of the DC-3 was ever found. In the carefully phrased accident report of the Civil Aeronautics Board, issued six months later, "*sufficient information is lacking in this case to determine the probable cause.*"

But, on the docks, in the airports, on the beaches, and in the taverns, wherever the old-timers met to discuss the mysteries of the seas and the skies, the pattern of the disappearances could be seen. The menace that haunts the Bermuda Triangle had struck again, claiming yet another victim. Those who knew anything of the sea knew about the terrifying mid-Atlantic region where ships (and now planes) had been vanishing for more than a century, vanishing without reason, in good weather, without sending cries of distress and without leaving a trace.

Veteran observers of the area knew about the British South American Airways airliner, the Star Tiger, that had vanished in January of the same year while approaching Bermuda from the Azores. Just as the DC-3 seemed destined to do a few months later, the Star Tiger sent an "all's well" message when nearing the end of a long, routine journey, then lapsed into silence. At the conclusion of the Star Tiger investigation, the Ministry of Civil Aviation stated that it had never encountered a more baffling problem. Because of the lack of evidence supporting any other theory, the Ministry suggested *that the mishap had occurred because of "some external cause."*

A few weeks after the loss of the DC-3 the Star Ariel, *sister ship of the* Star Tiger, *disappeared between Bermuda and Jamaica on a flight in calm, clear weather. The word spread quickly. It was time to break the jinx, to find out what was causing all the disappearances. A search such as never before seen, made possible by the fortuitous presence of a large U.S. Navy task force and a number of British ships and planes, spared no effort in the recovery attempt. But once again it was all in vain, for the* Star Ariel *had also flown into oblivion in the Bermuda Triangle.*

A line drawn on a map from Bermuda to Puerto Rico to Florida and back to Bermuda outlines the center of this area and gives it its name. Some of the disappearances have taken place outside the center triangle, and when they are all plotted on a map the triangle is expanded and distorted into almost a square or a kite shape. This is the sinister no-man's-land that is said to be creating such fear in the hearts of sailors and pilots that they refuse to discuss it with outsiders. Surrounded by the vacation lands of Bermuda, the Bahamas, and Florida, patrolled by the U.S. government and heavily traveled day and night, the region is in no way isolated. Although many vessels, both civilian and military, cross it daily without mishap, the number of disappearances is altogether beyond the laws of chance for such a relatively limited area.

On the afternoon of December 5, 1945, the strangest aviation drama of all time began as five Navy Avenger torpedo bombers took off from the Fort Lauderdale Naval Air Station on a short routine patrol that was to end in confusion, tragedy, mystery, and the apparent deaths of twenty-seven men. Although there was no evidence of bad weather, the flight leader radioed that all five planes were lost and unable to tell in which direction they were flying. A short time later communications faded out, never to be resumed. A rescue

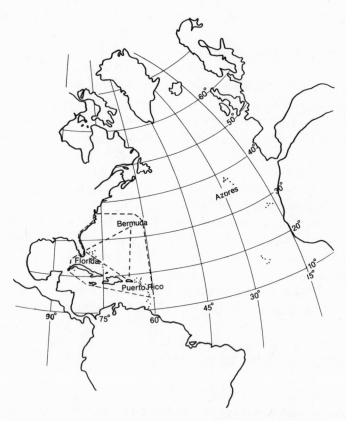

The Bermuda Triangle

plane immediately headed for the supposed area of the lost patrol, and it, too, vanished. The greatest search in aviation history lasted for five days, but no trace of the six aircraft was ever found. The Navy, after a lengthy investigation, admitted that it was more confused than before the inquest had begun. Authorities could only scratch their heads and wonder what it was that continued to strike again and again in the Bermuda Triangle. One Navy officer commented that "They vanished as completely as if they'd flown to Mars."

Many other incidents occurred in the 1940s. The City Belle *was found abandoned near the Bahamas in 1946, and the* Rubicon, *a ghost ship, drifted near the coast of Florida in October 1944, in excellent condition, but with only a dog aboard. Al Snider, an internationally famous jockey, vanished in March 1948 while on an afternoon fishing trip near the southern tip of Florida. In 1940 the* Gloria Colita *was found abandoned, but in excellent condition, near the western coast of Florida, in the Gulf of Mexico.*

Going back farther, the La Dahama *was sighted in the Bermuda Triangle in 1935, several days after another ship had reported watching it sink. In 1931 the Norwegian ship* Stavenger *disappeared in the Bahamas with forty-three men aboard, and the* Raifuku Maru *vanished on a calm day in 1925 after sending the message "Come quick, it's like a dagger! We cannot escape."*

The Carroll A. Deering *was discovered hard aground on Diamond Shoals in January 1921 with all sails set. Two cats were the only living creatures aboard. The strangest part of the incident is that a full meal was on the stove, waiting for a crew that would never arrive. The same year a dozen other ships vanished in the area. They left their ports on normal, routine voyages and all sailed the same ghostly path. Although their destinations were officially listed as Bermuda, Jamaica, Miami, and other such locations, they all arrived instead at the Port of Missing Ships.*

In 1918 the U.S. Navy, one of the favorite targets of the jinx, suffered a major loss. The Cyclops, *a 542-foot collier, sailed from Barbados for Baltimore with 309 men on board and was never seen or heard from again, despite a frantic search effort. It was the first radio-equipped ship ever to vanish, but it sent no SOS. After half a century the Navy admits that although many theories have been suggested, none satisfactorily accounts for the loss of the* Cyclops. *Compounding the mystery still further, two of her sister ships, the* Proteus *and the* Nereus, *disappeared in 1941 on almost the identical route.*

The victims have not always been nameless and faceless. In 1909 Joshua Slocum, at that time the world's best-known sailor, vanished while crossing the Triangle. Eleven years before he had gained enduring fame by being the first man to sail alone around the world. He and the Spray sailed south from Massachusetts one day and never emerged from the Bermuda Triangle. Those who knew him and the Spray did not consider it likely that the two were victims of any normal hazard of the sea.

The infamous history of the Bermuda Triangle extends far back into the last century, into the century before that, and then even farther, back to the first known traveler in the area, Christopher Columbus. Columbus sailed through the Sargasso Sea, another legendary twilight zone, and the Bermuda Triangle on his first voyage to the New World in 1492. His men were spooked by the strangeness of the Sargasso and unnerved by events as they crossed the Triangle—a bolt of fire that fell into the sea, unusual actions of the compass, and a strange light that appeared in the distance late one night.

Although records are scattered and incomplete, it is documented that four American naval vessels vanished without explanation between 1781 and 1812. In 1840 the Rosalie, a large French ship, was found deserted near Nassau, sails set, a valuable cargo intact, and everything in order. The Bella, a mystery derelict, was found in 1854. The Lotta, a Swedish bark, vanished near Haiti in 1866, followed two years later by the Viego, a Spanish merchantman.

One of the greatest mysteries of the sea is the strange disappearance of the Atalanta in 1880. She left Bermuda in January for England with a crew of three hundred cadets and officers and was never seen again. Despite a massive sweep by a large armada of ships sailing swaths across the ocean within sight of each other, not a scrap, a spar, or a lifeboat from the Atalanta was ever found.

The chain continued unbroken in 1884 when the Miramon, *an Italian schooner bound for New Orleans, glided silently into limbo. When the* Freya, *a German bark, was discovered abandoned in 1902, there was some speculation that an earthquake might have been the cause.*

The lurking menace of death should have been satisfied after all the victims it had claimed, especially the three airliners and the flight of planes in the 1940s, but airplanes and ships have continued to disappear up to the present day. The story is always the same: good weather conditions, no mechanical problems, routine radio reports, and then silence. So rarely is anything found in the vast, intensive search that follows that it comes as a surprise when any debris is recovered or a message is received.

One of these exceptions occurred in February 1953, when a Jamaica-bound British York transport sent an SOS while north of the Triangle. After the message ended abruptly without explanation a search was launched, but nothing was found. A London court later reported, "Cause unascertainable."

In March 1950 an American Globemaster vanished north of the Triangle and was followed several months later by the freighter Sandra. *It vanished one calm, tropical night with a load of insecticide.*

Incidents continued unabated: a Navy Super Constellation in 1954; the sulfur-laden Southern Districts *in the Straits of Florida in the same year; the* Connemara IV, *found derelict in the very center of the Triangle in 1955. In 1956, as if making up for a slow year, the jinx claimed a number of victims, including a Marine Sky Raider and a Navy patrol bomber with a crew of ten.*

An unusually high number of vanishments have occurred near Christmas, and experts have not yet discovered why the Triangle is especially ominous at that particular time of year. In December 1957 publisher Harvey Conover, one of America's best-known yachtsmen, and several relatives, left Key

West on the 150-mile trip to Miami in his racing yawl, the Revonoc. *Although their intended path would have always kept them in sight of land, they vanished forever.*

Meanwhile, planes were not being ignored. In 1962 an Air Force KB-50 rolled down the runway at Langley AFB, Virginia, and headed for the Azores with a crew of nine. Shortly after takeoff the tower received a brief, weak radio message that the tanker was in some sort of trouble. An extensive search once again produced no trace of any kind.

The U.S. Navy has lost two nuclear submarines, the Thresher *in 1963 and the* Scorpion *in 1968. Both ended their final voyages near the Triangle.*

1963 was a big year for the jinx. It started with the Marine Sulphur Queen, *a cargo ship specially refitted to carry molten sulfur. Bound for Virginia from Texas, it vanished off the tip of Florida after sending a routine radio message. With the exception of several life jackets, nothing from the vessel was found. The loss was highly publicized, as was the Coast Guard inquiry into the matter. Although a number of possible solutions have been suggested, no one alive knows what really happened.*

One of the most baffling aspects of the disappearances has always been the failure of searchers to find bodies. It would generally be expected that one or more would be washed ashore after a shipwreck, but this has never happened in the Bermuda Triangle. Since most of the incidents have occurred within sight of land, the absence of bodies is especially puzzling.

In July 1963 the Navy and the Coast Guard searched for ten days without finding a trace of the Sno' Boy, *a 63-foot fishing boat lost on an 80-mile trip from Jamaica. A month later two KC-135s were caught in a sky trap with eleven crewmen. At noon they radioed their position, then were never heard from again. When debris was located near Bermuda it was assumed that there had been a midair collision.*

But the finding of debris 160 miles away created a mystery. If there had been a midair collision, why were there two areas of debris? If the planes had not collided, why did they crash simultaneously? There is no satisfactory answer, and Air Force officials are still scratching their heads over the affair.

Puzzling disappearances continued. In 1965 an Air Force C-119 vanished while on a flight in good weather from Homestead AFB to Grand Turk Island. A strange, garbled message was received by the Grand Turk tower operator just about the time the plane should have been touching down. What desperate, last-minute information was the pilot attempting to relate before he crossed over into oblivion? There is speculation that one of the UFOs sighted by Gemini IV may have played a part in the loss.

In 1967 a number of vessels took one-way trips into the Bermuda Triangle. The year started when a Chase YC-122 cargo plane vanished into thin air on the 60-mile flight from Fort Lauderdale to the Biminis. The plane was carrying motion picture equipment for a Lloyd Bridges movie entitled, ironically, The Unkillables. *The year ended with the loss of two Florida men who had gone on a short boat ride to view the Christmas lights of Miami Beach from a mile out at sea. The Coast Guard received a call that the men were unable to run the engine because of a bent propeller, but that there was no danger of any kind; they simply would like a tow back to port. Nineteen minutes later the Coast Guard arrived at the location given by the men but found nothing of the boat that lived up to its name—the* Witchcraft.

In July 1969 five abandoned vessels were found during calm weather in the same general area. A Lloyd's spokesman exclaimed that this was "most unusual," especially considering the excellent weather. The next month Bill Verity, an experienced transatlantic voyager, vanished in the Triangle.

Unexplained incidents are still occurring: the freighters

Elizabeth and Caribe vanished in 1971; and in March 1973 the Anita, the largest cargo ship ever lost without a trace, sailed from Norfolk and was never heard from again.

Officially, the Navy, Coast Guard, and the Air Force deny the existence of strange forces in the area. Unofficially it is a different story. They admit that they are baffled, and that the few clues they do have only increase the mystery. A spokesman for the Navy said, "It looks almost like they [the missing vessels] have been covered by some gigantic electronic camouflage net. We know there's something strange going on out there, we've always known it, but there doesn't seem to be any reason for it all. We don't sneer at it a bit around here." For those who remain skeptical of the mysterious pattern, the record of disappearances is available for anyone to check. It takes only a few minutes.

Pilots avoid discussing the vanished planes with outsiders, and only reluctantly discuss them with each other. Crashes, although a touchy subject, are at least something that can be analyzed, something for which a cause can usually be found. Disappearances are another matter. It is possible for an airplane or a ship to go down occasionally without leaving a trace. It's possible but not very likely. There is almost always something, some debris or oil slick, to mark the spot. Pilots have no control over the situation, but can only continue to fly, hoping that their plane will not be the next victim. Despite their basic skepticism of unknown forces, pilots have encountered many strange phenomena. Compasses spinning wildly, severe turbulence during excellent weather, crooked radio beams, misbehaving gyroscopes, glowing windshields and instrument panels, and many, even stranger anomalies have been authenticated.

During the last century and a half more than forty ships and twenty airplanes have carried almost a thousand beings* into this misty limbo of the lost. Until the late 1940s each

---

* An estimate only, as bodies have never been found.

incident was merely a baffling individual event. But then the pattern became obvious: too many vessels were vanishing under similar circumstances in such a small patch of ocean. Investigators were not easily convinced—it was a long time before they conceded that something might be amiss with the area itself. Aviation and marine experts now strongly suspect that some phenomenon of the region, rather than a series of "coincidental" mishaps as the Navy suggests, may be responsible.

Accident investigators have ruled out the usual hazards such as sudden tropical storms; they do strongly suspect, however, that atmospheric aberrations and electromagnetic gravitational disturbances may be responsible. Some such force may have affected the compasses and silenced the radios of the five Avengers, then incapacitated the Mariner rescue plane when it entered the same zone. This incident, particularly the pilots' description of a strange sea and the inability to see the sun, as told in the Navy report, suggests some kind of atmospheric aberration, or "hole in the sky," an area, as yet unknown, that planes can enter but cannot leave. Many experienced pilots and sailors feel that the aberration theory is the only one that could account for events such as these— events that occur only occasionally, always without warning, often enough to be alarming, but irregularly, so that they cannot be predicted. Exactly what this aberration is and why it appears to be restricted to tropical waters such as in the Bermuda Triangle is not known at this time.

Some think the aberration may be a space warp, and that the missing vessels may have been entrapped in the fourth dimension. One prophet has predicted that one day the space warp will free all the vessels and they will return to their home ports with the skeletons of the crews. Another speculates that the crews may be alive, the same age as when they left, and will be able to reveal the secret of what lies beyond the shadowy edge of the Bermuda Triangle.

Perhaps time runs at a variable rate rather than at a con-

stant rate as has always been thought. If so, this would account for the many cases of ships and planes suddenly finding themselves hundreds of miles from where they were supposed to be for no logical reason. If the time flow varied enough from the standard rate, a vessel caught in such a trap might simply cease to exist in this world. Another possibility is that time does not always move in a straight line, but that parts of it occasionally break off and head away from the main flow, carrying with them whatever might happen to be in the area at the time. These vessels and their unfortunate occupants would be transported to the future or the past, or might be trapped in a parallel universe.

Some scientists feel that seaquakes, sudden shiftings of the ocean floor capable of causing waves up to 200 feet high, may be the most logical answer. Such waves could easily swallow a ship and would account for the absence of SOS's and of debris.

While the Navy and other experts dismiss the possibility that underwater volcanic activity and seaquakes are the cause of the losses, a number of scientists think that freak seas might be involved. Waves of 100 feet and more have been verified, and such a gigantic wall could easily roll even a medium-sized ship before it could send an SOS. Although not much is known about what causes such waves, it is suspected that powerful ocean currents or waterspouts may be factors. The flaw in this theory is that it takes a storm of some magnitude to produce a freak sea, and in none of the disappearances in the Triangle could the weather be called bad. Moreover, freak seas could not be responsible for the disappearances of planes. To account for plane losses, gigantic, invisible atmospheric waves not unlike those of the ocean have been postulated.

Aircraft occasionally encounter turbulence, not only in and near cumulonimbus clouds, but also in clear air. Extreme turbulence can actually disintegrate an aircraft, and may be the cause of some of the vanishments. Under careful examination, however, this theory also does not stand up. First, the weather was good when most of the disappearances occurred, and second, an aircraft that disintegrates leaves debris over a wide area.

Although most theories fail to account for more than a few of the incidents, there is one that does appear to make sense —that of magnetic anomalies. Compass variation is a phenomenon known even to the tyro pilot and sailor. The compass rarely points to true north, the north pole; it points instead to the magnetic pole, which is some distance away. In many places the variation is a significant factor that must be taken into account; if it is not, a vessel may well end up hundreds of miles from where it is supposed to be.

There are two places on the earth's surface where the compass does point to true north—the Bermuda Triangle and an area off the coast of Japan known as the Devil's Sea, which also has a high rate of disappearances. Between 1950 and 1954 at least nine ships vanished in the Devil's Sea. These were large freighters with powerful engines and radios, not merely small fishing boats. Only one was able to send an SOS. Extensive searches found a few small pieces of debris, but no survivors, bodies, or lifeboats. Alarmed, the Japanese government began a survey of the area, but all that was found was a new volcano. The eruption sank one of the research ships! The Japanese government then officially proclaimed the area to be a danger zone.

The U.S. Navy, in a classified operation known as Project Magnet, has been conducting an extensive geomagnetic survey, bringing up to date many measurements more than thirty years old. It is believed that the project may also be performing other functions, including listening for messages from outer space and investigating the theory of "reduced binding."

Wilbur B. Smith, an electronics expert who was in charge

of a 1950 study of magnetism and gravity made by the Canadian government, detected regions in the atmosphere where what he called "reduced binding" existed. These regions, he reported, were about 1,000 feet in diameter and extended to an unknown altitude; they either moved or faded away, only to reappear at another location. Smith found that "reduced binding" fields were often present where unexplained crashes had occurred. He theorized that while most planes would probably not be affected, others of a specific design and size might sustain enough of the force to be destroyed. It is possible that these forces not only affect aircraft and their compasses and radios, but also interfere with the human senses, causing vertigo and loss of spatial orientation.

Evidence has been presented that the Bermuda Triangle is merely a part of a larger problem region. This area, known as the Limbo of the Lost, includes the continental shelf north to New Jersey, the Gulf of Mexico, and the Atlantic Ocean east to the Azores.

Other researchers have discovered that the Bermuda Triangle and the Devil's Sea are only two of a number of anomalic areas spread across the globe. Mathematicians and engineers have found twelve such zones, named "Vile Vortices" for lack of a better term. These vortices are alleged to occur at the north and south poles and at five locations in each hemisphere. They were found to be equidistant from each other, and lines drawn on a globe from each vortex to those adjacent form a series of equilateral triangles. Scientists have not yet learned the significance of this pattern.

It was recently realized that the same geographic characteristics of the small sector of ocean known as the Bermuda Triangle that make it an ideal path for rocket launchings might also make it an ideal channel for landing approaches by vehicles from outer space. Perhaps a power source or signal device left in the area many centuries ago by a scouting party from another planet continues to send signals into

The Limbo of the Lost

space, showing the followers of the earlier explorers the best landing approach to this planet. The device might operate only occasionally, which would account for the fact that most ships and planes that traverse the area do so without incident. When the device did activate, however, the powerful beams might well be strong enough to affect navigation instruments and the human mind, and possibly even completely destroy any vessel unlucky enough to be in the way. Such a force could account for the many incidents that have occurred because of the apparent directional problems of the pilots, most notably in the case of the five Avenger bombers.

Increasing evidence that past civilizations have possessed knowledge and accomplished feats far beyond what scientists *previously thought possible supports the theory that earth was visited in ancient times by beings from outer space. It is considered unlikely that many of these achievements could have occurred without aid from an extremely advanced intelligence.*

The Coast Guard claims that the many incidents in the Bermuda Triangle are merely coincidence and that "there is nothing mysterious about disappearances in this particular section of the ocean. Weather conditions, equipment failure and human error, not something from the supernatural, are what have caused these tragedies." Most of the mishaps, according to the Coast Guard, occur because of the large number of people who brave the ocean in small boats while crossing to the Bahamas.

This statement does apply to those inexperienced boatmen who venture out in craft never intended for use in the open sea. But what about Joshua Slocum, Harvey Conover, and the many other expert sailors who have vanished? What of the lost airliners, the Air Force jets, and the five Avengers? They were piloted by men who knew their business and how to handle the roughest of conditions, yet they still vanished. The Coast Guard statement fails to account for the overwhelming majority of the disappearances.

The Bermuda Triangle continues to baffle officials. New theories are tried and discarded almost as quickly as vessels disappear. The only link that seems to exist between the missing vessels is that they were all crowded into the same small geographic confines. All explanations fail to explain why wreckage or bodies are never found and why the disappearances always occur during good weather. It may well be that man is not yet advanced to the point to be able to understand the forces that exist in the Bermuda Triangle.

1492

~~~~~~

Christopher Columbus, the Sargasso Sea, and the Bermuda Triangle

Christopher Columbus, the first known traveler through the Sargasso Sea and the area now known as the Bermuda Triangle, gave it an air of mystery that has grown as the years have passed. In his logs are descriptions of the weed-filled sea and reports of an erratic compass, a great flame of fire, and the appearance of a strange light at sea. Each incident frightened an already jittery crew and was to them a warning to turn back. Word of the unusual events spread among sailors everywhere, and the region soon acquired a reputation for being strange, a reputation that continues to this day.

When the astronauts began their quarter-million-mile journey to the moon in 1969 they had much more information about their intended voyage than Columbus had about his 3,000-mile trip in 1492. The astronauts were backed by thousands of technicians throughout the world, using the best computers and the best communications devised by man. They knew the exact time the journey would take and they were aware of and prepared for the many dangers they might encounter. When Columbus sailed from the Canary Islands with ninety men in three small ships he had almost no idea of what to expect. There were no charts to follow, no one to communicate with, no place to go for help, and no clue as to how long the trip would be or what dangers might be encountered.

The Sargasso Sea, an area with less wind, rain, and clouds than the rest of the ocean, is in the central part of the North Atlantic Ocean, stretching from 30° to 70° west and from 20° to 35° north.* It is almost as large as the continental United States, more than 2,000 miles long and 1,000 miles wide, and is bounded on all sides by currents which cause it to rotate slowly clockwise. Its name is derived from the Portuguese word for seaweed, *sargaço*.

The first sailors to cross the Sea feared they would soon run aground, as the presence of great masses of seaweed normally indicates that land is near. However, the ocean is several miles deep throughout the area. Many unusual creatures inhabit the Sargasso, either as recent stowaways on material that has drifted in, or as descendants of stowaways that have adapted to life on the weeds.

The horse latitudes, a belt of calm weather between latitudes 30 and 35, add to the strangeness of the area. The air in this region is often so still that sailors have been known to read all night on deck by candlelight, and sailing ships have been stranded there for months at a time.

Though Columbus reported the weed accurately, those who followed spread stories that inspired fear in all seamen. Sailors at that time were uneasy about traveling far from shore; they were not accustomed to being out of sight of land for extended periods. The yellow, brown, and green seaweed crawling with strange creatures and extending as far as the

---

* The North Atlantic Ocean extends south to the equator.

The Sargasso Sea

eye could see was terrifying to those sailing through it. Stories quickly grew, especially after ships sat becalmed for long stretches in the horse latitudes. Soon it was not the lack of wind that stopped them, according to the tales, but the thick mats of weed that supposedly grew up the sides of the ship, up the ropes and chains, and held them fast under the hot sun until all aboard died of thirst or starvation and the ship became a rotted hull manned only by skeletons and prevented from sinking by the seaweed tentacles. Borer worms, which thrive in tropical waters, sometimes did turn the sides of a becalmed ship into a rotted mass. The little things that crept along the mats of weed were transformed in the stories into monsters and giant squid that could haul a ship down to the depths of the ocean. The rumor grew that crews often died an agonizing death because there was no air to breathe.

Once debris of any sort has drifted into the relatively calm center of the Sargasso Sea it usually remains until it sinks, moving in enormous circles as a captive of the rotating pool. Plants carried by the surrounding currents drift into the center, where many continue to grow. It is suspected that much of the weed comes from the Gulf of Mexico, borne by the Gulf Stream, and from the Caribbean. Trees torn from riverbanks by tropical floods in Central America and the West Indies float in. Refuse from any river could eventually float to the Sargasso Sea. In 1968 it was reported that there was more oil and tar in the area than sargassum, coming from oil spills throughout the world.

Many derelicts have been found in the Sargasso, giving it the reputation of being a graveyard of ships. Several novelists have created civilizations in the center of the Sea. Here, according to the stories, countless wrecks, many of them hundreds of years old and full of treasure, pile up against each other. The residents of the floating kingdom, who all drifted in helplessly at one time or other, disdain the treasure since it is of no use to them. The Sargasso Sea, both in truth and in fiction, is a strange place.

The horse latitudes received their name when ships with horses aboard became stranded in the region. After a time of no rain and no progress, the supply of drinking water often grew dangerously low. Thirst-crazed horses occasionally broke away and plunged into the sea, or the weaker ones were thrown overboard to save the water for the better horses. Superstitious sailors believed that ghosts of the dead horses haunted the area.

On the evening of September 13 Columbus noticed that his compass needle no longer pointed directly to the north star, but instead pointed about six degrees to the northwest. That was the first time that such a variation had ever been noted. He watched the variation increase for the next few days, knowing that the crew would be alarmed should they learn of the new development. The other pilots also noticed it and their concern quickly spread to the crew, who became terrified. To them it seemed that they were entering a region where even the laws of nature were different. The sailors felt that some unknown force was causing the compass to betray them, and they feared that other mysteries might lie in wait as they sailed on into the strange area.

At this point those who write about this incident in relation to the Bermuda Triangle normally move on to some other subject, leaving the impression that there is indeed some strange force at work in the area. But the story does not really end here. Columbus reasoned that the needle did not point to the north star, as had always been thought, but to something else. The pilots and the crew, having respect for their leader's scientific skills, believed him, and their alarm subsided. More than three centuries later, Washington Irving, in his biography of Columbus, wrote, ". . . the explanation of Columbus, therefore, was highly plausible, and it shows the vivacity of his mind, ever ready to meet the emergency of the moment. The theory may at first have been advanced merely to satisfy the minds of others, but Columbus appears subsequently to have remained satisfied with it himself." Although Irving doubted that Columbus's theory was correct, Columbus did have the correct answer to the puzzle.

The compass needle points not to the north pole or to the north star, but to the north magnetic pole, which is presently near Prince of Wales Island, halfway between Hudson Bay and the north pole. There are, in fact, very few places on the surface of the earth where a compass points to true north; almost everywhere there is some variation, ranging from a few degrees up to as much as 180 degrees. Pilots, sailors, and hikers must be familiar with this now commonly known property of the compass, and it is a routine matter to add or subtract the required number of degrees to compensate for the variation in the area.

The "great flame of fire" that Columbus noted as having fallen into the sea was apparently a meteor. It did not cause any particular consternation among the crew, and was noted simply because of its size.

By the second week in October, the crew, pressing to turn back, was openly defiant to Columbus and his situation was desperate. For weeks they had been seeing land birds and plants and hopes were high that they would soon have a landfall. But each morning they would have nothing before them except open sea and more birds and plants. Clouds on the horizon were frequently mistaken for land, and sailors were so often crying out that they had seen land, only to raise and then dash the hopes of the crew, that Columbus declared that should anyone give such notice, and land not be discovered within three days, he would lose his claim to the reward promised to the first to view land.

By October 11 they had seen so many unmistakable signs that land was near that Columbus himself was watching from the deck. About ten o'clock at night he thought he saw a light in the distance, and fearing that he too was seeing things, called over one of the men. He also saw the light. Another man was called, but by then the light had vanished. Being uncertain, they did not raise the crew's hopes by sounding the news. Four hours later Rodrigo de Triana, aboard the *Pinta*, signaled that land was in sight. This time there was no doubt.

Historians have continued to speculate and to disagree about what the light might have been. A torch in a fisherman's boat or being carried by someone on shore or a group of luminous fish are some of the suggested causes. The most commonly accepted theory is that it was an illusion caused by extreme strain and wishful thinking.

The region that now includes the Bermuda Triangle was thus given an air of mystery by its first known navigator and his superstitious crew almost five hundred years ago. Columbus entered the information in his logbook in a matter-of-fact manner, but it was later exaggerated and sailors grew to fear that which they could not understand.

August 1840

Rosalie

In August 1840 the large French ship Rosalie *was found deserted but otherwise in perfect order near Nassau. Her sails were still set, and she appeared to have been abandoned only a few hours before being discovered. She had no leaks, carried a valuable cargo which was undamaged, and had only one living creature aboard—a half-starved canary in a cage. The whereabouts of the crew was never learned.*

Recent versions of the *Rosalie* incident are based on an account in a 1931 book named *Lo!*, written by Charles Fort, who spent a good part of his life searching old newspapers for bits of information to be used in "books that ask questions which orthodox science dares not answer." Fort wrote that he took his information on the *Rosalie* from a single article in the London *Times*.

London *Times,* November 6, 1840, p. 6:

SHIP DESERTED.—A letter from Nassau, in the Bahamas, bearing date the 27th of August, has the following narrative:—"A singular fact has taken place within the last few days. A large French vessel, bound from Hamburgh to the Havannah, was met by one of our small coasters, and was discovered to be completely abandoned. The greater part of her sails were set, and she did not appear to have sustained any damage. The cargo, composed of wines, fruits, silks, &c., was of very considerable value, and was in a most perfect condition. The captain's papers were all secure in their proper place. The soundings gave three feet of water in the hold, but there was no leak whatever. The only living beings found on board were a cat, some fowls, and several canaries half dead with hunger. The cabins of the officers and passengers were very elegantly furnished, and everything indicated that they had been only recently deserted. In one of them were found several articles belonging to a lady's toilet, together with a quantity of ladies' wearing apparel thrown hastily aside, but not a human being was to be found on board. The vessel, which must have been left within a very few hours, contained several bales of goods addressed to different merchants in Havannah. She is very large, recently built, and called the *Rosalie.* Of her crew no intelligence has been received."

Further research on the vessel proved to be difficult. The London *Times* carried no more articles on the ship, and the *New York Times* and the *Nassau Guardian* were not yet in existence. According to the British Library and the Library of Congress there are no libraries that now hold copies of the August 1840 newspapers from either Nassau or Havana. The Musée de la Marine in Paris had no information on the ship, which was reported to be French, but Lloyd's located two items that were tantalizing.

J. F. Lane, Assistant Shipping Editor, Lloyd's, August 15, 1973: I . . . regret that a search of Lloyd's Records has failed to reveal mention of any incident involving a vessel named *Rosalie* in the Bahamas in 1840.

However, I am enclosing extracts from Lloyd's Records which contain references to a vessel named *Rossini* which would appear to be the vessel in which you are interested.

Lloyd's List, September 25, 1840; Havana, 18th Aug. The *Rossini,* from Hambro to this port, struck on the Muares (Bahama Channel) 3rd inst.;* Crew and Passengers saved.

---

* Inst. stands for "instant," meaning "of the current month," or in this case, August.

Lloyd's List, October 17, 1840: Havana, 5th Sept. The *Rossini,* from Hambro to this port, which struck on the Muares (Bahama Channel) 3rd ult.* was fallen in with abandoned, 17th ult. and has been brought into this port a derelict.

There were enough similarities between the *Rossini* and the *Rosalie* to suggest they might be the same ship. The names were so close that one could have been mistaken for the other, especially if they were handwritten, which most messages were in 1840. The Nassau correspondent may have written *Rossini* but the *Times* editor may have mistakenly thought it was *Rosalie.* The route, in both cases, was Hamburg to Havana, and both vessels had been found near Nassau.

The dates are also very close. It was reported on August 27 that the *Rosalie* was brought into Nassau "within the last few days," and the *Rossini* was found on August 17 and towed to Nassau.

Hoping to obtain information that would indicate whether or not the two names applied to the same vessel, I contacted the Ministry of Education and Culture in Nassau. They were not able to find any mention of the *Rosalie,* but did locate the Vice Admiralty Court *Minutes* related to the *Rossini.* These proceedings, which lasted several months, were a series of meetings primarily concerned with the value and storage of the cargo, insurance claims, and other business, but they did contain a brief reference to the discovery of the ship and mentioned that it had been towed to Nassau.

Vice Admiralty Court *Minutes,* 1840, August 25: The Advocate and Procurator General appeared with Benjamin Curry and John Baptiste, the masters of the British wrecking vessels *Resolute* and *Seaflower,* and exhibited an affidavit detailing the curious circumstances connected with the finding of the above named vessel [*Rossini*], which was duly filed and entered.

---

* Ult. stands for "ultimo," or "in the preceding month."

From the phrase "curious circumstances," it appears that the authorities in Nassau did not know that the vessel had run aground two weeks before and that those aboard had been rescued.

Unfortunately, a search of the affidavits held by the Ministry did not produce the one giving the details of the discovery of the *Rossini*, which, if similar to those of the finding of the *Rosalie*, as described in the *Times*, would indicate the two were the same. As the situation now stands, there is reasonable doubt that the *Rosalie* incident is a mystery, but no definite proof one way or the other.

4

April 1854

Bella

One of the first mystery ships of the Bermuda Triangle was the Bella, *which vanished in 1854.*

There is not much information to be found on the *Bella*. Although it was British, the London *Times* did not mention the disappearance, and it is not listed in any of the many standard reference works on shipwrecks.

Lloyd's Register of British and Foreign Shipping of 1854 does list a *Bella,* built in Liverpool in 1852, and destined for Brazil, but does not say that it suffered an accident.

The ship is also mentioned in Harold T. Wilkins's *Strange Mysteries of Time and Space,* in a chapter about an Englishman named Roger Tichborne. The incident is in a book of such a title because of a mystery having to do with Tichborne's inheritance, and his disappearance on the *Bella* was only incidental to the main story. Unfortunately, Wilkins did not say where he found his information.

According to Wilkins, six days after the *Bella* left Rio de Janeiro in April 1854, bound for Jamaica, another ship, crossing the course the *Bella* was presumed to have taken, sighted debris in the water. A ship's long boat was upside down, and

The *Bella*

on its stern could be read, "*Bella*, Liverpool." The *Bella* itself
was not seen. The flotsam was brought back to Rio, and a
number of British and Brazilian steamships set out to hunt
for survivors but were unsuccessful.

It was assumed at the time that the *Bella* had capsized, as
it was overloaded to the point that the decks were carrying
cabin furniture in order to make room for more freight. Sudden squalls were known to have been in the area, and the
night before the long boat was found the weather had been
rather gusty. In Wilkins's account, no particular mystery surrounded the incident; the *Bella* was simply another ship that
failed to complete a voyage.

Wilkins did not say where the debris was found, but he did
say that it was discovered six days after the *Bella* had left Rio
de Janeiro. In the days of sailing ships a good freighter might

make 150 miles on a good day, possibly as much as 200 miles if all conditions were favorable. If the *Bella* had sailed for the full six days under optimum conditions, it could have been as far as 1,200 miles north of Rio when disaster struck. If conditions had been less favorable, or if it had not sailed all six days, it would have been found farther south.

The distance from Rio de Janeiro to the Cape of São Roque is approximately 1,200 miles, or just about as far as the ship might have traveled if all had gone well. The Cape is 2,000 miles from Barbados, and that is as close as the *Bella* could possibly have been to the Bermuda Triangle.

The Bermuda Triangle should not be given "credit" for the *Bella,* as it met its fate, whatever it might have been, in a different part of the world.

5

December 1872

Mary Celeste

No account of sea mysteries would be complete if it did not include the *Mary Celeste*. Although the boat was discovered drifting crewless between the Azores and Portugal, it is frequently mentioned in relation to the Bermuda Triangle.* All derelicts, no matter where they are found, are compared to it, and the ultimate mystery of any type is usually called the "Mary Celeste" of its field. Flight 19, the five Navy aircraft that disappeared off the coast of Florida in 1945, is often called the "Mary Celeste of aviation."

So many stories have been told about the famous derelict in the century since it was found that it is almost impossible to determine what is fact and what is fiction. Dozens of solutions to the mystery ranging from the very simple to the bizarre have been proposed, but no one knows, and no one ever will know, what actually took place.

The *Mary Celeste*, a 103-foot-long brigantine of some 282 tons, was found abandoned at sea by the *Dei Gratia* on December 4, 1872. The two ships had taken on their cargos in New York early the previous month; Captain Briggs of the

---

* It was found at 38° 20′ north, 17° 15′ west, to be exact, which is 590 miles west of Gibraltar.

Mary Celeste had sailed for Genoa on November 7, and Captain Moorhouse of the *Dei Gratia* sailed for Gibraltar on the fifteenth.*

When Captain Moorhouse sighted the other ship at sea a month later, the sails were set and it was sailing with the wind, but so erratically that a crew was sent to investigate. The boarding party found that the ship, which had been carrying Captain Briggs, his wife, daughter, and a crew of eight, was completely deserted. The only lifeboat was gone, and appeared to have been launched, rather than having been torn away.†

Descriptions of the condition of the ship vary considerably, but it was essentially in good order, and had not suffered severely from the weather, although some of the sails were slightly torn. Some versions of the tale have it that a meal was about to be served, others have the meal cooking on the stove, and still others have all the dishes washed and properly stored. Some of the stories are so detailed that the table was said to have been laid with half-empty cups of coffee (still warm), tea, eggs, bacon, bread, and butter. A vial of oil was supposedly sitting upright on a sewing machine, indicating that the seas had been calm, and a clock was still ticking on the wall.

The captain's personal effects were on board, and toys were on his bed, as if a child had been playing there. The cargo of 1,700 barrels of alcohol was intact, although there was 3½ feet of water in the hold. However, the ship's papers, except for the captain's logbook, were missing, as were the navigation instruments.

A sword was found hanging on the wall (or under the captain's bed) with blood (or rust) stains. Some versions of

---

* There is disagreement over the dates, but Charles Edey Fay, who took his information from original reports and is the most authoritative writer on the *Mary Celeste*, gives these.

† Some accounts have the boat still on the ship.

the story say there were blood (or wine) stains on the wood-
work and on the sails, while others do not mention blood at
all, even on the sword.

A six months' supply of food and water was on board.

The last entry in the logbook was on November 24, when
the boat was 100 miles west of the Azores. By the time it was
found, eleven days later, it was 500 miles to the east.

Captain Moorhouse's crew brought the brig into Gibraltar,
where he was awarded a small salvage fee after a lengthy
and controversial inquiry. The court was unable to determine
what had happened to the crew. Many versions of what had
happened were told, retold, and embellished. Captain Moorhouse and his crew were accused of being pirates, of having
seized the ship for its salvage value and disposing of its occupants. For a time it was rumored that Moorhouse had planted
some of his crew on the *Mary Celeste* in New York, and that
they had taken over the ship, killed the occupants, thrown
them overboard, and then waited for Moorhouse and the *Dei
Gratia* to catch up.

Another version was that the crew was discovered raiding
the cargo of alcohol. William A. Richard, then Secretary of
the Treasury of the United States, wrote an open letter that
appeared on the front page of the *New York Times* of March
25, 1873:

The circumstances of the case tend to arouse grave suspicion that
the master, his wife, and child, and perhaps the chief mate, were
murdered in the fury of drunkenness by the crew, who had evidently
obtained access to the alcohol with which the vessel was in part
laden.

It is thought that the vessel was abandoned by the crew between
the 25th day of November and the 5th day of December, and that
they either perished at sea, or, more likely, escaped on some vessel
bound for some North or South American port or the West India
Islands.

A simpler theory was that the ship had been caught in a storm and when it seemed about to sink it was abandoned by the crew, who then disappeared in the lifeboat.

Much has been made of a forehatch that was found open, and one theory is that alcohol fumes blew the cover off. Vapor resembling smoke poured out of the hold, leading Captain Briggs to believe the vessel was afire or about to blow up. The crew took to the lifeboat, taking care to attach a line to the ship, but the rope somehow became untied and allowed the *Mary Celeste* to sail away from the lifeboat and its hapless occupants.

Fiction writers have made good use of the incident, beginning with a young, unknown author named Arthur Conan Doyle, who wrote what was at the time an anonymous article in the January 1884 issue of *The Cornhill Magazine*, entitled "J. Habakuk Jephson's Statement." Doyle's story, which appeared eleven years after the event, was readily believed because much of it was very close to the truth or was deduced from true statements. He named his fictional ship the *Marie Celeste*, and many later writers have referred to the real ship by that name. Much of what is now told about the *Mary Celeste* is really from Doyle's *Marie Celeste*.

Since Doyle's time the proposed solutions have become even more ingenious. It has been suggested that food poisoning caused the crew to have delusions and that they jumped into the sea to escape some horrible hallucination; also that the cook poisoned everyone, threw the bodies overboard, and jumped in after them.

Barratry, a calculated scheme to defraud the owners of the ship, has been suggested as a solution. If the *Dei Gratia* had landed the crew of the *Mary Celeste* somewhere off the beaten path, then sailed into port with the story of the derelict, and collected the salvage money, the award could have been split among the members of both crews.

There was talk that the vessel's owner had arranged for

the crew to murder Briggs and his family and to sink the ship for the insurance, but that they somehow mishandled the job and lost their lives. The plan may have called for the crew to jump as the ship drove toward rocks near the Azores. An unexpected wind might have blown the ship to safety, allowing it to sail on as the crew drowned or was dashed to death upon the rocks.

It has been suggested that a waterspout, the seagoing cousin of the tornado, was responsible for the abandonment. Another theory is that a submarine disturbance caused the crew to panic and abandon ship. Yet another theory is that somewhere near the Azores the ship became stranded on a "ghost island," a shifting sandbar that comes and goes, constantly changing positions. The crew, thinking their position hopeless, took to the boat and were lost at sea. The sandbar then shifted again and set the ship free.

Many years after the event a man who professed to be the only member of the crew to survive claimed that the captain challenged the mate to a swimming race around the ship, and both were killed by a shark. As the crew looked on in horror the ship was struck by a huge wave that dumped all overboard. The ship stayed upright and sailed on alone while the crew, with the one exception, drowned.

Fifty years after the incident "confessions" were still being made by sailors claiming to have been members of the crew. None of the stories could be substantiated and today the fate of the occupants of the *Mary Celeste* is as much a mystery as the day the ship was found deserted at sea.

6

Winter 1880

Atalanta

On January 31, 1880, the British ship Atalanta *sailed from Bermuda with a crew of 290 cadets and officers. She disappeared en route to England, leaving not a trace behind.*

The first public notice that the *Atalanta* was overdue appeared in the London *Times* on April 13, 1880.* After that the search for the ship figured in the news almost every day for several months, and the disappearance commanded worldwide attention. The *Times* never lacked opinions, theories, hopes, and fears about the fate of the ship.

London *Times*, April 13, 1880, p. 6:

Seventy-two days having elapsed since the *Atalanta*, the sailing training-ship, was known to have left Bermuda on her return voyage to Portsmouth without intelligence having been received of her, it is feared that she may have been disabled by the lately prevailing high winds and driven out of her course. Although the Admiralty had previously ordered the *Wye*, store ship, to call in at the Azores . . . in search of the missing ship, their Lordships have since deemed it advisable to order the whole of the Channel Squadron [five ships]

---

* Many writers have erroneously called the ship the *Atlanta*.

The *Atalanta*

to . . . cruise first to the Azores, and thence to Bantry Bay [Ireland], with the object of picking up intelligence of the missing ship. The ships will open out within signalling distance of each other, by which means a large area of sea will be explored.

London *Times,* April 14, 1880, p. 2:
  When the *Atalanta* left Bermuda there were 109 tons of water on board, and an ample supply of provisions. The ship was in all re-

spects sound, possessed of unusual stability, and commanded by an officer of good judgment and high professional qualifications; but the unexpected delay in her arrival affords cause for anxiety for her safety, bearing in mind the many disasters which have occurred during the past two months, consequent on the very severe weather which has been experienced in the Atlantic. There is, however, still ground for hope that she may be only dismasted and may yet arrive in safety.

. . . It is just possible that, having had the misfortune to have her topmasts carried away by the easterly gales, which continued for nearly a month, the ship may have been driven off her course, and be at the moment laboring in the North Atlantic. An attempt has been made to connect [with the *Atalanta*] the copper-bottomed ship which is said to have been discovered bottom-up by the *Tamar*, . . . but this is utterly fallacious. . . . It would be impossible for the *Atalanta*, with her weight of water-tanks and 43 tons of ballast on board, to float in the circumstances stated. If she were once to turn turtle, she would sink with, alas! . . . alacrity. . . .

. . . It is feared by many people in Plymouth that the ship, bottom upwards, . . . is the missing vessel. There is much excitement here.

London *Times*, April 15, 1880, p. 10:

During the day more than 150 telegrams arrived [at the Admiralty] from various parts of the country from relatives of the crew and those on board, asking for information. . . . Their Lordships regretted they were unable to give any information. More than 200 persons also made personal inquiries at Whitehall during the day.

It may reassure some to be told that a vessel took 84 days in coming from Bermuda, whereas the *Atalanta* has not yet been more than 74 days.

The captain of the *Tamar* has sent a telegram . . . stating that during his last voyage he did not, as has been reported, pass a ship bottom upwards.

. . . This morning [Portsmouth] was thrown into a state of excitement by a rumour that the missing ship had arrived all safe at Falmouth. . . . [The report] was displayed at the newspaper offices and various shopwindows, [and] the dockyard gates were soon besieged by the anxious relatives and friends of those on board. . . . How-

ever, . . . a telegram from Falmouth was posted at the dockyard
stating that a merchant vessel called the *Atalanta* had certainly arrived in the harbour that morning, but that the rumour of the arrival of
Her Majesty's ship *Atalanta* was incorrect.

London *Times,* April 16, 1880, p. 5:
    . . . Although the absence of information continues to lead us to
a plentiful crop of rumours and speculations, the public will do right
to regard her for sometime longer as simply missing. Had she, as has
been surmised, foundered during a gale, or been burnt, or come into
collision with an iceberg, it is fair to assume that she would not have
been so completely wiped out of existence as not to have left some
floating wreckage behind to tell the story of her fate. . . . The popular theory still is that she has been dismasted, and has been helplessly driven out of her course, and consequently out of the track of
steamships. . . .
    The coral reefs in the vicinity of Bermuda are of an exceptionally
dangerous kind, extending . . . in some places more than ten miles
from the land. . . . These reefs shut in the islands on three sides
. . . and render access and departure from them an extremely peril-
ous undertaking. Should the *Atalanta* have gone to pieces upon this
coast . . . the wreckage would [by no means] be washed ashore;
on the contrary, it would most probably drift out to sea and be carried
eastwards by the Gulf Stream.

London *Times,* April 19, 1880, p. 6:
    On Saturday a report was bruited abroad to the effect that a life-
boat had been found, with the name *Atalanta* painted on the stern.
This was not confirmed, and even if it had been the boat could not
have belonged to the missing ship, as it is not a custom in the navy
to paint the names of the men-of-war to which they belong on the
stern or anywhere else.

London *Times,* April 20, 1880, p. 12:
    The gunboat *Avon,* from the Chile station, arrived in Portsmouth
Harbour yesterday. She reports that at the Azores she noticed im-
mense quantities of wreckage floating about . . . in fact, the sea

was strewn with spars, etc. The harbour at Fayal was crowded with dismasted ships, and wreckage was washed in continually during the five days the *Avon* remained. Nothing, however, seemed to indicate that a ship had gone down or broken to pieces. . . . Some of the officers of the *Avon* do not deem it impossible that the *Atalanta* has met with icebergs, but they reject the idea of her having "turned turtle."

London *Times,* April 21, 1880, p. 8:

. . . There can be no question of the criminal folly of sending some 300 lads who have never been to sea before in a training ship without a sufficient number of trained and experienced seamen to take charge of her in exceptional circumstances. The ship's company of the *Atalanta* numbered only about 11 able seamen; and when we consider that young lads are frequently afraid to go aloft in a gale to take down sail . . . a special danger attaching to the *Atalanta* becomes apparent.

London *Times,* April 26, 1880, p. 8:

There is no news to report with reference to the *Atalanta,* and even those hitherto most sanguine are beginning to lose heart. The Channel Squadron is now on its way to Bantry Bay, its searches at the Azores having evidently proved fruitless. . . . The public will probably not rest satisfied until an examination of the coasts of Greenland and Iceland has been made.

London *Times,* April 27, 1880, p. 10:

The crew of the *Tamar,* which arrived at Portsmouth to-day, were not aware that any anxiety was felt as to the missing training ship *Atalanta* until they arrived in England. . . . Among the passengers is an able seaman named John Varling* . . . who was invalidated from the *Atalanta* on the 3rd of January. . . . Varling's account of the performance of the training ship is far from reassuring, though the question will, of course, arise as to the value of his opinion. She is reported as exceedingly crank, as being overweight . . . and as having aroused the distrust of Captain Stirling. . . . She rolled 32 de-

---

* The *Times* spells the name "Verling" in some articles, and "Varling" in others.

grees, and Captain Stirling is reported as having been heard to remark that had she rolled one degree more she must have gone over and foundered. During the trying situation the peculiar weaknesses of the ship's company were brought prominently into notice. As, with the exception of two, the officers were almost as much out for training as the crew, Captain Stirling scarcely ever left the deck, and the work of shortening sail and sending down the spars was left to the able seamen on board, who, including marines (mostly servants), petty officers, and cooks, only numbered about 50 in a crew of 250. . . . The young sailors were either too timid to go aloft or were incapacitated by sea-sickness. . . . Varling states that they hid themselves away, and could not be found when wanted by the boatswain's mate. It took the ship 31 days to go to Barbados from Tenerife, . . . or about nine days [extra]. . . . The *Atalanta* left Barbados on Friday, the 9th of January, for Antigua, where they caught the yellow fever. Two men, whose names Varling cannot remember, had already died from the disease. . . . The ship called in at Bermuda on the 30th of January for water and provisions, and finally left for home on the 31st, since which time nothing has been heard of her.

London *Times,* May 10, 1880, p. 8:
The Channel Squadron, under the command of Admiral Hood, arrived at Bantry Bay this (Sunday) afternoon. The Admiral reports that nothing was heard of the *Atalanta* or anything belonging to her picked up.

London *Times,* May 18, 1880, p. 10:
To the Editor of the *Times*—
Sir: The reports of the captains of ships recently arrived all tend to confirm the previous accounts of a storm of unusual violence having prevailed in the Atlantic . . . in the probable track of the *Atalanta* from Bermuda.
To quote a few cases:
. . . the *Caspaer* was at Flores in a disabled state having been on her beam ends* . . . for 19 hours, in a gale, on February 12. Second

---

* A vessel is on its beam-ends when thrown over until the deck is almost vertical.

mate was killed, first mate broken legs, and two men seriously hurt. . . .

Ulster, from St. John's, was fallen in with . . . waterlogged and a complete wreck, crew at mastheads without food or water. . . .

A large ship abandoned and only mizen mast standing, a dangerous wreck to ships bound eastward, was passed. . . .

The following ships are also still missing: *Winnefred,* from New Orleans, December 30; *Devana,* from Bankok, October 1, and St. Helena, January 9; *Bay of Biscay,* from Rangoon . . . last seen on February 7.

We can gather from the above accounts, extracted from many other reports, some idea of the fearful weather encountered, and the havoc caused by these gales, and those who have experienced storms at sea, and know full well the dire effects of heavy water breaking on board a ship, the running into a half sunken wreck or iceberg on a stormy night in mid-Atlantic, can form some conclusion as to the fate of the *Atalanta.* . . .

I am, Sir, yours most obediently,
ALLEN YOUNG, Master Mariner

London *Times,* June 10, 1880, p. 5:

The Accountant-General of the Navy has received instructions from the Admiralty to post up the books of the *Atalanta* to the 4th. Inst. [of June], and the name of the training-ship will be forthwith removed from the Navy list. . . . Widows of officers will receive the award of the special pensions which is due them in consequence of their husbands having been drowned while in the performance of duty.

Captains continued to report the sighting of overturned vessels that might have been the missing ship. Messages were found in bottles and carved on barrel staves, but none appeared to be authentic.

Many theories were proposed—some to explain why the ship sank, others to explain why it was still afloat. Rumors spread quickly: it had been found capsized; it had sailed into Falmouth; it had struck an iceberg.

It cannot be said with certainty that no trace of the ship

was ever found. The ocean was filled with debris following the severe storms that wracked the ocean during February and March, and spars and masts carried no identification. Even the Navy lifeboats were unmarked. It may be that many eyes unknowingly saw parts of the *Atalanta*.

After many years the details of the incident, especially those of the weather and the other ships that disappeared at the time, were forgotten and the *Atalanta* came to be remembered as the ship that was lost in the limbo in 1880. The ship may have been lost far from the Bermuda Triangle, as only about 500 miles of its 3,000-mile journey were through it. Yet it is counted as a victim of the Triangle.

7

1881

~~~~~~

Ellen Austin and the Derelict

One of the weirdest cases of a derelict vessel occurred in 1881 when the British ship Ellen Austin *encountered a schooner in the mid-Atlantic. It had been abandoned but was still seaworthy. A small salvage crew went aboard and both vessels headed for St. John's, Newfoundland.*

A fog descended and the ships drifted apart. They met again several days later. Once again the schooner was deserted. The salvage crew, just like their predecessors, had vanished.

The basic story, which stops at this point, can be traced as far back as Rupert Gould's *The Stargazer Talks,* published in 1944. There are several other versions that begin where Gould left off.

One is that the captain of the *Ellen Austin* attempted to place another salvage crew on the derelict but no one would go and the vessel was left behind. The other is that another crew did go aboard, the vessels were parted by a squall, and the schooner and its second crew were never seen again.

Unfortunately, Gould did not cite his source, and his failure to mention the month of the occurrence made research difficult. I was not able to find the original report of the incident despite lengthy searches through the *New York Times Index,* the *Index to the Times* (London),* and Hocking. Lloyd's had no information. The Newfoundland public library in St. John's checked its files and the local paper, the *Evening Telegram,* for 1881 but could find nothing.

I checked, page by page, *The Newfoundlander* for 1881 and half of 1882 but had negative results even though that paper made a practice of describing interesting adventures of ships that docked at St. John's. There were many accounts of the travails of other vessels that journeyed that way. It is not likely that the story of the *Ellen Austin* would have been missed had the ship stopped at St. John's.

Rupert Gould was a skeptical and diligent researcher who made authentic attempts to solve the mysteries that he encountered. The incident may well have occurred as he said it did, but the variations that go beyond his account are fiction.

The *Ellen Austin*'s discovery will remain a mystery at least until someone locates the information that Gould used for his account. It may remain a mystery even after the source is discovered.

---

* Although there were no articles in the London *Times* about the *Ellen Austin* under the heading "Shipping Accidents," the item may be one of the hundreds of miscellaneous items under that heading. I was not able to check them all. Gould was English, so his source of information very likely was a newspaper from that country.

1866   1868   1884

Lotta   *Viego*   *Miramon*

In 1866 the Lotta, *a Swedish bark bound from Göteborg to Havana, vanished somewhere north of Haiti. Two years later the same fate was waiting for the* Viego, *a Spanish merchantman. The chain continued in 1884 when the Italian schooner* Miramon, *bound for New Orleans, disappeared.*

These are incidents for which, despite extensive research, I was not able to find any information. In some of the cases the problem was that the incidents, as they appear in the Legend, are very brief and almost devoid of details such as dates and routes. There is no proof that the ships disappeared in the Triangle, that they suffered their fates outside it, or that they even existed.

October 1902

Freya

   The Freya, *a German bark, was found deserted at sea on October 20, 1902. She had sailed from Manzanillo in the West Indies on October 3, en route to Chile, and was not seen or heard from again until she was found dismasted, lying on her side, and crewless. Her anchor was hanging free at the bow, and the captain's calendar was turned to October 4, indicating that disaster had struck soon after the ship had left port. The winds were known to have been light at the time.*

Lloyd's Register. Wreck Returns. 1900–1904. (Section entitled Abandoned at Sea) Number 446:

> *Freya.* 626 net tons. German.
> Point of departure: Manzanillo.
> Destination: Punta Arenas.
> Cargo: Ballast.
> Description of boat: Wood and bark.
> Circumstances and place: Near Mazatlán.
> Date of the disaster: Prior to October 21, 1902.

Nature, April 25, 1907, p. 610: "The Mexican Earthquake"

   Another great earthquake has been added to the series which has marked the recent increase in seismic and volcanic activity along the *Pacific coast of America. . . .*＊

Seaquakes are common in this region; sometimes they are felt by ships at sea though unnoticed on shore, and in at least one instance seem to have caused the loss of a ship. The story is a remarkable one. On October 3, 1902, the German barque *Freya* cleared from Manzanillo for Punta Arenas; nothing more has been heard of the captain or crew, but the ship was found, twenty days later, partially dismasted and lying on its side. There was nothing to explain the condition of the ship, but a wall calendar in the captain's cabin

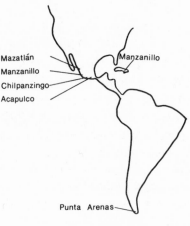

The *Freya*

showed that the catastrophe must have overtaken it on October 4, not long after leaving port, as was also indicated by the anchor being found still hanging free at the bow. Weather reports show that only light winds were experienced in this region from October 3 to October 5, but, on the other hand, severe earthquakes were felt in Acapulco and Chilpanzingo on October 4 and 5, one of which probably caused the damage to the *Freya* which led to its abandonment.

All the versions of the *Freya* story lead back, either directly or indirectly, to the 1907 article in *Nature;* no other source

＊ Italics mine.

has ever been reported. The article is primarily concerned with a series of earthquakes on the *west coast of Mexico*. In the one paragraph on the derelict, the cities of Manzanillo, Acapulco, and Chilpanzingo are mentioned, all of which are on the west side of Mexico. Mazatlán, where Lloyd's reports the derelict was found, is also on the Pacific side.

The confusion appears to have been caused by the existence of another city named Manzanillo, this one being a seaport on the southern coast of Cuba. The first writer who ascribed the mystery of the *Freya* to the Bermuda Triangle "mistakenly" assumed that the ship had sailed from the Cuban port rather than from the Mexican city of the same name.

The finding of the vessel north of its starting point is due to the action of the wind and currents after the ship was abandoned. It is not known what became of the crew, or whether the earthquake was in fact the cause of the wreck.

10

November 1909

Joshua Slocum and the Spray

Captain Joshua Slocum, the world's best known and most skilled sailor of the day, vanished in the Bermuda Triangle in 1909. He had previously won worldwide acclaim by being the first man to sail single-handed around the world. The voyage, which took several years in his superb yawl, the Spray, was finished in 1898. He was successful despite obstacles that would have defeated most ordinary men and boats. He outraced pirates near Morocco, survived storms that destroyed larger ships nearby, held entire tribes of savages at bay in the Straits of Magellan, and sailed on after his maps had been destroyed. He was stranded for a week in the doldrums of the Sargasso Sea, and was greeted upon his return to New York City, at night, by the worst storm of the voyage, a tornado that damaged much of the city.

Yet, this same man, who possessed the skill, courage, and stamina to defy successfully the worst hazards that nature could deal him, disappeared several years later on the relatively short journey through the Bermuda Triangle. He set sail from Martha's Vineyard on November 14, 1909, bound for South America, and was never seen again.

Many who knew Captain Slocum felt he was too good a

sailor, and the Spray *too good a boat, to have been defeated by any of the normal hazards of the sea.*

No one knows for certain what happened to Joshua Slocum and the *Spray*, despite the many stories and rumors that have grown since he disappeared almost seventy years ago. Some say that he was never seen again after departing on the trip that might have turned into another circumnavigation of the globe, while others report that he was seen in various ports along the way.

Many theories have been suggested to explain his disappearance. He may have finally met the gale that was capable of sinking him. The *Spray* might have caught fire. He may have been run down at night by a larger ship. It was not unusual for a small boat to be struck by a steamer in the busy coastal waters. A sailing boat's lights, normally dim, were sometimes hidden from view by the boat's own sails, and a large ship could easily crush a 37-foot yawl without anyone even feeling a bump. According to one of America's foremost writers of sea stories, Edward Rowe Snow, Slocum was run down by a 500-ton mail steamer near Turtle Island, Lesser Antilles, while en route to the Orinoco River.*

Descriptions of Slocum's health varied. His son, Victor, claimed that he was in the best of health, while others felt he was growing old. Slocum himself felt that his mind was not as sharp as it once had been, and he admitted to having an occasional blackout spell. It is possible that he fell overboard, either because of an accident or because of blacking out. He may have died a natural death and the boat eventually foundered either with or without his body still aboard.

The condition of the *Spray* was also debated and continues to be a subject of controversy among sailors. Slocum declared it to be completely seaworthy and able to sail for lengthy

---

* Edward Rowe Snow, *Mysterious Tales of the New England Coast.*

stretches with no one at the helm. He felt it had earned its reputation when it had completed its trip around the world. Others disagreed, saying that Slocum completed his epic voyage in spite of the *Spray*, not because of it; that his great skill carried him through situations where lesser men in the same boat would have failed. Expert sailors discouraged builders from imitating the lines of the *Spray*, claiming that it was a hazard to anyone lacking the skill of a Slocum. One sailor who saw the boat just before it sailed on its last voyage felt that it had aged along with its master. It was no longer neat and trim but dirty, smelly, and showing signs of wear and poor maintenance.

Some reports say Slocum was seen in various parts of the West Indies before he disappeared, and others state he was seen sailing up the Orinoco River long after he had been declared missing. It has been suggested that Slocum was unhappy with his wife and decided to deliberately vanish in order to spend his remaining days somewhere in peace.

The fate of Joshua Slocum and the *Spray* is truly a mystery of the sea.

11

March 1918

Cyclops

On March 4, 1918, the USS Cyclops, a 19,600-ton Navy collier, sailed from Barbados, West Indies, with a crew of 309 men and a cargo of manganese ore. The 542-foot ship, one of the largest vessels afloat, was bound for Norfolk,* but it failed to arrive. In spite of a massive search no trace was ever found. The ship did not send an SOS.

It was first thought that she had been torpedoed, but a search of German records after the war proved that submarines had not been operating in the area at the time. The Germans made a practice of broadcasting the destruction of large enemy ships, and no such announcement was made for the Cyclops.

It was suggested that she might have struck a mine, but it was later shown that none had been in the area. A mine strike normally allowed time to send an SOS, and at least some of the men would have been able to escape in life rafts. The lack of debris also spoke against a mine strike, as well as against the possibility of an internal explosion, which would have littered the ocean with wreckage and bodies.

---

* The destination has sometimes been given as Norfolk, sometimes as Baltimore. In either case the route across the Atlantic would have been the same, as both cities are in Chesapeake Bay.

Some felt that the ship had simply foundered, but others, including the Navy, emphasized that the weather had not been bad, certainly not bad enough to sink the large, seaworthy, eight-year-old ship. The captain, George W. Worley, had been in the Navy for twenty-eight years and had been the Cyclops's *commanding officer since her maiden voyage in 1910.*

After a lengthy investigation the Navy stated: "The disappearance of this ship has been one of the most baffling mysteries in the annals of the Navy, all attempts to locate her having proved unsuccessful. Many theories have been advanced, but none satisfactorily accounts for her disappearance." President Wilson said that "Only God and the sea know what happened to the great ship." One highly respected journal of the time, the Literary Digest, *even speculated that a giant squid rose out of the ocean, wrapped its tentacles around the* Cyclops, *and dragged it down to the bottom of the sea.*

Public announcement of the overdue ship was withheld until the middle of the next month.

Virginian-Pilot, April 15, 1918, p. 1:

AMERICAN NAVAL COLLIER PROBABLY LOST
FATE MAY BE ANOTHER MYSTERY OF SEA

Washington, April 14. The big American naval collier *Cyclops* . . . has been overdue in an Atlantic port since March 13. The navy department announced today that she was last reported . . . March 4, and that extreme anxiety is entertained as to her safety. . . .

The [Navy] statement follows: . . . "No well-founded reason can be given to explain the *Cyclops'* being overdue, as no radio communication with or trace of her has been had since leaving the West Indies port. The weather in the area in which the vessel must have passed has not been bad and could hardly have given the *Cyclops* trouble. While a raider or submarine could be responsible for her loss, there have been no reports that would indicate the presence of either in the locality. . . .

"It was known that one of the two engines of the *Cyclops* was injured and that she was proceeding at a reduced speed with one engine compounded. [But] even if her main engines were totally disabled, the ship would still be capable of using her radio plant.

"The search for the *Cyclops* still continues, but the navy department feels extremely anxious as to her safety."

Virginian-Pilot, April 16, 1918, p. 8:

Washington, April 15. . . . Officials refused to believe that the great 19,000-ton collier and the 293 lives she carried could have been wiped out without leaving a trace. Orders have gone out, therefore, for the searching vessels to "quarter" every rod of the route covered by the *Cyclops* and to visit every one of the scores of islands which dot that portion of the sea.

Navy officials frankly confessed that no theory yet advanced to explain the disappearance of the *Cyclops* . . . seemed plausible in the face of the facts. . . . An internal explosion might have destroyed the vessel's wireless and motive power at one instant, but surface wreckage would have remained to mark her grave.

The possibility that a sudden hurricane, not infrequent in those waters, might have first disabled and then engulfed the collier was admitted, but again it was pointed out that some evidence of the disaster must have been left in this case.

The search was discontinued in May, all efforts having been fruitless. The Navy calculated the stability of the *Cyclops* and concluded that the ship would have had an uncomfortable, quick, but not excessive roll. It might have been possible, they said, for the heavy ore to shift enough to cause a list and to submerge the deck edge; such a condition would have been dangerous under certain conditions of sea and weather. The Navy noted, however, that no unusual weather had been encountered by other vessels along the same route.

The Office of Naval Intelligence later listed the major theories that had been suggested to account for the loss.

1. The crew may have mutinied, seized the ship, and sailed off the usual trade route.

2. The American Consul General at Rio de Janeiro, a passenger who was accused of being pro-German, might have arranged to hand the ship over to the Germans.

3. The ship was torpedoed by a German submarine.

4. The cargo of manganese dioxide, highly incendiary under certain conditions, might have exploded.

5. The *Cyclops* may have foundered as a result of excessive strain from rolling.

6. Captain Worley, who was born in Germany, might have surrendered the *Cyclops* to the Germans or connived at her destruction by submarines.

The Navy could find no evidence to support any of the theories.

Many supposed clues to the loss have appeared over the years, but none were authentic. In 1919 the mother of one of the crewmen received a telegram from New York saying that he was safe and that the *Cyclops* was in a German port. A bottle message was found near Galveston that told of the *Cyclops* being torpedoed 1,000 miles east of Newfoundland. Both were investigated and found to be hoaxes.

In 1920 Lt. Commander Mahlon S. Tisdale provided evidence to support the theory that the ship had capsized. During a cruise on the *Cyclops* Tisdale discovered that the manhole plates on the topside tanks had all been left open. "I fought my way to the bridge and reported to the captain that someone had opened all of the topside tanks. He laughed at my earnestness and said that they were always left off in accordance with instructions from the navy yard. . . ."

Tisdale felt that on the *Cyclops*'s last voyage the cargo might have shifted and allowed the sea to rush into the open tanks, causing the ship to capsize.

"This could all occur in a few seconds and the ship would be bottom up before any one could abandon ship. . . . With everything secured for sea there would be little wreckage. . . . There would be no debris such as in the case of striking a mine or torpedo. There would be no time for an 'S.O.S.' There would have been no time for anything. The few men in the water could not have lived long of their own accord. Such small gear as did float off would have been lost in the vastness of the ocean long before the rescue vessels started their search."*

Although Commander Tisdale's explanation is one of the most commonly accepted solutions, there are many who disagree, saying that there are two important flaws in his argument. The first is that it assumes heavy seas, and reports consistently show that the weather was not bad. The second flaw is that his reasoning required that the manhole plates be left off.

Commander I. I. Yates of the Norfolk Navy Yard charged that Worley, who was known for his jokes, had pulled Tisdale's leg. "When Lieut. Commander Tisdale discovered the covers off the topside tanks the *Cyclops* was in a light condition, and it was immaterial whether the covers were on or off. In fact, in this condition the topside tanks are generally kept full of water [for ballast]."† Yates continued that there were no such orders from the naval yard and that Worley would not have sailed with the covers off while the ship was loaded.

The theory of a Captain Zearfoss was that "The *Cyclops* was sunk by her cargo. Manganese . . . has a tendency to settle down, grinding away whatever is below it. . . . I think

---

* Mahlon S. Tisdale, "Did the *Cyclops* Turn Turtle?" United States Naval Institute. *Proceedings*, January 1920, pp. 57–59.

† I. I. Yates, "Discussion," United States Naval Institute. *Proceedings*, April 1920, p. 604.

the end came suddenly when the bottom practically dropped out."*

Many Navy men felt that the *Cyclops*'s top-heavy super-structure had been the cause. Steel derricks, designed for the rapid loading and discharging of coal, towered high above the deck. If the ship were to list severely the top-heavy equipment would slow the recovery, the cargo might shift, and the vessel would quickly capsize. Partially filled holds, like the *Cyclops*'s, would be more likely to shift than would cargos in full holds. The flaw in this theory, like most of the others, was that it would happen only during bad weather.

By 1930 the *Cyclops* was still remembered well enough to garner the headlines when parts of a diary sent to the Navy revealed that four men "in enemy pay" had placed dynamite around the engine and had sunk the ship. At first the Navy felt that the diary might be genuine, but many points in the story were dubious, especially where it told of an enemy ship with 700 crewmen that remained in the area to clear away all the debris. The story quickly faded away, relegated to the status of an elaborate attempt at a hoax.

As recently as 1956 it was reported that the ship was seen to have blown up in the Straits of Florida "just before Easter" in 1918, but there was no explanation of why the report had been withheld for almost forty years, or why the ship might have been so far off course several weeks after it had been overdue.

In 1969 Conrad A. Nervig, who had served on the *Cyclops* on its last voyage to South America, suggested that in view of the known evidence he thought the ship had broken in half. "I was mystified at hearing a sound not unlike that caused by metal plates being rubbed together. . . . The ship was working to the extent that where steam or water pipes

---

* "Collier *Cyclops* Mystery Still Causes Speculation," United States Naval Institute. *Proceedings*, September 1923, pp. 1569–1570.

. . . were in contact with portions of the hull, the movement could be distinctly seen. . . . The deck amidships [was] rising and falling as if the ship were conforming to the contour of the seas. Later that day when I called it to the Captain's attention, he shrugged it off with a superior, 'Son, she'll last as long as we do.' "*

Nervig surmised that the task of loading the vessel might have been assigned to some young, inexperienced officer who confined the cargo to several of the amidship holds, accentuating the ship's inherent weakness. According to Nervig, this may have caused the ship to break in two and sink before an SOS could be sent.

The ship, however, had been properly loaded. It was done under the personal supervision of Captain Worley and foreman Manuel Pereira of the Brazilian Coaling Company, who had been in charge of loading vessels for many years. Pereira stated that the ship could have carried at least 2,000 more tons of ore without being endangered, and that the cargo had been well trimmed throughout the entire ship.

The *Cyclops* continues to be in the news, even apart from its role in the Legend of the Bermuda Triangle. It was the first large radio-equipped ship to disappear without sending an SOS and it was the largest Navy ship ever to be lost without a trace. Every March, the anniversary of its disappearance, its story is retold, the theories are rehashed, and its famous picture is shown yet another time. Its loss continues to be rightfully called the "most baffling mystery in the annals of the Navy."

Unlike other disappearances, pertinent new information continues to be received about the *Cyclops*. In the past few years there have been two important new developments in the case. The first occurred in 1968 when a Navy diver, Dean Hawes, discovered a ship while searching for the missing

* Conrad A. Nervig, "The Cyclops Mystery," United States Naval Institute. *Proceedings*, July 1969, p. 149.

nuclear submarine *Scorpion*. Hawes was stunned by the strange design of the vessel. Its bridge was high above the deck, supported by steel stilts. Upright beams like the skeleton of a skyscraper ran almost its entire length. Before he could explore the wreck, which was in 180 feet of water 70 miles east of Norfolk, he was forced to surface, and bad weather drove his ship from the area. Hawes later saw a picture of the *Cyclops* for the first time and is positive that it was the ship he had stood on. The wreck is located along the path that the *Cyclops* would have followed on its journey to Chesapeake Bay.

Hawes and Representative G. William Whitehurst of Virginia persuaded Navy officials to investigate, and divers were to attempt to relocate the wreck as a training exercise.

The announcement of the discovery of the wreck led to the second major break in the case. I was doing research on the *Cyclops* at the time, and its possible location immediately raised several questions in my mind. If the wreck is the *Cyclops*, what could have caused it to sink so close to its destination? Why had it not sunk earlier in the voyage when it was heavier because of its unburned fuel and thus more susceptible to capsizing or structural failure? The answer, I reasoned, had to be the one possibility that has steadily been denied since the time the ship disappeared; a storm had to have been responsible for the disappearance of the *Cyclops*.

Because of the disabled engine the ship's speed was only 10 knots, or about 240 nautical miles a day. It would have followed the 15-mile-a-day North Equatorial Current for about 1,300 miles until it met the Gulf Stream, which would then carry it as much as 120 miles a day for the remaining 500 miles. Based on these estimates, the *Cyclops* should have been where the sunken ship now lies after a little more than six days of travel. Since it had sailed from Barbados in the early evening of March 4, it should have been approaching Norfolk on the night of March 10.

I confidently decided that the newspapers, the Navy, and all the ships at sea had been wrong, and that there had been a storm near Norfolk that day that was strong enough to sink the ship. Since a north wind has a reputation for raising havoc with the Gulf Stream, the storm had probably come from that direction. A north wind strikes violently against the opposing flow of the current, turning it into a churning, thrashing torrent that has overwhelmed many a vessel. If there had

The *Cyclops*

been such a storm I felt that the wreck might very well be the *Cyclops*.

The National Climatic Center in Ashville, North Carolina, mailed the weather records for the east coast the same day they received my phone call. These records show that the wind blew hard in Norfolk early in March, reaching a top speed of 30 to 40 knots almost every day. On the eighth it died almost completely, but slowly began to build in strength the next morning. By 5:00 PM of the ninth, gale warnings had been issued from Maine to North Carolina. The wind came steadily from the southwest, increasing in strength until by 10:00 AM of the tenth it had reached 58 miles an hour. After noon the wind shifted, blowing from the northwest at 60 miles an hour. The speed varied between 40 and 60 until 5:00 PM, then remained near 40 for the rest of the evening, finally tailing off about midnight.

The storm had been widespread. Peak winds of 84 miles an hour struck New York City, where they caused one death, and the gale warnings had been extended south to Florida. The steamship *Amolco*, 375 miles northeast of Norfolk, was caught by the storm from noon of the ninth until the afternoon of the eleventh. It had to heave to to ride out the gale for the entire two days, and suffered $150,000 worth of damage.

Officer W. J. Riley of the *Amolco* later told a reporter for Norfolk's *Virginian-Pilot* that the Navy collier was probably caught "in the teeth of the gale," and he felt "positive the *Cyclops* was sunk during the raging of the high winds." Several seamen acquainted with the rolling tendency of the vessel seconded his opinion and added that it had probably sunk quicker than the lifeboats could be lowered.

Statements made just after the announcement that the *Cyclops* was missing suggest that the Navy thought the ship had been lost near the West Indies. The order to "visit every one of the islands that dot that part of the sea," and the opinion that a hurricane, "not infrequent in those waters," might have been the cause, indicate that the eyes of the investigators were focused so far away that they had not seen what had happened directly in front of their noses. The absence of any calls from the ship after it left Barbados also reinforced the idea that it sank early in its journey, near the West Indies.

Everyone was accustomed to strong spring winds, and

the storm, which was apparently worse at sea than it was on land, did not receive much publicity. The *Virginian-Pilot* mentioned it only in a half-inch notice on March 10, hidden at the bottom of page two between ads for Conkey's Buttermilk and the Couper Marble Works. It said only that gale warnings had been issued at 5:00 PM the previous day from Maine to North Carolina. There were no articles in later days that mentioned the storm of March 10.

Five weeks later when the headlines announced that the *Cyclops* was overdue, the wind that had gone almost unnoticed when it occurred had been forgotten. It was quietly tucked away in the Weather Bureau's statistics sheets where it would remain undiscovered for fifty-six years. No one at the time, including the Weather Bureau and the newspapers, thought to mention it to the Navy. Officer Riley and the *Amolco* were never heard of after the one small article in the Norfolk paper. The nation's attention was on the battlefields of Europe and the blackouts, morale, and Liberty bond drives at home, not on the lost Navy ship whose picture appeared on page one for a few days. As a result the story has always been that the weather "was not bad anywhere along the route."

Contrary to popular opinion, there never was an official inquiry into the disappearance. The Navy was fighting a war and could not take time out to examine the loss of every ship that occurred. Had there been an investigation, the weather information would surely have been discovered.

As of August 1974 it still was not known if the sunken ship off Norfolk is the *Cyclops*. On July 24 Lieutenant Douglas Armstrong, skipper of the *Exploit*, reported that he had located a ship in 190 feet of water, seventy miles northeast of Cape Henry, and had marked it with a buoy so divers could later identify it. I spoke with Hawes again on August 17, 1974, and learned that he had gone out with the Navy during the first week in August and watched on television as the ship was examined by underwater cameras. Because of construction differences, he could tell that it was not the same one he had found earlier.

No plans were then made for a concerted effort to locate the ship. However, the area is used by the Navy for training and requalifying divers, and it is likely that the ship that Hawes found will soon be found again and positively identified. It might very well be the *Cyclops*. In any case, the missing part of the puzzle, a substantial reason for the disappearance, has finally been found—the overlooked storm of March 10, 1918.

12

January 1921

Carroll A. Deering

The story of the *Carroll A. Deering* has been told so many ways that it would not be right to call any of them the Legend except for a very short version which goes something like this:

On a cold, gray, January dawn in 1921 the five-masted schooner Carroll A. Deering *was discovered hard aground on Diamond Shoals with all sails set. A meal was still on the stove but the only living things aboard were two cats. The crew was never found. That same year a dozen other vessels disappeared in the area and the government of the United States investigated the possibility that pirates or Soviet sympathizers had seized them.*

At the end of the lengthy investigation into the mystery of the Carroll A. Deering, *one government official stated, "We might just as well have searched a painted ship on a painted ocean for sight of the vanished crew."*

Many versions stop at this point, but several continue on, giving the full story of the *Carroll A. Deering*, or as much as could be learned.[*]

---

[*] Some of the past writers have erroneously called the schooner the *Carol Deering*.

Virginian-Pilot, Tuesday, February 1, 1921, p. 3:

The *Carroll A. Deering,* a five-masted schooner, went aground off Diamond Shoals Sunday night, according to advices from coast guard stations of that vicinity. The derelict was sighted today, and lifeboats . . . were manned to go to the assistance of the stranded craft.

A heavy sea was beating over the shoals, making the undertaking of the surfmen extremely hazardous. They arrived within 400 yards of the schooner—close enough to observe that the vessel had been stripped of her lifeboats and that there were no signs of life aboard.

Virginian-Pilot, Saturday, February 5, 1921, p. 4:

Last night it became definitely known that the schooner which was abandoned with all sails set . . . was the *Carroll A. Deering.* . . . She was boarded . . . and a casual inspection of the schooner convinced them that she could not be saved. Her seams had been ripped open by the constant playing of the waves, and her hold had been weakened beyond hope of repair by the disintegrating processes of the water. . . .

When she started on her South American trip last September she was in command of Captain Merritt, one of her owners, the other owner being G. G. Deering, after [whose son] the boat was named. A few days out and Captain Merritt was taken ill and was forced to put back. . . .

Captain Wormwell, a [66-year-old] veteran of the sea, but who had retired three years previously, was sent to take command. He made the trip down successfully and got back as far as Diamond Shoals, as far as present information is indicative, before meeting with a mishap. How the ship happened to be abandoned, with all sails set and with apparently no damage to her, is still as much of a mystery as ever. No word has been received from Captain Wormwell or any other member of his crew.

Mutiny has been suggested as one reason for the ship's strange plight, but it has been discounted very largely even as a conjecture. The beach where the ship came to grief has long been known as "the graveyard of seamen," and it is thought by some that an ugly squall came up when the *Deering* reached a point off there, that the crew, knowing by tradition the dangerous situation in which they found themselves, became panic-stricken and attempted to make for shore in life-boats. The theory is that either the life-boats in which they set out were upset by the gale, which was known to be raging, or that they were picked up by [another] ship. . . .

No new developments occurred and the derelict and its crew faded from the news, only to return several months later as the main element in an incident with overtones of an international conspiracy.

New York Times, June 21, 1921, p. 1:

The crew of an American ship is missing, and what seems to be conclusive evidence has been obtained that the men were taken as prisoner to another vessel and carried away to parts unknown, if they were not murdered.

A second American ship is long overdue, and two other American ships are unaccounted for under circumstances that lead to the belief that their disappearance is in some way connected with the capture of the crew of the first-mentioned vessel.

The United States Government has undertaken to solve these mysteries of the sea, which, in the opinion of officials today, point either to old-time piratical methods off the Atlantic Coast or the seizure of the vessels for the benefit of Soviet Russia.

Officials concede that it is difficult to believe that acts of piracy could be committed in and near the territorial waters of the United States in this day, but the evidence is such that they are unable to escape the suspicion. . . .

The State Department, . . . the Treasury Department, through its Coast Guard, . . . the Navy, . . . the Department of Commerce, . . . [and] the Department of Justice . . . [are] working on the theory that all these mysterious incidents are interrelated.

Several months ago the five-masted schooner *Carol Deering* [sic] of Portland, Me., was found abandoned off Diamond Shoals, North Carolina, with all sails set and her officers and crew missing. . . . Evidence indicated that she had been abandoned in a hurry for no conceivable reason, for the vessel was in good shape, with plenty of food. In fact, it was apparent that she had been abandoned when a meal was about to be served. Her small boats were gone, however.

A little later a bottle came ashore near where the ship was found, and in it was a note . . . which read as follows:

"An oil-burning tanker or submarine has boarded us and placed our crew in irons. Get word to headquarters of company at once."

The crew of the *Deering,* including the Captain, numbered twelve men, and not a trace of them has been discovered. . . . The writing found in the bottle has been compared with the penmanship of her missing mate, and handwriting experts have declared that there is no question that the mate wrote the message.

The steel steamer *Hewitt* of Portland, Me. . . . is also missing. . . . She might have been off Diamond Shoals about the time the *Deering* went ashore, and the authorities believe that she is still afloat, intact.

At the Department of Commerce today the statement was made that two other American steamers had disappeared under circumstances that led officials . . . to believe that they had not foundered, and it was openly admitted that they suspected that the ships had been the victims of pirates [or] Soviet sympathizers. . . . The names of these vessels could not be ascertained, and officials were extremely hazy as to details of their disappearance.

New York Times, June 22, 1921, p. 1:

The names of three other vessels which have disappeared off the Atlantic coast of the United States in mysterious circumstances were added by the Department of Commerce today to the list of those . . . more or less related to the supposed kidnapping of the crew of the American schooner *Carroll A. Deering.* . . . It is not asserted that all the missing vessels were the victims of pirates or possibly Bolshevist sympathizers . . . but the fact that all these vessels disappeared at about the same time, and that none of them left a trace is considered significant. . . .

Ordinarily ships that disappear leave some trace either in the way of boats, wreckage or dead bodies, but it is said that none of the ships added to the list today left any trace whatever. . . .

For some reason the Department of Commerce officials were unable to identify the two other vessels whose disappearance excited suspicion. . . .

The State Department . . . instructed consular officials of the United States at ports in various parts of the world to keep a lookout for the *Deering*'s missing crew and a mysterious vessel on which they were supposed to have been made prisoner. . . .

The department's statement throws suspicion on the conduct of a steamer which passed the Cape Lookout Lightship soon after the *Deering*. . . .

". . . On Jan. 29, 1921, the . . . *Carroll A. Deering* . . . passed Cape Lookout lightship, North Carolina, and on Jan. 31, 1921, it was found a few miles north of that point in such condition that there is every suspicion of foul play having occurred. . . .

". . . A man on board other than the Captain hailed the lightship and reported that the vessel had lost both anchors and asked to be reported to his owners. Otherwise the *Deering* appeared to be in very good condition. A short time [later] a steamer, the name of which cannot be ascertained . . . was asked to stop and take a message for forwarding, and, in spite of numerous attempts on the part of the master of the lightship to attract the vessel's attention, no response to his efforts was received."

New York Times, June 22, 1921, p. 10:

Senator Hale of Maine, who first asked for a Government investigation of the disappearance of the *Hewitt* and of the *Deering*'s crew, advanced today the theory that mutiny and not piracy was the explanation of the sea mysteries. . . .

"I think it will be found to be a plain case of mutiny in at least one of the cases," said Senator Hale. "Possibly the mutinous crew of one vessel boarded the other to get a navigator."

New York Times, June 22, 1921, p. 10:

It was the courage, persistency and detective skill of Mrs. W. B. Wormwell, wife of the Captain of the schooner *Carroll A. Deering* . . . which resulted in the evidence being gathered that has convinced the authorities at Washington that the schooner had been raided by Reds or pirates. . . .

Facing skepticism, and at times ridicule, this New England seaman's wife . . . obtained samples of the handwriting of the members of the *Deering*'s crew and convinced herself that the note [in the bottle] was written by the engineer, Henry Bates. . . .

To establish this she obtained . . . samples of [his] handwriting, and submitted those, with the note found in the bottle . . . to three handwriting experts, all of whom agreed that the writing was identical.

[Mrs. Wormwell] said tonight that, in her opinion, Bates, who was the most intelligent member of her husband's crew, wrote the note in his engine room, where he had the paper and the bottle.

The New York Police Department revealed on June 23 that a year before they had discovered that the United Russian Workers of the United States and Canada had made plans for members to seek employment on steamers, mutiny if possible, and sail the ships to Soviet ports. It was recalled that several vessels about that time had had trouble with their crews, and that the *William O'Brien*, which had to put back to port because of a troublesome crew, sailed the next day and was never seen again.

Despite the views of the various departments of the government, the New York police, and Captain Wormwell's wife, the piracy theory began to meet criticism. The most telling objections came from another department of the United States government.

New York Times, June 24, 1921, p. 2:

Weather Bureau officials came forward tonight with the theory that some of the dozen or more ships reported to have disappeared mysteriously in the North Atlantic may have been lost in the series of unusually severe storms which are known to have swept that area in the first weeks of February, 1921.

Records . . . show that a storm, accompanied by winds of up to 90 miles an hour, swept the North Atlantic lanes about Feb. 6, covering a section measuring 1,000 miles in length. This storm continued three days. Again on February 15, a storm suddenly arose in mid-ocean and raged for 72 hours.

The disappearance of the entire crew of the schooner *Carroll A. Deering* . . . might be explained by the theory that they attempted to leave her in their boats and were lost. . . .

. . . A number of ships . . . passed through some of the February storms and reached port only after sustaining damage.

Insurance underwriters suggested still another theory. Although the shipping business was then in a slump and owners

were suffering tremendous losses, many continued their insurance policies at artificially high rates. Insurance men
called the situation a "moral risk" time and found that the
number of sinkings began to increase.

An editor of *Lloyd's List* derided the bottle message, saying
that many years' experience had shown that such missives
were almost invariably frivolous. Another Lloyd's spokesman
said that the weather in the area had been extremely severe
at the time, and also that pirates would not have needed the
lifeboats which were missing from the *Deering*.

Lloyd's also suggested that the *Deering* crew, after abandoning ship, may have been picked up by the *Hewitt*, which
later went down with all hands. When the severe Atlantic
weather was considered, Lloyd's said, the number of vessels
reported missing was not exceptional.

By July the piracy "hysteria," as it was then being called,
had died down, and the simpler theory of the Weather
Bureau prevailed. The final blow came when it was announced that the bottle message was a fake.

Christopher Columbus Gray, the man who had reported
the discovery of the bottle, admitted that the note which had
started the piracy turmoil had not come from the *Deering*,
but from fishermen on the North Carolina coast.

For most of the world, the controversy and the mystery had
ended, but for those who pursued the story of the *Carroll
A. Deering* still further, it was just beginning to get interesting.*

It was learned that Captain Wormwell had confided to a
friend that both the mate and the second mate were worth-
less, and that the crew was drunken and unruly. On the return trip the mate had been jailed in Barbados, but the
captain had managed to have him released in time to leave
for home.

---

* See Edward Rowe Snow's *Mysteries and Adventures Along the Atlantic
Coast.*

On Saturday, January 29, the schooner was sighted off Cape Lookout, North Carolina. A number of the crewmen were congregated on the quarterdeck, which was normally reserved for officers, and a red-headed sailor with a foreign accent shouted to the crew of the Lookout Shoals Lightship that both anchors had been lost in a recent gale, and that they would like it reported ashore. The radio in the lightship was out of order, but when the men tried to pass the message on to the next vessel, a steamship, their attempts to hail that vessel were ignored. The mystery steamship, as it came to be known, has led to many questions. It was never determined what ship it was, or why it ignored repeated signals from the lightship. Some felt that it may have been a pirate ship or a rumrunner, and others claimed it was the *Hewitt*. Some versions have it that a tarp was draped over the side of the ship, covering the name.

Two mornings later the *Deering* was found abandoned about fifty miles to the north, its lifeboats gone, sails set, and an evening meal on the stove. Two cats were still aboard.

Most of the luggage and clothing was missing, as were the captain's large trunk, grip, and canvas bag. Had he abandoned the ship in an emergency, he would not have taken these heavy objects.

A navigation chart on the table appeared to have been marked by Captain Wormwell to a certain point, after which the writing changed. Several pairs of rubber boots were found in the cabin, indicating that other men had been there, and it appeared that someone had been sleeping in the cabin's spare room.

Many questions still remain in the mystery of the Ghostship of Diamond Shoals.

Were the members of the crew involved in a mutiny, or in murder? Were they unruly and drunken, or have stories grown after the fact, based on a few isolated episodes?

Why was the crew on the quarterdeck, an unusual place to congregate, and why did someone other than the captain send the message to the lightship? Was the captain ill at the time? Was he on the ship? Why didn't the crew say anything about the captain if he was sick or gone? If he was all right, why wasn't he there? Why had someone else been marking the chart in the captain's room?

Despite the apparently bogus bottle message, could pirates or rumrunners have been responsible for the disappearance of the crew? Did government officials, wishing to avoid an international incident, coerce Gray into falsely admitting a hoax?

Was the mystery steamer the *Hewitt?* Did the steamer and the schooner meet somewhere between Cape Lookout and Diamond Shoals? Was there collusion between the two crews? Was a sick Captain Wormwell transferred to another ship, which later foundered?

What took place on the *Carroll A. Deering* between the time it passed Cape Lookout and when it was found, stranded and empty, several mornings later? Could it have happened as the Coast Guard assumed, that the captain and crew abandoned what they felt was a doomed ship, only to be lost at sea in their lifeboats?

The story of the *Carroll A. Deering* is unique in maritime history, and it can truly be said that the more that is learned about it, the more mysterious it becomes.

As for the schooner itself, it was declared to be an unsalvageable menace to navigation and was dynamited several weeks after the stranding. The stern section was never seen again, but the bow washed ashore on Ocracoke Island the following summer. It remained there until 1955, when hurricane Ione, which played another role in the Legend of the Bermuda Triangle, swept it back to sea. Remnants later washed ashore and may still be seen in various shops in Hatteras as tourist attractions. The bell and lights from the vessel were returned to Bath, Maine, where they were kept by the town's most famous resident, Carroll A. Deering.

13

April 1925

Raifuku Maru

"It's like a dagger! Come quick," the frantic voice pleaded over the wireless. "Please come, we cannot escape." Then the cries from the Raifuku Maru* faded away into the stillness of the tranquil sea. Other ships in the Bermuda Triangle were puzzled as to why a ship would send such a message on so calm a day. Nothing has ever been heard or seen of the freighter or its crew since that April morning in 1925.*

Dictionary of Disasters at Sea During the Age of Steam:†

The Japanese steamship *Raifuku Maru* left Boston on April 18th, 1925, for Hamburg with a cargo of wheat. Shortly after leaving port the steamship encountered very heavy weather and by the morning of the 19th was in distress. An S.O.S. call was sent out which was picked up by the White Star liner *Homeric,* 34,356 tons, Capt. Roberts, 70 miles distant. Shortly afterwards another message was received stating that all lifeboats had been smashed. A last message in broken English, "Now very danger. Come quick," came just before the *Homeric* sighted the derelict. The liner drove through the mountainous seas at a speed of 20 knots to the spot indicated, lat.

---

* The ship's name is usually misspelled *Raiuike Maru* in the Legend.

† Charles Hocking compiled his *Dictionary of Disasters* . . . from the files of Lloyd's Register of Shipping, London, which published the book.

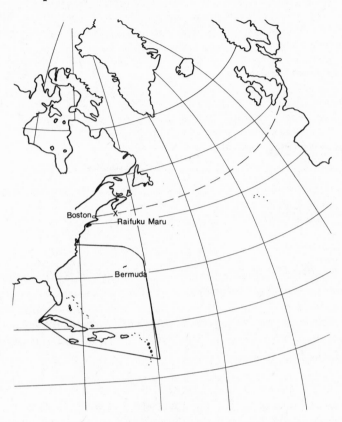

The *Raifuku Maru*

41° 43′N., long. 61° 39′W. [400 miles directly east of Boston, and 700 miles north of Bermuda], to find the *Raifuku Maru* with a list of 30 degrees and quite unmanageable. Approaching as near as she dared the liner stood by in the hope of picking up survivors, but none could survive in such a sea, and all 48 of the crew were drowned.

14

December 1925

Cotopaxi

In 1925 the cargo ship Cotopaxi *disappeared on a voyage from Charleston to Havana.*

Although the *Cotopaxi* is frequently mentioned in the Legend, no information other than its route and the year it vanished has ever been given.

Lloyd's Weekly Casualty Reports. December 11, 1925, p. 355, Overdue Vessels: COTOPAXI. Jacksonville, Dec. 1. Steamer *Cotopaxi,* which left Charleston on Nov. 29 for Havana, with coal, reported to-day that she had water in the hold and was listing badly, but did not send out a distress call.

Lloyd's Weekly Casualty Reports. December 18, 1925, p. 396, Overdue Vessels: COTOPAXI. London, Dec. 9. The following information, dated Dec. 8, has been received: Radio efforts [to] locate steamer *Cotopaxi* and [the] cutter search [are] unavailing.

Lloyd's Register. Wreck Returns. 1925–1926:
Cotopaxi, 2351 gross tons, U.S. Registry. Steel, screw. Charleston, S.C. to Havana. Cargo: coal. Left Charleston November 29, 1925. In wireless communication December 1 and not since heard of.

The dates in the information from Lloyd's provide a clue to the reasons for the ship's troubles.

New York Times, December 2, 1925, p. 17:
JACKSONVILLE, FLA., Dec. 1 (AP). While the west coast [of Florida] was still in the grip of a receding storm tonight, on the east coast storm warnings had been hauled down and the work of repairing the damage was started. . . .

The tempest temporarily paralyzed tropical shipping, but only one ship sent out a call for assistance. The Munson steamer *Red Bird,* bound for Havana, ran into trouble in the high seas . . . and dropped anchor to await an opportunity to enter Miami's harbor.

Three planes were swept out to sea at Daytona Beach but no one was injured in the mishap. . . .

The storm was described by Weather Bureau observers as "phenomenal."

By the next day the gale, which caused heavy damage along the southern Atlantic seaboard, swept into New York with a velocity that at times reached 65 miles an hour.

Although the *Cotopaxi* was not mentioned in the newspapers, it was at sea in the path of the gale that forced many ships to seek refuge and caused massive damage to harbors and cities.

15

March 1926

Suduffco

The freighter Suduffco *sailed south from New Jersey and vanished in the Bermuda Triangle. At the end of a lengthy search a company officer said that the ship might as well have been swallowed by a giant sea monster.*

Like the *Cotopaxi*, the *Suduffco* is usually included in the Legend of the Bermuda Triangle, but details are seldom given.

New York Times, April 8, 1926, p. 2:

The Transmarine Corporation of Port Newark, N.J., announced yesterday that it had requested the Navy Department to search for its freighter *Suduffco*. Officials of the company fear for the safety of the freighter.

The *Suduffco* sailed from Port Newark for Los Angeles on March 13. She carried a crew of twenty-nine and a mixed cargo of 4,000 tons, including a large shipment of steel pipe. She was due at the Panama Canal on March 22 or 23, but since she sailed no word has been heard from her.

The *Suduffco* was proceeding down the coast at a time when the coast was swept by storms.

Despite a month-long search, no trace of the *Suduffco* was ever found. The captain of the Cunard liner *Aquitania,* which was approaching New York as the *Suduffco* was leaving, reported that the voyage had been made in the "worst seas I have ever known," and that gales like tropical cyclones had held the ship back.

16

October 1931

~~~~~~

Stavenger

In October 1931 the Stavenger, *a Norwegian vessel with forty-three on board, vanished near Cat Island in the Bahamas.*

The loss of a ship with forty-three men on board is not likely to be overlooked, yet the best sources of shipping information are not able to verify the disappearance.

There was no information on the *Stavenger* in the *New York Times,* the London *Times,* or Hocking's *Dictionary of Disasters at Sea.* Lloyd's has no information on it, nor was there anything in the *Nassau Guardian.*

In response to a query from me, the Norwegian Maritime Museum in Oslo wrote:

As to the disappearance of a Norwegian ship named *Stavenger* (*Stavanger?*)* no traces have been found in the official list of Norwegian ships lost at sea 1931.

We have also checked the weekly lists of movements of Norwegian vessels October and November 1931 without result. . . .

---

* The name of the ship is apparently slightly misspelled in the Legend, although the minor variation would make no difference in finding information on it. One of Norway's largest cities is Stavanger.

Of the ships named *Stavanger* and registered in *The Norwegian Veritas* 1931, . . . none . . . are struck off the list in 1932 or 1933. It seems there must be a mistake some place, either of the name or the year.

The Norwegian Director General of Shipping and Navigation also responded:

We regret not to be able to find any ship with that name. . . . The only ship with a similar name—S/S *Stavanger* with signal letters L D T N—was registered in 1925. As this ship—however—was totally wrecked in 1957 it cannot be the same ship.

There were several weather disturbances in the Bahamas at the time. The *Nassau Guardian* of October 14 told of a "tropical disturbance of small diameter and moderate intensity . . . about 100 miles east or east-southeast of Nassau . . . accompanied by a very strong wind . . . [of] forty miles an hour." Cat Island is approximately 125 miles east-southeast of Nassau.

On October 21 the *Guardian* reported "a distinctly rising wind that was blowing quite a gale."

It could be that a ship named *Stavanger* encountered problems during one of these disturbances and that incomplete reports or incomplete research led later writers to assume that it had sunk.

It does not appear that a ship named either *Stavenger* or *Stavanger* sank anywhere during the early 1930s.

April 1932

John and Mary

> *In April 1932 the Greek schooner* Embircos *found the two-masted* John and Mary, *of New York registry, abandoned fifty miles south of Bermuda.*

New York Maritime Register, March 9, 1932, p. 15:

John & Mary (Fishing schooner). Motor [vessel] *Tide Water Associated* which left NY March 6 for Las Piedras [Venezuela] picked up the crew of schr. *John and Mary* of New York in lat. 38 58 N, lon. 69 50 W [point A on map].*

New York Maritime Register, April 27, 1932, p. 9:

John & Mary (Br aux sc)—New York, Apr. 19.—Stmr [steamer] *West Quechee* reports by radio that on April 16, while in lat. 31 29, lon. 63 29 [point C on map], boarded the *John & Mary,* auxiliary two-master schr of New York, which was abandoned on March 8 [at point A on map]; the derelict's hull was found in good condition but engine was damaged by explosion.

An explosion in the engine or engine room caused the abandonment 600 miles northwest of Bermuda and 270

---

* At least one previous account reported the rescue but erroneously called the vessel the *Tidewater* and gave the position as 36°58′N, 69°50′W, which is approximately 150 miles south of the correct position.

The *John and Mary*. A, abandoned March 8; B, sighted by the *Embircos?*; C, boarded by the *West Quechee*.

miles east of Cape May, New Jersey. Thirty-nine days later, when the vessel was sighted by the *West Quechee*, it had drifted to a position approximately 100 miles southeast of Bermuda, an example of how derelicts can drift toward the Bermuda Triangle from other areas.

I was not able to find any information about the discovery

of the *John and Mary* by the *Embircos,* which supposedly took place fifty miles south of Bermuda (point B on map).

Although it is not stated in the *Maritime Register,* it appears that the *West Quechee* towed the derelict to port for repairs. According to *Merchant Vessels of the United States,* the *John and Mary* then foundered off Cape May on July 9 of the same year. All six persons on board were rescued.

18

August 1935

La Dahama

A ghost ship haunted the sea near Bermuda in 1935. The La Dahama, masts trailing overboard and skylights smashed, rested on the gentle swells as the men of the Aztec boarded and inspected her. There seemed to be no reason for her abandonment, as plenty of food and water was on board, and both lifeboats were intact. Taking charge of the captain's log, the men returned to the Aztec and sailed on to England, where they related the mystery of the derelict. To their amazement, they learned that the Rex, an Italian liner, had rescued the crew of La Dahama several days before the Aztec had discovered her, and then all on board the Rex had watched the La Dahama plunge into the sea! It was a ghost ship that the Aztec had found, risen from a watery grave.

New York Times, August 28, 1935, p. 1:
The rescue of the crew of five men from the sinking auxiliary schooner yacht *La Dahama* of Philadelphia by the Italian liner *Rex* was told yesterday in a radio message from Staff Captain Alberto Ottino. . . .

"Noon today, Lat. 37.57 N., Long. 51.55 W., we met American yacht *La Dahama* of Philadelphia, sixteen tons, ownership Welsh, flying distress signal with five men aboard. Crew taken off. Yacht abandoned in sinking condition because of water seeping through." (Signed) "Ottino."

The position given approximately is 1,037 miles southeast of the Ambrose channel Lightship and right on the track of vessels bound from New York for the Mediterranean.

New York Times, August 30, 1935, p. 19:

Five men who were rescued last Tuesday from the foundering schooner *La Dahama* of Philadelphia, were landed in New York yesterday by the Italian liner *Rex,* which made the rescue.

All of the men were in good health and not affected by the five-day storm which gradually tore the sixteen-ton vessel to pieces, flooding her and preventing the men on board from sleeping or eating anything except canned fruit and other cold stores.

The men were Albert R. G. Welsh, Philadelphia sportsman and owner of *La Dahama;* Captain Lars M. Larsen, master; and three seamen. . . .

When the *Rex* sighted the schooner's distress signals flying shortly before noon on Tuesday the sea was calm and the schooner was not in immediate danger, although Captain Larsen said she would not have survived another blow. If the *Rex* had not come along the schooner would have gone down in another two days, and the five men, exhausted by constant manning the pumps and inadequate food, would have had to put out in a small dinghy. . . .

On Aug. 18 they cleared Bermuda and had several days of fairly good sailing. Then they ran into a violent storm from the southwest. The wind ripped the foresail away. Then both masts went, and the ship was helpless as her auxiliary engine had already been disabled. Water seeped in rapidly for the next four days.

Lookouts on the *Rex* sighted *La Dahama* before the weary men knew that rescue had arrived. . . . An eighteen-man crew put out in a motor lifeboat and took off the schooner's men, their personal effects, and as much of the vessel's navigating equipment as possible. The rescue took only 50 minutes.

The *La Dahama*

London *Times,* September 10, 1935, p. 9:

RESCUE IN ATLANTIC
MYSTERY OF ABANDONED YACHT SOLVED

While the captain and the chief officer of the Elders and Fyffe ship *Aztec* were relating at Avonmouth yesterday the discovery by them in the Atlantic of an abandoned yacht, information was received in London that the owner and a crew of five from the yacht had been picked up on August 27 by the Italian liner *Rex.* . . .

On September 1 the abandoned yacht was discovered by the British ship *Aztec* about 700 miles north-east of Bermuda. She was boarded by a party from the *Aztec,* who found the two masts trailing overboard and the skylights smashed. There was plenty of food and water and both lifeboats were intact, but there was nothing to show when or how the crew had abandoned her. Captain Carden, of the British ship, took charge of the log-book, the last entry in which was dated August 23, reading, "Wind south-east; carrying full sail; 8AM, passed British steamer *Thurland Castle.*" The previous day's entry recorded a split foresail.

The *Rex* discovered the schooner about 875 miles northeast of Bermuda. The *Aztec* found her five days later about 700 miles northeast of Bermuda. Neither location could be considered as being in the Bermuda Triangle, or even anywhere near it.

The passengers on the *Rex* did not watch the yacht sink, they left it in a "sinking condition" in a calm sea. The captain said the boat would not float more than two days, but the water was so still that it lasted at least five days, when it was discovered by the *Aztec*. It was not then a resurrected ship, but merely a derelict about to sink.

19

February 1940

〰〰〰〰〰〰〰〰〰〰〰〰〰〰〰〰〰〰〰〰〰〰〰〰〰〰〰〰〰〰

Gloria Colita

The schooner *Gloria Colita, of St. Vincent, British West Indies, was found mysteriously abandoned 200 miles south of Mobile in the Gulf of Mexico. There was no apparent reason for the desertion as the seas were calm and everything was in order.*

Times-Picayune (New Orleans), Monday, February 5, 1940, p. 1:

A 125-foot schooner, adrift, crippled, and unmanned in the Gulf of Mexico under unexplained circumstances, was taken in tow about 150 miles south of Mobile, Ala., Sunday by the Coast Guard cutter, *Cartigan.*

The schooner, the *Gloria Colita* of St. Vincent, British West Indies, had sailed from Mobile January 21 with a cargo of lumber for Guantanamo, Cuba, the Coast Guard said.*

What befell the schooner and her crew since then remained just as much a mystery when the *Cartigan* reached her at 9:45 A.M. Sunday as when the derelict was first reported Saturday afternoon by a passing steamer. . . .

The *Cartigan* reported that the foresail on the *Gloria Colita* was

---

* Previous accounts of this incident have misspelled the names of the boats, calling them the *Gloria Colite* and the *Cardigan.*

The *Gloria Colita*

still set but torn, that her other sails were down, the deck a mass of wreckage and the steering gear disabled. . . .

The Coast Guard said it was possible that the schooner had been buffeted by a storm, but could advance no explanation for the absence of the crew.

Times-Picayune, Tuesday, February 6, 1940, p. 1:

Planes and ships of the Coast Guard searched a wide area during the day for the crew of the waterlogged mystery schooner *Gloria*

Colita, but the blue waters of the Gulf of Mexico Monday night still concealed the fate of the nine men. . . .

The Coast Guard, towing the *Gloria Colita* to Mobile, reported a skiff had been found upside down in the Gulf, but there was no definite indication it had belonged to the ill-fated schooner.

With planes from its Biloxi station flying over the area by day and three ships, the *Triton, Tampa,* and *Boutwell,* searching the waters, the Coast Guard hoped to find survivors if they are adrift in a small boat or on wreckage in the Gulf. The chances, however, are slim that any are still alive. . . .

Her rigging in tatters and her deck awash, the *Colita* was sighted Saturday afternoon by a passing vessel. . . . There was no one aboard and the lifeboat was gone, Chief Boatswain Sven Halvorsen, commanding the *Cartigan,* radioed. "From the general condition of the vessel, the deck cargo of lumber shifted and parted the main rigging," he said. . . . "The ship has taken a severe punishment."

Times-Picayune, Wednesday, February 7, 1940, p. 1:

The battered, unmanned schooner *Gloria Colita,* found in the Gulf of Mexico Saturday, was towed to port at Mobile, Ala., Tuesday night as officials planned a hearing for today to determine what befell ship and crew. . . .

When the *Gloria Colita* sailed from Mobile she was laden with a cargo of lumber for Guantanamo, Cuba. For the next two days, according to reports of the weather bureau in New Orleans, storm warnings were up in the area through which she should have sailed.

The Coast Guard reported Tuesday night that the schooner's three masts were still standing when she was picked up, but that the rigging was in shreds and her rudder and steering apparatus shattered. The deck cargo of lumber was missing, but that in the hold was intact. The hold was nearly filled with water, it was added. . . .

Tuesday . . . Coast Guard boats scoured the Gulf in an area thought likely to yield some clue as to the fate of the missing crew.

Times-Picayune, Thursday, February 8, 1940, p. 1:

MOBILE, ALA., Feb. 7 [AP]. Captain Halvorsen discounted the belief that the hold of the schooner would be found to contain bodies of her crewmen. He expressed the opinion that "they were swept overboard."

At the same time, the United States weather bureau here pointed out that its maps indicate a severe disturbance in the Gulf a few days after the *Gloria* left here on January 21. Storm warnings were ordered up on the 22nd from Port Eads, La., to Valparaiso, Fla., and on the 23rd another storm was located in the Gulf just south of Apalachicola, Fla.

Times-Picayune, Sunday, February 11, 1940, p. 20:

GULFPORT, MISS., Feb. 10. After sighting the vessel at daybreak, volunteers from the *Cartigan* boarded her, only to find that she had neither captain nor crew and that the lumber cargo on deck was swishing about with the swaying of the waterlogged derelict. . . . Captain Halvorsen said he had no doubt that the vessel's crew was swept overboard and were drowned during the storm of January 22 and 23.

20

November, December 1941

Proteus, Nereus

The story of the Cyclops *continued many years later when two of her sister ships vanished without a trace while on very nearly the same route as their older sister. The* Proteus *left the Virgin Islands late in November 1941, followed several weeks later by the* Nereus. *Both were bound for Norfolk. Had it not been for Pearl Harbor, the double disappearance would probably have been as big a story as the loss of the* Cyclops *a quarter-century before.*

Although the United States was not then fighting Germany, a check of naval records after the war revealed that there were only a few German vessels in the area at the time, and that none had reported having sunk any such ships.

The following information is from the U.S. Navy's *Dictionary of American Naval Fighting Ships* and Charles Hocking's *Dictionary of Disasters at Sea During the Age of Steam.*

The Newport News Ship Building and Dry Dock Company began construction of the 522-foot colliers in 1911, and they were commissioned in 1913. They transported coal, oil, men, and stores to Navy ships until they were decommissioned in the early 1920s. Both remained inactive in Norfolk until they were struck from the Navy List in December 1940 and sold to Saguenay Terminals, Limited, of Ottawa, to be used for hauling bauxite from the Caribbean to the United States and Canada. Bauxite is the main source of aluminum, which is essential to the aircraft industry.

The *Proteus* left St. Thomas, Virgin Islands, on November 23, 1941, headed for Portland, Maine. It never arrived, and no trace was ever found. Subsequent German reports show that it was probably a war casualty on November 25.

The *Nereus* left St. Thomas for the same destination on December 10, 1941, and also was lost without a trace. The Navy assumed that it had been torpedoed by a German U-boat.

21

October 1944

Rubicon

On October 22, 1944, a Navy blimp reported a derelict off the coast of Florida. Several hours later, two Coast Guard cutters were on the scene and found that the only living creature aboard was a dog. The ship, the Rubicon, *was in excellent condition except for a missing lifeboat and a broken hawser hanging over the bow. The personal effects of the crew were still on board and there was no clue as to why no one was on the ship. It appeared to be a case of a new* Mary Celeste *just off the Florida coast.*

New York Times, October 23, 1944, p. 21:

ONLY DOG IS FOUND ON A DRIFTING SHIP

Cuban Cargo Craft, Floating Off Florida,
Recalls Story of the *Marie Celeste* [sic]

HER LIFE BOATS ARE GONE

Vessel is Towed into Port—Some Think
Hurricane May Have Carried Her to Sea

MIAMI, Fla., Oct. 22 [UP]. A maritime mystery reminiscent of that which for a long time involved the *Marie Celeste* [sic] is recalled in the finding of a Cuban cargo ship adrift in the Gulf Stream with a dog the only living thing aboard.

Possibly a victim of the Caribbean hurricane, the vessel was sighted yesterday by a Navy blimp which notified the Coast Guard here. Two boats were sent from Miami to investigate, and found that she was the *Rubicon,* of about ninety gross tons.

Her lifeboats were gone, but the personal effects of the crew were still aboard. A broken hawser* was hanging over her bow. Early reports did not indicate whether the lifeboat moorings had been cut, broken or slipped.

The investigating boats reported by radio while towing the *Rubicon* . . . that she was apparently in excellent condition. . . .

No indication of the fate of the vessel's crew was found in a study of the ship's log, where the last entry was dated September 26, when she put into Havana Harbor. The *Rubicon* had apparently been trading along the Cuban coast before that time.

It was believed by some that any crew members stationed aboard had gone ashore when the hurricane winds hit Havana, leaving the dog, and that the ship's moorings gave way.

Although the headlines and the first paragraph are attention-grabbers, the remainder of the article, particularly the last paragraph, seems to clear up any mystery.

There were no later articles to confirm or deny that the ship was set adrift by the hurricane. This lack of follow-up contributed somewhat to the *Rubicon*'s being listed as a mystery.

---

* A hawser is the rope or cable used to moor a ship to the dock.

22

December 1945

~~~~~~

Flight 19

At 2:10 PM, *December 5, 1945, five Avenger torpedo bombers roared down the runway of the Fort Lauderdale Naval Air Station and winged their way into the greatest aviation mystery of all time, an event that was later to be called the Mary Celeste of the sky. Flight 19 was scheduled for a routine patrol—160 miles straight east, north 40 miles, then 120 miles directly back to base. Total time was estimated to be two hours. Avengers normally carried a crew of three, counting the pilot, but one man failed to show that day. Perhaps it was coincidence, possibly it was due to a premonition, but in any case it saved his life. The other fourteen crewmen were not to return.*

According to later testimony each plane had been carefully preflighted and held a full load of fuel. All equipment, engines, compasses, and instruments were in good working order. Extensive radio gear was in each plane, including ten communication channels and homing devices which showed the heading to take to return to base. Each plane carried a self-inflating life raft and each man wore a Mae West life jacket. The pilots and crewmen were all experienced. The weather was excellent.

The first message from the patrol came at 3:45, the time they were to have requested landing instructions. Instead, they sent a strange message.

"Control tower, this is an emergency," the worried voice said. "We seem to be off course. We cannot see land . . . repeat . . . we cannot see land."

"What is your position?" the tower asked.

"We're not sure of our position," replied the patrol leader. "We can't be sure of where we are. We seem to be lost."

How could that be? the tower operators asked each other. Flight conditions were ideal.

"Head due west," came the orders from the tower.

There was a long silence. Then the patrol leader came in, alarm evident in his voice. "We don't know which way is west. Everything is wrong . . . strange . . . we can't be sure of any direction. Even the ocean doesn't look as it should!"

The tower operators were puzzled. Even if a magnetic storm had affected all the compasses the pilots still should have been able to find their way home. By flying directly toward the sun, which was then approaching the horizon, they would have crossed the coast very near the base. From the messages it appeared that the sun was invisible to them.

Time passed as the tower men heard the pilots talking to each other. They were confused and scared but they were keeping together.

Shortly after 4:00 the leader, obviously panicked, abruptly turned the flight command over to one of the other pilots, indicating that a very grave situation existed.

At 4:25 the new leader called the tower. "We're not certain where we are. We must be about 225 miles northeast of base . . . it looks like we are . . ."

Then . . . silence.

A giant Martin Mariner flying boat with a crew of thirteen immediately took off for Flight 19's last estimated position. Equipped with full survival and rescue gear, the plane was able to land on the roughest of seas. The tower called the Avengers to let them know help was on the way, but received no reply.

The Mariner sent several routine radio reports indicating that it was approaching the position of the five Avengers but could not yet see anything. Then, an ominous silence pervaded the tower as the controllers waited for further messages from the rescue plane. None ever came.

The controllers tried frantically to re-establish contact but it was fruitless. The rescue plane had gone the same route as those it was supposed to rescue.

Other planes were sent, ships were dispatched, and a general alarm was raised. The positions of the patrol and the Mariner were thoroughly searched but nothing was found except the calm, empty sea.

At 7:04 PM a Miami tower operator intercepted a faint message from far, far away. "FT . . . FT . . ." Those were the call letters of Flight 19, which no one else would have been using. Yet it was two hours after the flight must have run out of fuel.

Coast Guard and Navy vessels searched throughout the night, but no signal flares shattered the still, dark scene. The portable radio units designed to transmit automatically upon contact with water were never heard.

The next day a vast search began in earnest. Three hundred planes and twenty-one ships criss-crossed the sea and sky; land parties searched the Florida coastline, the Keys, and the Bahamas, but not a clue was uncovered from the sea or from any beach, jungle, or mountain. The search continued for weeks; all areas were checked again and again. Although the hope of finding survivors faded, searchers continued looking for some trace of the aircraft that might hint at their fate. Nothing was ever found.

Military experts were completely baffled. Six airplanes and twenty-seven men—how could they possibly have vanished in such a small area?

If they had run out of fuel the Avengers would have floated at least long enough to enable the crew to launch the self-inflating rafts. The men were well trained in sea survival procedures, and the equipment was capable of keeping them alive for many days in the open sea. But running out of fuel would not explain the confusion earlier in the flight, nor would it explain the strange messages. It would not account for the loss of the Mariner.

Each plane was well equipped with radio gear. Why was there no SOS, either before or after they were down? Why didn't the Mariner send one?

One suggestion was that the winds might have blown Flight 19 off course. Had a wind shift occurred they might have been driven far to the south. But then they would have been over the myriad islands of the West Indies and always within sight of land, or over the Great Bahama Bank, a vast shallow area where the airplanes would have been found even had they sunk.

If by some quirk of fate there had been a five-plane midair collision, debris would have covered a wide area and would surely have been seen.

A waterspout could not have been the cause, as they are easily seen and avoided.

Why did the Mariner vanish as it approached the lost patrol's last position? One ship observed an explosion in the air at 7:50 and found an oil slick, but that was more than three hours after the Mariner's disappearance.

The members of the Naval Board of Inquiry, after an extensive investigation, concluded that they "were not able to even venture a good guess as to what had happened." Another officer said, "They vanished as completely as if they'd flown to Mars. We don't know what the hell's going on out there." A Navy bulletin issued at the end of the search required all ships and airplanes to remain on the alert for clues to the disappearance. That order has never been rescinded; it is still in effect today!

There are many more questions that should be raised. Why were all the compasses erratic? Did the same force that threw them off also silence the radios? Did the Mariner disappear when it entered the same zone as the Avengers? Why did the sea seem strange and why was the sun invisible? Why was there no debris, no oil slick, not even a telltale pack of sharks? It is inconceivable that six airplanes and twenty-seven men could vanish and fail to leave a trace behind. But vanish they did. In the Bermuda Triangle.

The Navy investigation of the incident took several months, and the subsequent report* was more than 400 pages long. I have thoroughly examined the report many times and have concluded that the key to understanding what occurred lies in the radio communications with the pilots. These messages do not appear together in the report but are scattered throughout—some are in the testimony of witnesses while others are in the logs of the communication stations. I have arranged them in order as they occurred that day, along with pertinent testimony and various facts and opinions of the Board.

To make the account more readable, several changes have been made.

The time of day, given some places in the report as Eastern Standard Time on the 24-hour clock and in other places as Greenwich Mean Time, has been converted in every instance to Eastern Standard Time on the 12-hour clock.

The names of the various stations and planes have been standardized. For example, Port Everglades Radio, also referred to in the report as Air Sea Rescue Task Unit Number 4, ASRTU#4, and NHA-3, is always shown here as Port Everglades. Similarly, plane TBM-3, BuNo. 23307, Squadron

---

* *Board of Investigation into five missing TBM airplanes and one PBM airplane convened by Naval Air Advanced Training Command, NAS Jacksonville, Florida, 7 December 1945, and related correspondence.* Washington, D.C.: United States Navy, 1946.

Number FT-28, is shortened in this account to its call sign, FT-28.

The "cast" of the drama of Flight 19, and the radio stations and bases that played a part, are as follows:

LT. CHARLES C. TAYLOR, a flight instructor and the leader of Flight 19. FT-28 was the call sign of his plane.

CAPT. EDWARD J. POWERS, JR., a Marine student pilot undergoing advanced navigation training in Flight 19. FT-36 was his airplane.

ENSIGN JOSEPH T. BOSSI, student pilot, flew FT-3 as a part of Flight 19. (There were two other students on the flight.)

LT. ROBERT F. COX, a senior flight instructor at Fort Lauderdale Naval Air Station, was in radio contact with Flight 19 for a short time. He flew FT-74.

LT. WALTER G. JEFFREY, the pilot of Training 49, the Martin Mariner search plane that disappeared.

LT. GERALD E. BAMMERLIN, the pilot of Training 32, the search plane that left Banana River Naval Air Station the same time as Training 49.

Fort Lauderdale Naval Air Station (NAS), 20 miles north of Miami, the departure and intended returning point of Flight 19.

Port Everglades, the Air Sea Rescue Task Unit at Fort Lauderdale.

Dinner Key, a seaplane base at Miami.

Banana River Naval Air Station, now Patrick Air Force Base, near Cape Kennedy.

Navy Board of Inquiry Report

The Loss of Flight 19

Fact 1: [The five TBMs] departed at approximately 2:10 PM, 5 December 1945, as Flight 19 on an authorized navigation training flight from U.S. Naval Air Station, Fort Lauderdale, Florida.

Flight 19: The proposed route

Fact 2: Flight 19 [was assigned] navigation problem No. 1 which is as follows: (1) . . . fly 091 degrees [east] distance 56 miles to Hens and Chickens Shoals to conduct low level bombing [then] continue on course 091 degrees for 67 miles, (2) fly course 346 degrees [north] distance 73 miles and (3) fly course 241 degrees [west-southwest], distance 120 miles, then returning to . . . Fort Lauderdale.

Fact 16: Charles Carroll Taylor, Lieutenant, U.S. Naval Reserve . . . was the authorized and assigned instructor in charge of Flight 19.

Facts 4–7: Edward Joseph Powers, Jr., . . . George William Stivers, . . . Forest James Gerber [and] Joseph Tipton Bossi [were the four other pilots].

Facts 8–12: [Each plane except Gerber's carried three men, counting the pilot. Gerber was one man short.]

Fact 18: . . . Stivers, . . . Powers, . . . Gerber [and] Bossi . . . were naval aviators undergoing instruction in VTB Type Advanced Training.

Fact 19: [Eight of the nine crewmembers] were undergoing Advanced Combat Aircrew Training in VTB type aircraft.

All the pilots, except Taylor, and all the crewmen, except one, were students in training.

Testimony of Lt. Robert F. Cox, flight instructor Fort Lauderdale NAS: I was flying around the field at approximately 3:40 PM. . . . I heard some planes or boats. One man was transmitting on 4805 [the channel used by training flights] to "Powers." That is the word he used and he didn't give any recognition. The party calling asked "Powers" what his compass read a number of times and finally said, "I don't know where we are. We must have got lost after that last turn."

During this time, at approximately 3:45 PM, I called Operation Radio, Fort Lauderdale, and notified them that either a boat or some planes were lost. They Rogered my message.

Also, I called, "This is FT-74, plane or boat calling 'Powers,' please identify yourself so someone can help you."

I received no answer. Later he called and asked if anyone had any suggestions. I called again, giving my identification as FT-74, and he answered, giving his as MT-28.

I said, "MT-28 this is FT-74, what is your trouble?" MT-28 came back, "Both my compasses are out and I am trying to find Fort Lauderdale, Florida. I am over land, but it's broken. I'm sure I'm in the Keys, but I don't know how far down and I don't know how to get to Fort Lauderdale."

I said, "MT-28, this is FT-74, put the sun on your port wing if you are in the Keys and fly up the coast until you get to Miami, then Fort Lauderdale is 20 miles further, your first port after Miami. The air station is directly on your left from the port. What is your present altitude? I will fly south and meet you."

MT-28 replied, "I know where I am now. I'm at 2300 feet. Don't come after me."

I called, "MT-28, Roger, you're at 2300. I'm coming to meet you anyhow."

I then received a call from Fort Lauderdale asking if it was FT-28 or MT-28, and after calling MT-28 again I learned that it was FT-28 and relayed this message to Fort Lauderdale.

I then received a message from FT-28, "Can you have Miami or someone turn on their radar gear and pick us up? We don't seem to be getting far. We were out on a navigation hop and on the second leg I thought they were going wrong so I took over and was flying them back to the right position, but I'm sure now that neither one of my compasses are working."

I called FT-28, "You can't expect to get here in ten minutes. You have a 30 to 35 knot head or cross wind. Turn on your emergency IFF gear [to make the plane's image brighter on a radar screen], or do you have it?"

He replied that he didn't. I then told him to turn on his ZBX gear [tells which direction to head to return to base], but received no comment. I repeated and still received no answer. Fort Lauderdale and Port Everglades also tried to get him to turn it on. I don't know whether they got an answer or not. Fort Lauderdale suggested I tell FT-28 to have one of his wingmen take over the lead and I did this. I received no direct answer, but heard some transmission about radar or something.

I then called FT-28, "Your transmissions are fading. Something is wrong. What is your altitude?"

He replied, "I'm at 4500 feet."

At this point my MHF (ATC transmitter) went out and I had no power for transmission on that frequency. The frequency we had been using was 4805 kilocycles, so I tried to contact him on all nine channels of VHF and finally got Navy Lauderdale on No. 7. As his transmissions were fading he must have been going north. I believe at the time of his first transmissions he was either over the Biminis or the Bahamas. I was about forty miles below Fort Lauderdale and couldn't hear him any longer. . . . After that I came in and landed. . . .

Question: In what direction were you flying during the period when FT-28 transmissions became progressively weaker?

Cox: South and slightly southwest.

Question: What was your approximate geographical position when the signals from FT-28 faded out altogether?

Cox: I was approximately twenty-five miles south of Miami. . . .

Question: Did you observe the state of the sea?

Cox: Yes, sir. The sea was very rough. It was covered with white caps and long white streamers. The visibility was very good in all directions, except directly west.

After Cox's transmitter failed Port Everglades was able to establish contact with Taylor.

4:25. Port Everglades to Taylor: Radio check, can you read us?

4:25. Affirmative. We have just passed over small island. We have no other land in sight.

Testimony of Commander Richard Baxter, Assistant Operations Officer, District Coast Guard Office, Seventh Naval District, Miami: In my estimation [the planes] were near Walker Cay [40 miles north of Grand Bahama Island] when they thought they were over the Keys.

4:26. Taylor: Am at angles 3.5 [altitude 3500 feet]. Have on emergency IFF. Does anyone in the area have a radar screen that could pick us up?

4:26. Port Everglades to Taylor: Roger. Stand by.

4:28. Port Everglades to Taylor: Suggest you have another plane in your flight with a good compass take over the lead and guide you back to the mainland.

Taylor: Roger.

Port Everglades: We were able to pick up particles of messages between Flight Leader (FT-28) and other planes in the flight concerning their estimated position and compasses, however as best we could tell, due to poor reception, no other plane ever assumed the lead.

4:31. Taylor to Port Everglades: One of the planes in the flight thinks if we went 270° [west] we could hit land.

4:39. Port Everglades to Fort Lauderdale via phone: In as much as FT-74 [Cox] has run out of communication with FT-28 [Taylor] by proceeding south, I think that this flight is lost somewhere over the Bahama Bank and suggest that the Lauderdale Ready Plane be dispatched guarding 4805 Kcs on a course of 075° [east-northeast] and try to establish communication with FT-28. And if the Ready

Plane can pick up FT-28 better as he proceeds on this course we will be sure that the flight is lost over the Bahamas. Ready Plane could also act as relay on the frequency as it is becoming more difficult to pick up FT-28.

4:45. Taylor to Port Everglades: We are heading 030° [north-northeast] for 45 minutes, then we will fly north to make sure we are not over the Gulf of Mexico.

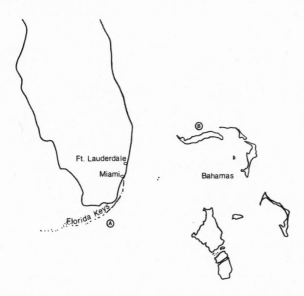

Flight 19: Estimated position about 4:00. *A,* Lt. Taylor's estimate; *B,* the probable position.

4:45. Port Everglades to Dinner Key: Are you able to get a bearing on FT-28?

Dinner Key to Port Everglades: Negative—advise him to send continuously on 4805 Kc, we cannot pick up his IFF.

Testimony of Lt. Commander Donald J. Poole, Flight Officer, NAS, Fort Lauderdale: Port Everglades had contact with FT-28, Lieutenant Taylor, at this time, 4:45 PM, so I immediately notified them to instruct FT-28 to fly 270 degrees [west], also to fly toward the sun. I know this was transmitted because I listened over Operations radio. I do not know that it was ever acknowledged. Port Everglades also instructed FT-28 to change to 3000 kilocycles, Channel 1 [reserved for emergencies] but this was never done by FT-28. I had a pilot in the ready plane warming it up, but was hesitant about sending it out until I had some information as to where to send it.

4:47. Fact 27: The Gulf Sea Frontier and Eastern Frontier HF/DF nets were alerted to obtain all possible bearings on transmissions from FT-28, who was transmitting on 4805 kilocycles.

Opinion 16: Unsatisfactory radio communication on 4805 kilocycles was due to interference from Cuban broadcasting stations, static, the presence of a steady carrier note, and atmospheric conditions during this time.

Opinion 20: Difficulty was experienced in obtaining the HF/DF bearings on the aircraft of Flight 19 . . . because of interference on 4805 kilocycles.

4:49. Port Everglades to Dinner Key: Have you been able to get a bearing on FT-28 yet?

Dinner Key: Negative.

Port Everglades: We request you alert the DF [Direction Finding] Net up the coast and have them attempt to pick up this lost flight. Please let us know if you have any success.

Dinner Key: Wilco.

4:51. Fort Lauderdale to Port Everglades: If possible advise FT-28 to turn on his ZBX [homing device]. (Attempted to relay to FT-28 at 4:52 with no success.)

4:56. Port Everglades to any plane in flight with FT-28: Turn on your ZBX. (No reply.)

Testimony of Lt. Commander Poole: At approximately 5:00 PM I heard two different students unidentified as to plane or person, make the following statements: "If we would just fly west we would get home." The other transmission that I heard was, "Dammit, if we would just fly west we would get home."

5:07. Taylor to planes in flight: Change course to 090° [east] for 10 minutes.

5:09. Unidentified: How long have we gone now? Let's turn and fly east two degrees. We are going too damn far north instead of east. If there is anything we wouldn't see it.

5:09. Fort Lauderdale advised Port Everglades via phone that the Lauderdale Ready Plane was held on the ground and would not go out.

5:11. Unidentified: You didn't get far enough east. How long have we been going east?

5:14. Hello [Port Everglades], this is FT-28, do you read? Over.

5:15. Taylor to Port Everglades: I receive you very weak. We are now flying 270° [west].

Port Everglades: Roger.

5:16. Taylor to Port Everglades: We will fly 270° until we hit the beach or run out of gas.

5:20. Port Everglades to Taylor: If you can change to Yellow Band (3000 Kc) [emergency frequency] please do so and give us a call. (No reply after 3 attempts.)

5:20. Rough Crash Log: Communications with T-28—come in strong and fade—Port Everglades unable to get any messages through to T-28—Fort Lauderdale can hear planes talking to each other—apparently still flying 270°.

5:22. Taylor: When first man gets down to ten gallons of gas we will all land in the water together. Does everyone understand that?

5:24. Taylor to Port Everglades: I receive you very weak. How is the weather over Lauderdale?

Port Everglades: Weather over Lauderdale clear. Over Key West CAVU [ceiling and visibility unlimited]. Over the Bahamas cloudy, rather low ceiling, poor visibility. (No reply.)

5:30. Taylor to planes in flight: Is that a ship on the left? (Unable to read reply.)

5:33. Taylor to Port Everglades: Can you hear me?

Port Everglades: Hear you strength three, modulation good. (No reply.)

5:34. Port Everglades to Taylor: Can you change to 3000 Kcs? (No reply after 3 attempts.)

Testimony of Lt. Samuel M. Hines, Operations and Tower Duty Operator, Fort Lauderdale NAS: There was very much static on 4805 kilocycles from 4:10 until 5:30 at which time, in addition to the static, music from Cuban broadcasting stations interfered with reception. The lost planes from 4:10 until 7:04 PM alternately came in loud and clear and faded beyond audibility. The receiver at Port Everglades was able to receive transmissions which Operations Radio did not hear, and vice versa. . . . Operations Radio [Fort Lauderdale] was unable to get a Roger on any message sent to the planes.

5:50. Taylor to Port Everglades: I can hear you very faintly. My transmission is getting weaker.

5:52. Fort Lauderdale to Port Everglades via phone: At 5:51 all stations along the coast were alerted to be on lookout for FT-28 and his flight.

5:52. Miami to all Air Sea Rescue Stations via teletype: All stations Banana River South light up to greatest extent possible.

5:54. Port Everglades: Did you receive my last transmission? Change to 3000 Kcs.

5:55. Taylor: I cannot change frequency. I must keep my planes intact.

By this time it was completely dark.

5:59. Unidentified: Cannot change to 3000 kilocycles, will stay on 4805 kilocycles.

Fact 28: At approximately 6:00 PM, 5 December 1945, an approximate HF/DF fix was obtained on FT-28 placing FT-28 within a one-hundred-mile radius of 29 degrees, 15 minutes, north, 79 degrees, 00 minutes, west, at 5:50 PM.

The position of Flight 19 had been calculated! It was over the Atlantic Ocean somewhere north of the Bahamas and east of New Smyrna, Florida. At this time the position had only been calculated; it had not yet been transmitted either by teletype to other stations or by radio to the planes. The fix was only approximate but if Taylor could be informed of it he had only to head west and Flight 19 would reach the coast.

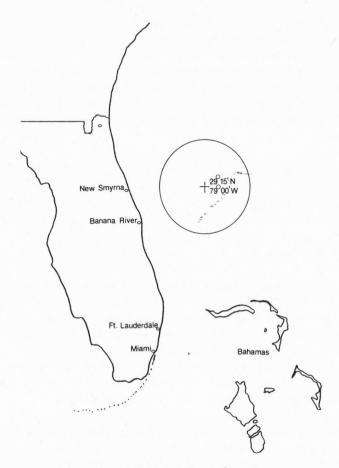

Flight 19: The 5:50 calculated position

6:02. Unidentified: We may have to ditch any minute.

6:03. Taylor to Powers: Do you read?

6:04. Taylor: Do you read?

6:05. Taylor to Powers: This is Taylor—We are over—Don't you think—

6:06. Unknown: Should be able to see a light—

6:07. Port Everglades to Taylor: Do you read me?

6:09. Port Everglades: Do you read me? (Long Count.) [One, two, three, four, five, six, seven, eight, nine, ten.]

Opinion 36: The courses flown by Flight 19 subsequent to 6:07 PM are undetermined.

6:10. The 5:50 HF/DF evaluated position was telephoned to the tower at Fort Lauderdale.

The fix still had not been transmitted either by teletype or by radio.

Opinion 21: The Air Sea Rescue . . . teletype was out of commission south of Banana River during the critical period of the evening.

6:15. Unidentified: Negative—what course are we on— We are over the Gulf. We didn't go far enough east—How long we been on this course— I suggest we fly due east until we run out of gas, we have a better chance of being picked up close to shore—

Opinion 17: The leader of Flight 19 in FT-28 was uncertain as to in which direction lay the Peninsula of Florida and this uncertainty influenced his later decisions.

6:17. Taylor to Powers: What is your course? (No acknowledgment.)
6:21. Miami to Banana River via teletype: Our DF [direction finding equipment] gives fix on flight as 29° N—79°W, which puts them north of original presumed position. Will you alert fields north of you as far as Jacksonville. (This message was not Rogered for.)

Testimony of Commander Claude C. Newman, Officer in Charge, Port Everglades:

Question: Was Port Everglades in communication with any of the lost TBMs when you intercepted the coordinates of the high frequency direction finder fix at 6:21 PM?

Newman: No, sir. We had been out of two-way communication for approximately one hour.

Question: Lacking two-way communications, was there any attempt made to transmit the HF/DF fix to the aircraft in difficulty by means of so-called "blind" transmission?

Newman: No, sir.

Testimony of Commander Richard Baxter, U.S. Coast Guard, Seventh Naval District, Miami:

Question: Which of these [Air Sea Rescue] stations were available and suitable for transmitting the evaluated fix to the TBMs?

Baxter: In my opinion, none of those stations were satisfactory at that time of day on 4805 kilocycles.

6:24. Port Everglades to Banana River via phone: Have all stations . . . attempt to contact FT-28 on 4805 Kc and advise him to maintain course of 270°. This is serious as planes have been lost since 4:21 PM and their gas should be out by 7:30. The TWPL [teletype] System is out north of here. Also alert Dumbos [search planes] in your area.

Fact 30: The 5:50 HF/DF evaluated position was transmitted on the . . . teletype net . . . at approximately 6:36 PM.

Opinion 22: No Air Sea Rescue activities engaged in assisting Flight 19 were in successful communication with the flight after the receipt of the evaluated fix.

Opinion 23: No activity associated with assisting Flight 19 made blind transmissions or radio broadcasts of the 5:50 evaluated position to any aircraft of that flight.

6:37. Unidentified: What course are we on now?

6:43. FT-3 [Bossi] to FT-28 [Taylor]: [Indistinguishable.]

6:44. On 4805 Kcs. Conversation garbled. Could hear FT-3 [Bossi] give his call.

6:44. Port Everglades to Bossi: Good, come in please.

6:48. Port Everglades to Bossi: We are reading you very weak. Come in please.

6:50. FT-3 this is Port Everglades, over.

7:04. FT-3 [Bossi] called FT-28 [Taylor]. No acknowledgment.

Rough Crash Log: Last transmission from the flight (T-3 calling T-28). No answer.

7:46. FT-28, FT-28, this is NSO, NSO, NSO. How do you read me, over. [NSO is Miami Radio.]

7:49. FT-28, FT-28, this is NSO, NSO, NSO. How do you read me, over.

7:54. FT-28, FT-28, this is NSO, NSO, NSO. How do you read me, over.

7:59. FT-28, FT-28, this is NSO, NSO, NSO. How do you read me, over.

Opinion 39: The fuel supply of the aircraft in Flight 19 should have permitted them to remain airborne until approximately 8:00 PM.

8:13. Air Sea Rescue Crash Boat, Fort Lauderdale, on Bimini Patrol, to Port Everglades: We are still trying to contact FT-28 on 4805 Kcs. Negative results.

8:13. Port Everglades: You may secure for tonight.

8:37. Coast Guard Message: All ships area east Florida coast east to 74 degrees be on alert for five planes considered to be down.

9:52. FT-28, FT-28, this—how do you hear me, over. (Heavy interference.)

9:56. FT-28, FT-28, this is—how do you hear me, over. (Heavy interference.)

The Loss of the Search Plane

Testimony of Lt. Charles W. Johnson, Operations Duty Officer, Banana River Naval Air Station: As operations duty officer, I sent planes Training No. 32, and Training No. 49 on the assigned search. . . . I briefed Lt. Bammerlin [pilot of Training No. 32] and Lt. Jeffrey* [Training No. 49] as follows: Bammerlin was to take off and fly direct to 29 degrees north, 79 degrees west [the 5:50 fix of Flight 19], and

---

* A number of accounts of this incident erroneously name either Lt. Harry G. Cone or Lt. Robert F. Cox as the pilot of the missing search plane.

then conduct an expanding square search. Lt. Jeffrey was to take off and fly up the coast to latitude 29 degrees north and then east to longitude 79 degrees west, where he would contact Lt. Bammerlin and then would also conduct an expanding square search. . . . They were to send CW reports every hour . . . [and] were also to guard 4805 kilocycles which was the voice frequency of the TBMs.

Testimony of Radioman Second Class Vernon D. Clary, Communications Department, NAS, Banana River: Just prior to 7:30, Training

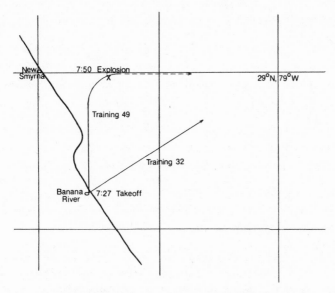

Flight 19: The route of the Martin Mariner

49 sent his departure report. . . . Training 49's first position report was due at 8:30 PM. When he failed to call base at 8:35 PM, the operator attempted to contact him. The operator called him continually for an hour and still failed to get an answer.

Testimony of Commander William J. Lawrence, Commander, U.S. Coast Guard, NAS, Banana River: At 9:12 PM I received information from the Joint Operations Center, Miami, that an explosion was observed by the SS *Gaines Mills* at a position 28 degrees, 59 minutes north, 80 degrees, 25 minutes, west at 7:50 PM. . . . The explosion had been reported as serious and the burst of flames had lasted for several minutes. It was assumed that it could possibly be Training No. 49 with which we were attempting to establish communication on 3000 kilocycles, but had not been able to do so. The explosion was reported to have been observed at 7:50 PM, exactly 23 minutes after Training No. 49 had taken off. The position of the explosion given was 45 nautical miles from Banana River seaplane area.

. . . The master of the SS *Gaines Mills* stated that a plane appeared to catch on fire in the air and quickly hit the water and explode and that an oil slick and debris had been seen by members of the ship's crew. The officer in charge of the New Smyrna surface craft reported later that he did not see any of the debris and that if any had been located the sea was too rough to permit picking it up. . . . No wreckage was seen other than reported by the SS *Gaines Mills* who failed to pick it up because of rough seas.

Testimony of Lt. Gerald E. Bammerlin, pilot of Training 32, NAS, Banana River: After takeoff we [Training 32] proceeded to [the 5:50 fix] and commenced an expanding square search. . . . When we first arrived in the area . . . at about 8:15, the ceiling was approximately eight to twelve hundred feet overcast, occasional showers, estimated wind, west, southwest, 25 to 30 knots, and the air was very turbulent. The sea was very rough [and] whitecaps were visible below. . . .

About 9:45 we were instructed to proceed to a position about 25 miles east of New Smyrna to investigate an explosion reported by a tanker. With the strong headwinds, it required about an hour to arrive on that scene. . . . We commenced an expanding square search at the position of the reported explosion, investigating numerous radar targets and visually observed lights, all of which were proved negative. . . .

The weather and sea conditions 25 miles east of New Smyrna upon our arrival were ceiling estimated 1,000-2,000 feet, wind estimated west, southwest, about 25-30 knots, air very turbulent but, as I recall, we encountered no rain showers. The sea was very rough.

Testimony of Commander William T. Murphy, U.S. Coast Guard, Miami: We received a dispatch from the USS *Solomons:* "Our air search radar showed plane after takeoff from Banana River last night joining with another plane [Training 32], then separating and proceeding on course 045 degrees at exact time the SS *Gaines Mills* sighted flames and in exact spot the above plane disappeared from the radar screen and never reappeared."

Opinion 53: Training 49 [the Martin Mariner] exploded in the sea for reason or reasons unknown in the approximate position of 28 degrees, 59 minutes north, 80 degrees, 25 minutes west.

Many factors contributed to the loss of Flight 19, the most important of which was the failure of Lieutenant Taylor's compasses. The report stated that none of the planes had clocks, but it was not known if the men carried watches. Because of Taylor's frequent questions about the time, it appears that he did not have a watch, and there is no better way to become disoriented than to fly for an unknown amount of time in an unknown direction.

Taylor had transferred to Fort Lauderdale not long before the flight, and his unfamiliarity with the Bahamas could account for his erroneous assumption that he was over the Florida Keys. Taylor could not decide whether he was over the Atlantic Ocean and east of Florida, or over the Gulf of Mexico and west of the peninsula. As a result he changed direction a number of times, led the men back and forth, and progressively moved farther north of the Bahamas.

The second major factor that prevented the flight from being saved was Taylor's refusal to change his radio to the emergency channel. This resulted in his inability to maintain radio contact with the ground stations. He apparently feared that if the planes attempted to change channels but were unable to get together on the new frequency, they would be out of communication and would not be able to "find each other" again on the radio.

Transfer to 3000 kilocycles would have provided a channel undisturbed by interference from other planes and from the Cuban broadcasting stations. It would also have permitted stations closer to the flight to have contacted them, since all radio stations were equipped with the emergency channel, but very few could transmit or receive on the training frequency. The use of the emergency channel would also have permitted the direction-finding stations to have found the flight's position much earlier.

The third factor in the disappearance was the weather. Although it had been "fair" when the planes took off, it rapidly deteriorated. Search planes reported extreme turbulence and unsafe flying conditions, and one ship in the area reported "high winds and tremendous seas." Flight 19 was not a group of experienced veterans touching down on a calm sea in the middle of a sunny afternoon—it was one disoriented instructor and four student pilots attempting to ditch at sea on a dark, stormy night. It was a hopeless situation.

The strange quotations attributed to the pilots by the Legend do not appear in the Navy report, nor does the report suggest that the tower operators were particularly puzzled or alarmed.

The dilemma was not that the men couldn't tell in which direction they were going, but rather that they couldn't decide which direction was the proper one to take. They weren't sure which side of the Florida peninsula they were on, and continually changed direction, usually taking a heading of east or west. Another time they flew north, as Taylor said, to be sure they were not over the Gulf of Mexico.

Although Taylor did allow a plane with a good compass to fly the lead position, he did not panic during the ordeal, nor did he ever turn command of the flight over to one of the students.

It has frequently been said that it is inconceivable that the airplanes could have vanished in such a restricted area. According to the official report, however, they flew around, lost, for more than four hours before finally running out of fuel.

They went down in the Atlantic Ocean somewhere east of the United States and north of the Bahamas. Their travel was not restricted in any way.

The loss of the Martin Mariner is considered mysterious because the plane supposedly vanished within a few minutes after Flight 19 was last heard from. The Legend has the flight's last call coming at 4:25 PM and the Mariner taking off and vanishing shortly thereafter in a clear, sunlit sky as it was about to enter the zone where the Avengers disappeared. The 7:50 explosion, according to the Legend, came about three hours after the plane had disappeared; therefore the explosion and the disappearance of the Mariner could not have been related.

In reality, the Mariner took off at 7:27 PM, and the explosion took place on a dark, stormy night, exactly where the airplane should have been after 23 minutes of flight. It was the only plane missing besides the five Avengers, and officials, who did not hear about the explosion until 9:12, immediately assumed that it was the search plane that had failed to make its scheduled 8:30 position report. Mariners were nicknamed "flying gas tanks" because of the fumes that were often present, and a crewman sneaking a cigarette, or a spark from any source, could have caused the explosion.

In the Legend the impression is given that the Mariner was the only rescue plane on the way to aid the missing flight. It almost seems as if the "menace of the Triangle" were swatting the first intruder away from its domain. Other search planes, in the Legend, took off only after the Mariner had disappeared.

The missing plane was not the only searcher, however. It was not even the first one to take off. The Dinner Key (Miami) Dumbo was in the air at 6:20, but its antenna quickly iced over and it was unable to communicate. Search planes left Vero Beach at 6:45 and Daytona Beach at 7:21. Training 32 and 49 did not leave Banana River until about

7:30. Other planes took off still later, and a number of ships were also sent to the scene.

The Navy Board of Investigation did not profess to be baffled, as the Legend claims. It listed fifty-six "facts" and fifty-six "opinions" based on the fourteen days of testimony. Among them were Opinion 37, that "the aircraft of Flight 19 made forced landings in darkness at sea east of the peninsula of Florida sometime after 7:04 PM," and number 38, that "the state of the sea . . . was rough and unfavorable for a water landing."

One part of the Legend is that upon terminating the search the Navy issued orders for all vessels crossing the area to continue to watch for debris and survivors and that "the order is still in effect to this very day!" It almost makes it seem as if the Navy still had hopes of finding something after all these years. Such is not the case. It is standard procedure as a part of the announcement of the termination of every search to include the phrase that travelers in the area should remain on the alert. The statement is never canceled as it is, in fact, part of an order canceling a search.

A recent addition to the story is that Lieutenant Taylor asked to be replaced before the flight took off but that the request was denied. Therefore, says one account, "it is *thought* [that] he *might* have been sick or *possibly**° intoxicated."†

In the report, Lt. Arthur A. Curtis, Aviation Training Officer, Fort Lauderdale Naval Air Station, testified as follows:

Q. Did you notice anything unusual about the behavior of the pilots in this flight?
A. Yes, Lieutenant Taylor did ask me to find another instructor to take his place, giving me no particular reason except that he did not want to take the hop.

° Italics mine.
† Robert Marx, "The Bermuda Triangle: Mystery or Myth?" *Argosy*, February 1974, p. 55.

Q. At what time did Lieutenant Taylor make this request?
A. To the best of my knowledge, it was about 1:15.
Q. What was your action on this request of Lieutenant Taylor?
A. I said I would not be able to get him a relief.
Q. Do you know Lieutenant Taylor's movements from that time until the flight was dispatched?
A. I do not know, sir.
Q. Did you observe any unusual behavior of Lieutenant Taylor?
A. No, sir.
Q. Did he seem normal in all respects?
A. Yes, sir.
  None of the parties to the investigation desired further to examine this witness.

The request was not mentioned again in the report and it does not appear in the list of Facts or the list of Opinions as having a bearing on the incident. It seems unlikely that the investigators would not have pursued the matter further had there been the faintest possibility that Lieutenant Taylor had been physically or emotionally impaired. On the contrary, a page was added to the report on October 14, 1947, in which the Navy absolved Taylor of all blame for the loss, saying that "some unexpected and unforeseen development of weather conditions must have intervened; that Lieutenant Taylor realized at an early hour that an emergency existed; that he promptly took charge, kept his flight together, and thereafter valiantly attempted to bring the flight home in the face of [the] most difficult flying conditions."

Many factors prevented Flight 19 from being saved: the failure of Lieutenant Taylor's compasses; failure of the one radio channel Lieutenant Cox needed to continue communicating with the flight; the refusal to let Cox use a ready plane; bad radio reception; the delay in sending out rescue planes; the approach of night and the invasion of bad weather; the inability to locate the flight promptly with radio bearings; the failure to broadcast the position of the fix once it was known; the failure of the teletype system; the icing of the Dinner Key Dumbo's antenna; the military discipline that kept the group together even though several of the pilots knew they were headed the wrong way; the fact that Flight 19 was the last flight of the day. Had any one of these factors not prevailed, the flight might have ended differently. One or more of the planes might have made it back, and the event would quickly have been forgotten, rather than becoming known as the strangest flight in the history of aviation.

The most tragic part of the incident is that when Lieutenant Taylor first reported his predicament, he was, according to later testimony, over the reefs and cays just north of the Bahamas. Flight 19 was almost exactly on course when the pilots decided they were lost!

23

December 1946

City Belle

*Exactly a year to the day after the disappearance of the
Avengers and their rescue plane, another mystifying incident
occurred in the Bahamas. The schooner* City Belle, *out of
Nassau and bound for Grand Turk Island, was found deserted
at sea on December 5, 1946.*

*She was perfectly seaworthy, and everything was in order,
even to the lifeboats still hanging in their places. For some
inexplicable reason an inquest was never held, and the* City
Belle *was quickly forgotten. Had the case been pursued it
might have been found to be as baffling as the* Mary Celeste
or the Carroll A. Deering.

Nassau Guardian, Thursday, December 5, 1946, p. 2:
It is thought that the heavy winds experienced this week caused
the passengers and crew of the *City Belle* to abandon the sloop when
she was en route from Nassau to Turks Island. It was reported to the
Port Officer this morning . . . that the sloop had been sighted between Hog Cay, Exuma, and Sandy Cay. There were no signs of any
passengers or crew. We have been unable to have the rumour confirmed that an American crash boat had picked them up. The sloop's
cargo was said to be intact.

Several other small boats are believed to have encountered difficulties during the recent stormy weather, but no details are yet available.

Nassau Guardian, Saturday, December 7, 1946, p. 4:

It was announced today by the Post Officer that seven survivors of the Schooner *City Belle,* which was found abandoned between Hog Cay and Sandy Cay, have been located by an American crash boat. . . . It is understood that the survivors were taken to the American base in Exuma. Further details, it is hoped, will be available on Monday.

The *Nassau Guardian* did not follow up on the story, so the survivors' accounts of the mishap are not known. Despite this unfortunate gap the coverage was adequate to show that the incident, as it was told in the Legend, was inaccurate and sensationalized.

The newspaper reports also contradict the frequently stated observation that the weather has never been bad during an incident, and that there have never been survivors in the Bermuda Triangle.

24

1947

Superfortress

In 1947 an American Superfortress bomber strangely vanished 100 miles off Bermuda. After an extensive search failed to find a trace, Air Force officials speculated that a tremendous current of rising air near a cumulonimbus cloud may have caused the bomber to disintegrate.

I was not able to find any original information on this "vanishment," but a logical explanation is included in the Legend itself. A cumulonimbus, or thunderhead, cloud contains both updrafts and downdrafts which may be in excess of 200 miles an hour.

An airplane passing through or near such a cloud could be rapidly subjected to alternating up- and downdrafts, and conceivably could encounter both at the same time, at opposite extremes of its length or breadth. Although airplanes are built to withstand severe turbulence, like all other machines there is a limit to how much stress they can endure. Beyond that point the weakest part of the structure will fail.

The points on any airplane that are most likely to give way are the empennage, or tail section, and the attachment of the wings to the fuselage. Under sufficient stress one or more of these sections could either bend or shear off, causing a completely uncontrolled spin and a crash.

Pilots treat cumulonimbus clouds with respect and normally fly through them only inadvertently.

25

January 1948

Star Tiger

In the early morning hours of January 30, 1948, the Star Tiger, a Tudor IV owned and operated by British South American Airways, radioed the tower at Bermuda to give a position report, state that all was well, and announce that its arrival would be on schedule. That was the last message ever heard from the large airliner. A search began before daylight; ten ships and more than thirty airplanes methodically covered all parts of the ocean that the plane could possibly have reached.

Although the weather was excellent when the disappearance occurred and during the first part of the search, no oil slicks, bodies, or debris were found. Toward the evening of the second day bad weather moved in and the planes were grounded. Ships continued an unsuccessful search for several more days before admitting defeat.

A lengthy investigation conducted by the Ministry of Civil Aviation concluded that "no more baffling problem has ever been presented for investigation," and that the "fate of the Star Tiger must remain an unsolved mystery." The court could only hint that "some external cause must have overwhelmed both the men and the machine."

The following information on the last flight of *Star Tiger* is a condensation of the report of the investigation conducted by the Ministry of Civil Aviation of Great Britain.*

The Tudor IV Type of Aircraft

The Tudor IV is an all-metal monoplane . . . propelled by four liquid-cooled reciprocating engines. . . .

The aircraft carries two identical wireless-telegraphy transmitters, which have a range of several thousands of miles and three wireless telephony transmitter-receivers having a range of about 200 miles. . . .

[It] carries four inflatable rubber dinghies [which are] equipped with appropriate emergency rations and distress equipment, and with a radio transmitter. . . .

Maintenance of "Star Tiger"

[From] an examination [of the maintenance records] relating to "Star Tiger" . . . two matters have emerged. . . . Certain defects re-appear regularly in the records, indicating not only that they were not rectified en-route, but also that major checks at the maintenance base failed to eliminate them. Secondly, the aircraft not infrequently took off on passenger-carrying flights over long distances with not unimportant defects unremedied. The records suggest that there was a lack of spare-parts at stations along the route, and that, on some occasions, time was not allowed for full servicing and testing. . . .

The Route

The journey . . . was from London to Havana. The first stage in the schedule was from London to Lisbon, where an overnight stop

---

* Great Britain. Ministry of Civil Aviation. *Report of the court investigation of the accident to the Tudor IV. Aircraft "Star Tiger" G-AHNP, on the 30th January, 1948.* (Cmd. 7517) London: His Majesty's Stationery Office, 1948.

The *Star Tiger*

was to be made. The second stage was from Lisbon to Santa Maria [Azores] where the aircraft was scheduled to re-fuel and to set off . . . for Bermuda. . . . The route lies entirely over the ocean; no islands or land masses are crossed. . . .

In the average conditions of wind which prevail in the winter . . . the aircraft, after completing the 1960 nautical miles flight to Bermuda has insufficient fuel remaining to proceed to any other airport. . . .

. . . There are no observation-ship stations along the route. . . . Furthermore, there is in the area little commercial shipping from which data can be obtained. The weather along the route must therefore be inferred from observations taken on the land-masses and islands of America, Europe and Africa and from such data as aircraft on the route supply. The reliability of forecasts is not as high as it is in areas where more complete data are available. . . .

The accuracy of forecasting particularly of wind and cloud is only moderate. . . . It is a fairly common experience to encounter head winds which are much stronger than those forecast, particularly in the winter months. . . .

Apart from the uncertainties of the winds, the route is not difficult for flying. It is a warm weather route, and there are no serious troubles with, for example, icing. . . .

Use is made of astronomical navigation [astral] methods, based on sextant observation of the stars. . . . In good conditions a star-fix . . . is unlikely to be in error by more than about 15 miles. Dead-reckoning navigation . . . is supplementary to stellar [astral] navigation.*

The Crew

. . . There can be no question that [the crew] formed an able and experienced team. The witnesses who knew Captain McMillan were unanimous in their appreciation of his high qualities. . . . Radio Officer Tuck was described as most experienced and capable. . . . All these officers had previous experience on the Bermuda route, but they had not previously flown together as a crew.

The Last Flight of "Star Tiger"

"Star Tiger" left London Airport on her last trip on 27th January, 1948. . . . A failure of the cabin heating apparatus and trouble with one of the compasses . . . were remedied during the scheduled overnight stop at Lisbon. . . .

---

* Dead reckoning is calculating the *approximate* position based on the *estimated* wind velocity and direction and the *estimated* speed and course of the vessel. Should any of the factors differ from the estimate, the calculated location could be significantly in error.

At the Azores Captain McMillan received an adverse report from the Meteorological Office . . . and decided to stay overnight. . . . Another aircraft of the British South American Airways Corporation was awaiting a favourable opportunity for taking off for Bermuda. This was the Lancastrian G-AGWL, commanded by Captain Griffin. . . . On the next morning [the two commanders] went together to the Meteorological office . . . and ultimately decided to fly with one hour's interval between them. . . . The strength of the adverse headwinds had lessened and . . . they [proceeded] at a height of 2,000 feet . . . affording a less effective adverse wind component . . . [and taking] the aircraft below cloud base. . . . "Star Tiger's" flight plan . . . gives the flight time as 12 hours 26 minutes and the estimated time of arrival at Bermuda at 3.56 A.M. the next day. . . .

Trouble had again developed on the flight from Lisbon with the same compass and [it] was remedied [at the Azores]. . . .

Captain McMillan appears to have taken a full load of petrol. . . . [He] instructed . . . "fill her to the gills" and the . . . total all-up weight was [a 936-pound overload].

This overload was soon reduced by fuel consumption and cannot of course have had anything to do with the disaster. Captain McMillan's insistence on full tanks does, however, indicate that he fully appreciated the difficulties occasioned by the prevalent headwinds. The winds on this route not infrequently contain such a headwind component as to prevent a Tudor aircraft with full tanks from reaching Bermuda . . . and the headwinds did from time to time increase en route beyond the forecast strength. . . . Twice before on westward trips "Star Tiger" had had to divert to Gander in Newfoundland on account of headwinds, and . . . another Tudor IV had encountered winds so much stronger than forecast that it had arrived with its petrol gauges showing "nil" and its commander had alerted the air sea rescue organization and had prepared to "ditch" his aircraft. . . . The incident had received not a little publicity and must have emphasized the necessity of carrying all fuel possible on this leg of the flight.

The Lancastrian took off from Santa Maria at 2.22 P.M. on 29th January and "Star Tiger" followed at 3.34 P.M. The Lancastrian touched down at Kindley Field, Bermuda, at 4.11 A.M. the next day, having had an uneventful crossing. "Star Tiger" was never seen again. She had been heard, however, frequently during her flight. . . . Radio conditions appear to have been good. . . . The prescribed hourly position reports were duly sent out by "Star Tiger" down to the last one at 3 A.M. . . . There are three matters dealt with in these messages which call for comment.

The first of these concerns the height above sea level at which the aircraft was flying. This is an important matter because of course the lower the altitude the less opportunity there is for dealing with any emergency which might upset the stability of the aircraft. The flight was planned to take place at a height of 2,000 ft. throughout the passage. . . . [However,] the record keeping was not of a high order, [and] it is impossible to say with certainty at what height the aircraft was flying when communications ceased.

The second matter . . . relates to the rule . . . that the radio station guarding any aircraft must not allow more than 30 minutes to elapse without contact. . . . Nevertheless the radio logs show that [at one time Bermuda] did not make contact [for] 55 minutes, [and another time there was] an interval of 42 minutes. These incidents may not be without significance when the final loss of contact is considered.

The third matter concerns weather information. . . . Winds . . . in all zones except the last were stronger than the Santa Maria forecast. . . . [The Lancastrian's] estimated time of arrival at Bermuda had accordingly to be recalculated [and] was one hour [later] than planned. . . . At 1.26 A.M. the Lancastrian navigator obtained an astral fix which showed him that he was considerably off course. He was then [where] the Azores forecast was "winds light and variable." . . . In fact he was experiencing a south westerly wind of some 48 knots, and . . . during the preceding hour he had been carried approximately 68 miles north of his intended track. . . .

Two facts emerge from [these] signals; firstly, the . . . delays in obtaining a reply. . . . Secondly, the unreliability of forecasts on the crucial portion of this route.

Apart from [that] there was nothing out of the ordinary in the messages passing to and from "Star Tiger." . . . She had amended her flight time . . . from the original estimate of 3.56 A.M. to 5 A.M. . . . Her hourly position reports . . . showed a normal progress and although it is clear that she, like the Lancastrian, had been taken off course by the change of wind, her position report at 2 A.M. showed that her navigator had been able to obtain an astral fix, so that that position was a known one, and not obtained by dead reckoning alone. . . . Up to 3 A.M. on January 30th, therefore, it is a reasonable inference from the known facts that "Star Tiger" had had a steady and uneventful flight. Her officers had received and acknowledged the Bermuda weather forecasts . . . but they had not (unless they overheard) received the revised winds transmitted at the Lancastrian's request at 2.42 A.M.

"Star Tiger" was heard twice after the transmission at 3.2 A.M. of her 3 A.M. position report. At 3.4 A.M. her operator requested a radio bearing from VRT [Bermuda]. . . . The request was repeated at 3.15 A.M. and . . . the VRT operator was able to give a first class bearing of 72°. He advised the aircraft accordingly and obtained an acknowledgement of receipt. This was the last signal heard from "Star Tiger."

. . . In the vicinity of the last known position of "Star Tiger," and in any area in which she is likely to have flown thereafter, the weather was stable, there were no atmospheric disturbances of a serious kind which might cause structural danger to an aircraft, and there were no electrical storms.

The moon had risen at 1 A.M. . . . Cloud base [was] just above 2,000 feet. It was broken cloud, assessed at six-tenths, but increased in intensity towards Bermuda; the Captain of the Lancastrian had seen stars through gaps in cloud until within 90 miles from destination. He had first seen the powerful marine lights of Bermuda when 25 miles from it.

The VRT operator . . . admitted the two occasions when contact with the aircraft was lost for 55 and 42 minutes respectively. . . . "I had other traffic on the air at the time—that may be the reason." His log, however, showed that he was not busy at the time, and he added, "I imagine the air was filled with signals from other stations," which may have been the case. . . . However . . . on neither of these two occasions did the operator declare the emergency which his written instructions required him to declare after a 30 minute loss of contact.

Mr. Richards last communicated with "Star Tiger" when he gave the bearing at 3.15 A.M. At 3.50 A.M. when 35 minutes had elapsed without a signal from the aircraft, he called her again. He got no reply. . . . He asked [Bermuda Approach] Control if they had made contact. They had not. He called "Star Tiger" again at 4.5 A.M. Again there was no response. Fifty minutes had now gone by since the last contact. He could not remember if he informed the [BSAA] Corporation of loss of contact, but said he probably had. The tele-printer sheets . . . contain no record of any such message. At 4.40 A.M. [12.40 A.M. local time] he called again, again without response, and then, 95 minutes after the last contact, he declared a state of emergency. . . .

Mr. Richards was asked whether by 4.40 A.M. the loss of contact had not caused him considerable anxiety. He answered: "No, he was not due till 5 A.M."

Energetic steps were taken once the emergency was declared. At 4.55 A.M. the Search and Rescue Section of the U.S. Army Air Force at Kindley Field was alerted, and by 7.16 A.M. [3.16 A.M. local time] a Fortress aircraft equipped with a radar scanner was in the air. During the next day 25 other aircraft took part in the search. All areas of the sea where it was conceivable that "Star Tiger" might have come down were scanned. The search went on until nightfall on February 3rd. Altogether 104 flights were undertaken and a total of 882 aircraft-hours was flown. . . . There were a number of false alarms both of radio messages and of objects sighted in the water: all were investigated, without result. Extremely bad weather prevailed throughout the greater part of the search. . . . After five days of continuous and intensive effort the search had to be aban-doned. . . . No trace of the loss of "Star Tiger" was found and no trace of wreckage or of any other object connected with her has since been seen.

Analysis of the Possible Causes of the Accident

There is good reason to suppose that no distress message was transmitted from the aircraft, for there were many radio receiving stations listening on the aircraft's frequencies, and none reported such a message. Thus there exists first the possibility [of] a failure of the aircraft's transmitting installation. There may then have hap-pened an accident . . . which the aircraft's crew were unable to report. . . . The aircraft may have failed to find Bermuda before her fuel was exhausted, being deprived of the navigational information which depended on radio. . . . The alternative hypothesis is that an accident occurred with such rapidity that no distress message could be sent, or that no such message was thought to be necessary until, as it proved, it was too late.

A total failure of the radio transmitting equipment due to any cause other than a failure of the D.C. electric power supply is extremely unlikely, for the equipment is duplicated. . . . Normal types of breakdown are guarded against adequately.

The D.C. power supply is provided by two independent generators which also charge a storage battery. . . . Only a total failure involving both the generators and the battery, would effect a failure of radio. . . . The possibility of such an occurrence is remote. . . .

A total failure of radio is thus most unlikely. . . . Had the radio failed shortly after 3.15 A.M. the navigator would have [had to find] Bermuda, which was then distant some 340 nautical miles and 2½ hours' flying time, without the aid of radio bearings and without such information on the state of the wind as might have been obtained by radio. His target was in a small group of islands, equipped with powerful marine lights around the coast, the visibility of which . . . was about 30 miles in all directions. He had about 3¾ hours in which to find his target before the exhaustion of his fuel.*

. . . Proceeding on [the 3:15 bearing the navigator] would set a course which, in the wind conditions actually prevailing, would have brought him within some 30 miles of Bermuda by 5.30 A.M. . . . The aircraft could hardly have failed to find the island in a short time, in the conditions of visibility which prevailed.

The possibility that failure of power would interfere with the aircraft's course-keeping can be discounted, for though the magnetically controlled gyroscopic compass would cease to operate, there are also available two bowl compasses of high accuracy. . . . †

---

* This is misleading. Since he was 2½ hours away he would have only 1¼ hours to search once he was in the area.

† This is a very questionable deduction by the Court. Bowl compasses are not always highly accurate and are subject to several types of error. They are especially difficult to use in turbulent air. Although one of the compasses was repaired in Lisbon it failed again on the trip to the Azores and the report does not state if it was then repaired or replaced.

Thus it appears that, had the navigator been forced to work without data other than those which he had available at hand, it is very probable that the aircraft would have reached Bermuda. . . .

There would accordingly appear to be no grounds for supposing that "Star Tiger" fell into the sea in consequence of having been deprived of her radio, having failed to find her destination, and having exhausted her fuel.

Causes That Can Be Eliminated

Constructional Defects. There are no grounds for supposing that in the design of the Tudor IV aeroplane, or in the manufacture of the particular Tudor IV aeroplane "Star Tiger," there were technical errors or omissions, judged against a standard of agreed good practice.

Meteorological Hazards. Nor are there any grounds for supposing that the loss of "Star Tiger" was caused by any meteorological hazard. . . .

Errors of Altimetry. There is little possibility that the aircraft flew into the sea as a result of an error in the indication of height. . . .

Mechanical Failure of Engines. The failure for mechanical reasons of one engine is a possibility, but the aircraft could fly entirely safely on three engines, and, indeed at her weight at the relevant time, on two. . . .

Causes That Cannot Be Eliminated

Fire. . . . The occurrence of fire . . . is now very rare. Every precaution is taken in design to prevent it, and this type of aircraft is well supplied with fire extinguishing devices. . . . Had any serious fire occurred . . . it is unlikely that a distress message would not have been transmitted . . . [unless] a fire occurred as a separate event after a radio failure; this requires the coincidence of two improbabilities. . . .

Loss of Control. . . . When flying at a fairly low altitude such as this, the time available for the recovery from any loss of control is not great.

Loss of Engine Power. . . . There remains the possibility that the engines were starved of fuel. . . . Not only is it very unlikely, but [a shortage of fuel] would certainly be noticed [earlier in the flight].

Conclusion

In closing this Report it may truly be said that no more baffling problem has ever been presented for investigation. In the complete absence of any reliable evidence as to either the nature or the cause of the disaster to "Star Tiger" the Court has not been able to do more than suggest possibilities, none of which reaches the level even of probability. Into all activities which involve the co-operation of man and machine two elements enter of very diverse character. There is the incalculable element of the human equation dependent upon imperfectly known factors; and there is the mechanical element subject to quite different laws. A breakdown may occur in either separately or in both in conjunction. Or some external cause may overwhelm both man and machine. What happened in this case will never be known and the fate of "Star Tiger" must forever remain an unsolved mystery.

The disappearance of the *Star Tiger* thwarts all explanation as each of the suggested solutions seems too unlikely to have occurred. It is truly a modern mystery of the air.

Although the reason for the plane's loss is unknown, the failure to find any trace of it cannot be considered a mystery. The weather was deteriorating during the latter stages of the flight, winds were increasing, the aircraft's fuel reserve was diminishing, and the sea was growing boisterous. The chances for a successful ditching on a rough sea in the dark are not good, and debris is not as frequently left at a crash scene as might be supposed, especially during poor weather. The *Star Tiger* could have gone down as many as five hours before the radar-equipped Fortress arrived in the area, and as many as eight hours before daylight, when other search craft joined in.

UFO-oriented writers have made much of the phrase in the concluding section of the Board's report, "some external cause may overwhelm both man and machine," apparently thinking that the Court may have considered the possibility that a UFO was responsible, but lacked the courage to openly express such a theory. In the context of the report, an "external cause" could be anything other than the human or the mechanical element, such as the weather.

It should be noted that although the Court concluded that many of the possible causes of the disappearance were extremely unlikely, *it did not declare that any of them were impossible.* Had there been a total radio failure, however unlikely such an occurrence might have been, the loss of the navigation equipment combined with the strong winds and the low fuel supply would have created a critical situation that allowed almost no margin of error. In any case, whatever happened to the *Star Tiger* will forever remain a mystery.

26

March 1948

Al Snider

Al Snider, internationally famous jockey, and two friends anchored their rented cabin cruiser in the shallow water near Sandy Key, off Florida's southern tip, and rowed a short distance away in a tender to fish for a few hours. They never returned to the cruiser.

The Coast Guard began a search with the aid of more than a thousand men and hundreds of boats and airplanes. The rowboat was found several days later near a small island sixty miles to the north, but it was empty.

After the Coast Guard ended its search Snider's wife and friends contributed money to be used for further searching, and rewards totaling more than $15,000 were offered for the discovery of the men or their bodies. Despite the incentive no trace of the three men was ever found.

Miami Herald, Sunday, March 7, 1948, p. 1, col. 4:
   By Arthur L. Himbert. A new wind velocity record for March was established here during the 24-hour period ending at noon Saturday, the Miami weather bureau reported. The old record . . . was shattered at 7:23 P.M. Friday when a sustained velocity of 48 miles an hour was recorded. . . .

Small craft warnings, hoisted from Melbourne south around the Florida Keys late Friday, were ordered continued for another 24 hours. . . .

During the peak winds Friday night, limbs were blown from trees, several windows were broken . . . and a small launch was swamped in the Intercoastal waterway.

Miami Herald, Sunday, March 7, 1948, p. 1, col. 6:

A 38-foot Coast Guard picket boat braved "extremely heavy" seas Saturday to rescue four Cubans from the 170-ft. barge *Virginian,* as mountainous waves pounded it to pieces on the north jetty of Government cut. . . . The waves tossed it up and down like a cork. . . .

. . . The *Virginian* was swept inshore by 15-foot waves churned up by the northeaster which hit the Miami area Friday night. . . . The picket boat almost capsized when a huge wave hit it broadside. . . . The *Virginian* was carrying a crane, a bulldozer, an ambulance chassis and other cargo. . . .

Meanwhile, the Coast Guard was searching with planes and boats for a 16-foot outboard tender of the yacht *Evelyn K,* which failed to return to the keys Friday night. Three men were aboard, but their names were not known.

Miami Herald, Monday, March 8, 1948, p. B1:

By John Woempel. Navy, Coast Guard, and civilian planes and boats were searching Sunday for three fishermen, including one of the nation's leading jockeys, Al Snider* of Miami Springs, who have been missing two days in Florida Bay. About 30 planes scoured the wide expanse of water and islands south of the tip of the Florida peninsula as far west as the Dry Tortugas Saturday and Sunday. The men were reported lost in a small boat Friday while 50-mile-an-hour winds churned the bay. . . . They had set out at 5 P.M. Friday from the yacht *Evelyn K.,* which had been anchored near Craig, a town on the overseas hwy. No one has seen them since. . . .

Searchers, spurred on by a $15,000 reward, continued their efforts for several weeks, although hampered by choppy seas

---

* Previous writers have erroneously spelled his name "Snyder."

and high winds. Hopes for the men zoomed when the plywood skiff was found near Everglades City, 60 miles north of Sandy Key, in an area of mangrove trees and swamps known as the Ten Thousand Islands.

The boat was found right-side-up. The floorboards were cracked, the engine had been pushed overboard, and it appeared that someone had attempted to lash himself in with a rope. The Coast Guard and the Navy, who had pulled out several days before, re-joined the search, along with hundreds of volunteer boatmen, pilots, and ground searchers with bloodhounds.

Many possible clues were discovered but all proved to be negative. Three footprints were found to be those of a small girl who lived nearby. A message written in the sand was not believed to have been written by the men, and arrows pointing in opposite directions had been made, it turned out, by local fishermen. An investigation of a "circling buzzards" clue uncovered two dead pelicans.

Nothing was ever found to show that any of the men had reached shore.

The Legend failed to mention one "small" point about the disappearance of Al Snider—the gale that struck the small skiff as the men were fishing in the dark.

27

December 1948

〜〜〜〜〜〜〜〜〜〜〜〜〜〜〜〜〜〜〜〜〜〜〜〜〜〜

DC-3

One of the eeriest of all the disappearances in the Bermuda Triangle took place in the early morning darkness of December 28, 1948. A DC-3 passenger plane chartered for a flight from San Juan, Puerto Rico, to Miami vanished within sight of its destination. The weather was excellent, the pilots were experienced, and there had been no sign of mechanical problems. Captain Robert Linquist, copilot Ernest Hill, and stewardess Mary Burks were returning twenty-seven passengers, including two infants, to their homes after a short Christmas vacation. The passengers were still in a holiday mood and singing Christmas carols as a tail wind gently wafted the airliner along its way. At 4:13 AM, as the glow of the city's lights began warming the horizon, Linquist contacted Miami Control, stating that he was approaching the field from fifty miles south, that all was well, and that he would stand by for landing instructions.

Then, whatever fate had decreed for them happened immediately and decisively—so quickly that there was not even time for a distress call. The tower radioed landing instructions but Linquist did not acknowledge. While on its final approach to the field, almost within reach of land, the plane had simply vanished.

A *massive search began within a few hours. The weather was ideal. The seas were clear and calm, and so shallow in most of the area where the plane had last reported that large objects could be seen on the bottom. Hundreds of ships and planes scoured the ocean from San Juan to Florida, covering the Caribbean, the Everglades, Florida Bay, the Gulf of Mexico, the Keys, Cuba, Hispaniola, and the Bahamas. Not a trace of evidence was found, not even a life jacket, a bit of debris, an oil slick, or any of the packs of sharks and barracuda that always appear at the scene of a disaster. To this day nothing has turned up to shed a ray of light on the mystery.*

Civil Aeronautics Board. Accident Investigation Report. *Airborne Transport, Inc. Miami, Florida, December 28, 1948:*

History of the Flight

At [10:03 PM],* December 27, 1948, NC-16002 departed from Isla Grande Airport, San Juan, Puerto Rico, for Miami. . . .

Eleven minutes after takeoff the flight called the airport control tower. The control tower did not receive the call but it was intercepted by CAA Communication at San Juan, to which the flight reported that it was proceeding to Miami, Florida. . . . CAA Communications at San Juan was unable to contact the flight again, although numerous attempts were made. At [11:23 PM], the Overseas Foreign Air Route Traffic Control Center at Miami, Florida, received a radio communication from NC-16002 stating it was flying at 8,500 feet . . . and that it estimated its time of arrival over South Caicos at [12:33 AM], and Miami at [4:05 AM], December 28, 1948.

The New Orleans Overseas Foreign Air Route Traffic Control Center intercepted a position report from NC-16002 at [4:13 AM], which stated it was 50 miles south of Miami. This was the last known contact with the aircraft. Unsuccessful attempts were made to contact the flight by CAA Communications from San Juan, Miami, and New Orleans.

_____

* All times have been changed from the 24-hour clock to civilian time.

The DC-3

The Civil Aeronautics Board . . . was notified . . . at [8:30 AM] that NC-16002 was considerably overdue. . . . When it was definitely determined that the aircraft was missing, the United States Coast Guard was alerted and an extensive search was immediately started. . . .

Investigation

On December 27, 1948, at approximately [7:40 PM], NC-16002 landed at San Juan, Puerto Rico, after difficulty with the landing gear.* Captain Linquist reportedly said that when the landing gear was lowered, the landing gear warning lights indicated that the gear was not locked. A repair agency on the airport . . . was asked to examine the aircraft's batteries. They were found to be discharged with the water level low. Advised that it would take several hours to recharge the batteries to their proper operating capacity, the Captain

---

* The same crew had flown the plane from Miami to San Juan that day.

asked the mechanic to add water and return them to the aircraft without charging. The landing gear warning light system was reported as malfunctioning but was not repaired.

At [8:30 PM], the crew of NC-16002 filed an IFR flight plan from San Juan to Miami . . . and the Captain stated the aircraft was in good working order. However, one hour later the . . . aircraft was having battery trouble and [was] delayed. Due to this delay, the flight plan became invalid. . . . At approximately [9:15 PM],* NC-16002 taxied to the end of Runway 27 and . . . the tower was unable to contact it by radio. The Chief of the Puerto Rican Transportation Authority . . . proceeded to the aircraft where he was advised by the crew that the aircraft's receiver was functioning properly but that due to weak batteries the transmitter was not. After conferring with the crew and then with the tower by means of the emergency car radio, the Chief of Aviation authorized the flight to make a VFR takeoff. It was agreed that the flight would remain in the vicinity of San Juan until sufficient power was produced by the generators to transmit. If this was accomplished, a new IFR flight plan was to have been filed and the flight could proceed to Miami. The flight departed at approximately [10:03 PM]† and eleven minutes later advised CAA Communications at San Juan it was unable to contact the tower and was proceeding to Miami on an IFR plan. Messages were intercepted from the flight while enroute, but further attempts to contact the flight relative to the flight plan and to ascertain its position were unsuccessful. . . .

Captain Linquist had flown the San Juan-Miami run for Airborne Transport, Inc., as copilot but this was his first trip as captain for that company. However, he had flown the route for other companies and had had military experience in the area.

Analysis

No examination of the wreckage was possible, as the aircraft is still missing. . . . At the time of departure from San Juan the aircraft's transmitter was not functioning, due to discharged batteries.

---

* The report gave this time as 22:15 [10:15 PM], an obvious error since the plane took off at 10:03.

† The report had this time as 23:03, an error which conflicted with other information in the report.

There was no report of any malfunctioning of any part of the aircraft other than the electrical system. . . .

It is known that the aircraft's transmitter was operating at [4:13 AM] . . . when . . . New Orleans . . . intercepted a position report which stated the flight was 50 miles south of Miami. It is possible, however, that some failure of the electrical system occurred subsequent to this transmission, making the aircraft's radio and automatic compass inoperative. It is also possible that the pilot may have been in error as to his reported position. Since the aircraft had fuel for 7½ hours of flight, and since the last message was intercepted approximately six hours and 10 minutes after takeoff, an error in location would be critical.

A review of the weather . . . indicated a change in wind direction from northwest to northeast as the flight neared Miami with no change in wind velocity from what was forecast. Without crew knowledge of this change, the aircraft could have drifted to the left of the course some 40-50 miles. This information was broadcast from Miami at [12:15 AM], but it is not known whether the flight received it.

Probable Cause

The Board lacks sufficient information in this case to determine the probable cause.

Flight Personnel

Pilot R. E. Linquist, age 28, held an airman certificate with a commercial pilot and instrument rating. . . . He had a total of 3,265 flying hours.

Copilot E. E. Hill, age 22, held an airman certificate with a commercial pilot and instrument rating. . . . He had a total of 197 flying hours.

The Aircraft

NC-16002 was a Douglas DC-3. It was manufactured June 12, 1936, [and] had a total of 28,257 hours.

Although the CAB did not solve the mystery of the DC-3, its report provides important information. The Legend emphasizes the swiftness of the disaster—the suddenness of the loss of contact between the tower and the plane. However, the report indicates that because of battery problems the transmitter had not worked properly on the ground at San Juan or early in the flight. It appears that the problem continued throughout the flight, since a number of fruitless efforts were made to establish contact with the plane while it was en route.

Any number of problems might have arisen within the hour and a half between the plane's last call and the time when the fuel tanks ran dry. More electrical trouble might have developed, and a plane at night without lights, instruments, or navigation equipment is a helpless creature. Linquist might have attempted to let someone know of his difficulties but failed because of the faulty transmitter.

Although the weather was good, it may have been an important factor in the loss. Linquist's information was that early in the flight there would be a light wind from the southwest, and later, from the northwest. He would have corrected for the expected wind by heading slightly to the left of his intended course. As the plane approached Miami the wind shifted, coming from the northeast. Although it was not a strong wind it could have caused the plane to drift 40 or 50 miles to the left of course, according to the CAB, if the pilot was not aware of the change. The DC-3 may have drifted so far south that it missed the southern tip of Florida and flew off into the Gulf of Mexico.

Neither the CAB report, the *Miami Herald*, nor the *New York Times* states that Linquist had reported seeing the lights of Miami. Previous writers made that assumption. They believed Linquist was 50 miles south because he said he was, then deduced that since he was that close he was within sight of the city.

Despite the Legend, the DC-3 never was in contact with Miami Tower. According to the December 29 *Miami Herald,* "The New Orleans station advised district Coast Guard headquarters in Miami. . . . The message from the DC-3 was not heard here."

A position report is never exact. It is only an estimate. A position fix at sea was a difficult feat in the 1940s, the days of low-frequency radio ranges. Even today, with more modern equipment, the Coast Guard assumes that all position reports contain an error factor. Before the use of omni ranges and DME (distance-measuring equipment) there were no precise methods of plotting an exact position, in terms of either distance or direction. Positions were estimates based on calculations that depended on the indicated air speed, the altitude, the barometric pressure, the outside air temperature, the estimated wind direction and speed, the weight of the plane, and the time in flight. Calculations were aided by celestial navigation if conditions permitted, but the process was only approximate. When Linquist said he was 50 miles away it was only an estimate. He could easily have been 100 miles out. Toward the end of a long flight pilots often report themselves closer in than they really are.

Similarly, when a pilot says he is south of a given point he is giving an approximation only. Linquist might have been somewhere in a southerly direction at the time, but he was not necessarily directly south.

If the DC-3 had flown a direct course from San Juan it would have approached Miami on the path indicated by the dotted line in the map shown below. A report from 50 miles out should have been made from point B (on the map), which is southeast of Miami. If he was, as he stated, 50 miles south (point A), he would have been considerably off course. Cumulating all these approximations and possibilities for error, the DC-3 probably was somewhere within the pie-shaped area when it went down. It conceivably could have been so far from Miami that it was even outside that area.

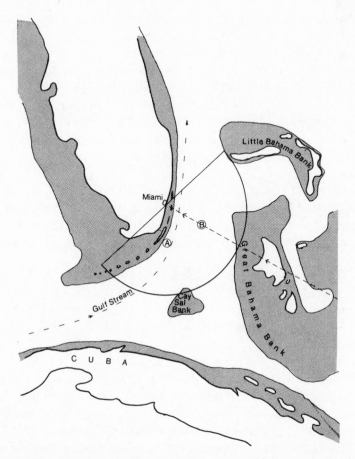

The DC-3 approaches Miami. *A*, 50 miles south of Miami; *B*, 50 miles from Miami, on course. Shallow areas are gray.

According to the Legend it is strange that search planes and ships were not able to find the downed plane in the water south of Miami, which is only about twenty feet deep. Although an object as large as an airplane would be impossible to miss, no one has ever reported finding an old DC-3 in the area.

Nautical charts reveal that much of the water south of

Miami is shallow (gray on the map). There is a 10- to 15-mile-wide area off the coast of Florida as well as another large, shallow area to the east, the Great Bahama Bank. Between them, however, the ocean drops off sharply to a depth of 5,000 feet in the Straits of Florida, through which flows the turbulent Gulf Stream. Only a very small portion of the area is shallow; the remainder is well beyond sight and reach. The DC-3 might still have been sinking and drifting north in the Gulf Stream as the search for it began many miles to the south.

The condition of the pilots should also be considered. By the time of their last report they had been in operation about twenty hours, most of it in the air. It had been a very long day, and their judgment and calculations could have been affected by fatigue.

The plane would have gone down by 5:45 AM at the latest, as it would then have been out of fuel. It could even have gone down as early as 4:15. In any case Linquist would have had to ditch at sea in the dark, very possibly demolishing the plane. If any traces had been left behind the chance of their being found would have been almost nil because of the turbulence and swiftness of the Gulf Stream. Since the first search plane could not have reached the area before 9 or 10 AM the Stream had a minimum of three hours and a maximum of about six in which to disperse any oil or debris.

The exact cause of the loss will never be known, but there are several important factors in the case that are not mentioned in the Legend.

28

January 1949

Star Ariel

On January 17, 1949, the Star Ariel, a British South American Airways Corporation airliner, vanished under conditions similar to those under which her sister ship, the Star Tiger, had disappeared almost exactly a year before. The four-engine plane took off from Kindley Field, Bermuda, with seven crewmen and thirteen passengers into a beautiful morning sky on a flight to Jamaica. An hour later Captain McPhee radioed a routine flight report to Bermuda: "We are at cruising altitude, the weather is good. Expected time of arrival at Kingston as scheduled." The Star Ariel was never heard from or seen again.

The plane was known to have been on course at the time of her last radio call, and the navigational equipment assured that she would remain on or near the proper path. Had the plane sustained structural failure and crashed, debris would have been strewn over a large area. Had a ditching occurred on a sea known to have been very calm, there should have been some survivors. At the very least, the two life rafts would have been automatically ejected from their compartments in the wings and would have been found. Yet the intensive search, performed in excellent weather, was all in *vain. Not a trace of the plane or its passengers was ever found.*

An investigation by the Ministry of Civil Aviation was not able to shed any light on the cause of the disappearance.

According to the report of the Ministry of Civil Aviation,* the airplane had 10 hours' fuel on board for the 5½-hour flight. It was flying with a tail wind and carrying a relatively light load. The weather was excellent and the plane was above the freezing level, making icing out of the question.†

The crew was well qualified. Captain McPhee had 4,200 hours of flight time, including almost 2,000 in command of BSAA aircraft, and extensive experience on the route on which he disappeared. The other officers were experienced, and the radio operator in particular was known for his outstanding skills.

The four Rolls-Royce engines had all performed well in the past, and there was no reason to suspect that they were at fault. De Havilland propellers were in use, and they had never failed in the history of the Tudor. The aircraft carried complete navigation equipment, including several receivers and transmitters, direction finders, a radio compass, and radar.

Safety equipment included three inflatable dinghies, each with room for fifteen to eighteen people and equipped with distress and sailing aids, first aid equipment, and a radio transmitter. The radio in the dinghy stored inside the airplane carried an automatic SOS transmitter that had an estimated range up to 75 miles. A switch in the nose of the aircraft operated automatically should the aircraft strike water, caus-

---

* Great Britain. Ministry of Civil Aviation. Civil Aircraft Accident. *Report on the loss of Tudor IVb Star Ariel G-AGRE which disappeared on a flight between Bermuda and Kingston (Jamaica) on 17 January, 1949.* (M.C.A.P. 78) London, His Majesty's Stationery Office, 1949.

† Ice can build up on a plane only near the freezing level. Above that altitude the water particles are frozen and will not stick to the aircraft.

ing the dinghies to be ejected from their compartments and inflated. Life belts for all passengers and the crew were stowed on board, and in addition to the regular doors, five emergency exits could be used for escaping from the cabin.

Structural failure was all but ruled out as a cause of the disappearance because the past performance of the Tudor IV suggested that it was most unlikely. The plane had successfully flown more than 350 hours with no problems, and meteorologists were certain that there could not have been turbulence along the route. Had a structural problem occurred the amount of pressurization in the airplane at the cruising level of 18,000 feet would have been so slight that it probably could not have led to disintegration of the aircraft.

While the possibility of sabotage was not entirely eliminated, no evidence was found that it played a part in the loss.

According to the weather report of HM Meteorological Office there were no weather complications of any kind. There were some clouds along the route, but they were well below the cruising altitude. Visibility was unlimited above the clouds and only slightly restricted below them.

Although the exact cause of the loss of the *Star Ariel* will never be known, there is some significant information in the report that does not appear in the Legend.

At 9:32 AM,* 51 minutes after takeoff, Captain McPhee called Bermuda:

"I departed from Kindley Field at 8:41. My ETA at [Kingston] is 2:10 PM. I am flying in good visibility at 18,000 feet. I flew over 150 miles south of Kindley Field at 9:32. My ETA at 30° N is 9:37. Will you accept control."

The second message . . . was originated by G-AGRE [*Star Ariel*] at 9:42. . . . It read: "I was over 30° N at 9:37. I am changing frequency to MRX [Kingston]." This was acknowledged. The ac-

---

* All times, regardless of location, have been converted to local Bermuda time.

knowledgment was for the Captain a complete clearance to change frequency to Kingston.

At 1:52 PM [4 hours and 10 minutes after the last message and 18 minutes before *Star Ariel*'s estimated time of arrival] messages were originated by [Kingston] to . . . Bermuda, requesting information about G-AGRE and pointing out that the aircraft had not been in contact with Jamaica since the time of its departure from Bermuda. . . .

Thus Kingston raised the first warning at 1:52, which signal was received at Bermuda at 2:23 and passed to "Approach Control" at 2:30. . . .

At 2:45 Nassau reported . . . that G-AGRE had not contacted Kingston and was now overdue and requested information.

At 2:54 a message was sent from B.S.A.A.C. [Bermuda] by teleprinter that nobody had any information on G-AGRE and that all concerned were being alerted.

At 3:05 B.S.A.A.C. Operations Bermuda [ordered a] search action to be taken by G-AHNJ (Tudor IV) which had landed at Nassau at 1:43 en route from Kingston to Bermuda.

At 5:08 a message was sent from New York Air Sea Rescue to U.S.A.A.F. Bermuda planning all-out search. . . .

. . . G-AHNJ, which took off [from Nassau] at 4:25 PM for Bermuda, was instructed to search along the presumed track of [*Star Ariel*]. The track was bisected at a position 27° N 69° W at 7:05 PM and G-AHNJ landed at Bermuda at 9:20 PM. . . . At 4:47 PM an aircraft flew . . . from Bermuda to a point 500 miles along the course and did a 1-mile lattice search all the way back. The same evening another aircraft flew the entire route from Bermuda to Guantanamo (Cuba).

The *Star Ariel*, which was last heard at 9:42 AM, could have gone down immediately after that message, and most likely was down at 11:00 AM, when its next position report was well overdue. Although the official report does not tell what time searchers arrived the following morning, it would have been too dark for a visual sighting until at least 7:00 AM, or approximately twenty hours after the *Star Ariel* prob-

The *Star Ariel*

ably went down. Even if the liner had stayed airborne until late in the afternoon without sending position reports, it would have been down at least twelve hours before it could have been sighted, had any of it remained to be seen.

B.S.A.A.C. Operations Officer: The inclusion of the passage [changing to Kingston frequency] in the last position report is unusual. The aircraft was at that time only 150 miles out of Bermuda on [the] 1,100 mile flight to Kingston, and in my experience aircraft on this route do not attempt to work [Kingston] until they are abeam Nassau. . . . It strikes me as most extraordinary that G-AGRE should [transmit that it was transferring to Kingston] before establishing satisfactory radio contact with [Kingston]. . . . I also cannot understand why [Bermuda] did not take any action . . . in regard to an aircraft last reported only 150 miles out of their station, as Regulation Procedure requires that flight watch be maintained until the aircraft is approximately at the midpoint of its journey and that control may not be relinquished until satisfactory radio contact has been established with the station ahead. . . .

B.S.A.A.C. Local Representative [Kingston]: The fact that the aircraft had not made any contact with [Kingston] was no cause for immediate concern as the usual procedure for aircraft at position 30° N is to . . . work Nassau . . . until approximately midway in the flight from Bermuda to Kingston when they contact [Kingston].

Kingston was informed by cable that *Star Ariel* would be making contact, but there was no concern over the absence of a call because of knowledge that radio conditions were unusually poor that day. Kingston assumed that the plane would continue to contact Bermuda until it came within range. Kingston did not know that the *Star Ariel* had signed off from Bermuda and Bermuda did not know that the plane had not established contact with Kingston.

The possibility of an aircraft signing off from one frequency and not reporting on the new one does not appear to have been guarded against by any of the procedures laid down by the highest authorities up to this time.

This oversight caused the long delay in realizing that the plane was out of contact, and the search was not begun until it was too late to reach the suspected ditching or crash area until after dark. Had there been an established procedure for the transfer of control, searchers could have been at work early in the afternoon, rather than by dawn of the following day.

Opinion: Through lack of evidence due to no wreckage having been found the cause of the accident is unknown.

Although the Tudor IVs were successfully operated in the Berlin airlift, they were never used to carry passengers after the loss of the *Star Tiger* and the *Star Ariel*.

An artist's conception of the Sargasso Sea, an area of mystery and legend since the time of Columbus. Courtesy of The Mariners Museum, Newport News, Virginia.

Joshua Slocum. Courtesy of Percy E. Budlong and The Mariners Museum, Newport News, Virginia.

The *Cyclops,* a Navy collier, sailed from Barbados on March 4, 1918 with a cargo of manganese ore and a complement of 309 men. The ship was never seen again. U.S. Bureau of Ships.

Joshua Slocum and the *Spray*. Slocum left Martha's Vineyard in the *Spray* on November 14, 1909, bound for South America. He never completed the journey. From "Sailing Alone Around the World," New York: Century, 1900.

The launching of the *Carroll A. Deering* on April 4, 1919. The schooner was discovered crewless and hard aground on Diamond Shoals on the morning of January 31, 1921. Courtesy of The Mariners Museum, Newport News, Virginia.

The *Nereus* under construction. The ship left the Virgin Islands on December 10, 1941, headed for Portland, Maine, and was lost without a trace. U.S. Bureau of Ships.

he *Proteus* left the Virgin Islands on November 23, 1941, headed for ortland, Maine. It failed to arrive and no trace was ever found. Navy epartment.

Five Navy Avenger torpedo bombers disappeared while on a flight from Fort Lauderdale, Florida, on December 5, 1945. The loss is the best known of all the incidents in the Bermuda Triangle. Navy Department.

Closeup of an Avenger. Navy Department.

A Martin Mariner similar to the one that was lost while searching for the five Avengers. Navy Department.

A B-29 Superfortress. In 1947 an American Superfortress vanished 100 miles off Bermuda. Officials speculated that it may have been disintegrated by air currents near a cumulonimbus cloud. Official U.S. Air Force photo.

Al Snider on Citation. Snider and two fishing companions were lost in Florida Bay in March 1948. He had been scheduled to ride Citation in the Kentucky Derby. Courtesy of Keeneland-Cook.

A B.S.A.A. Tudor IV, similar to the *Star Tiger* and the *Star Ariel*, which were lost in the late 1940s. Flight International photo.

A DC-3. On the morning of December 28, 1948, Airborne Transport N-16002, a DC-3, reported that it was 50 miles from Miami, approaching for a landing. It failed to arrive and could not be found. U.S. Army Air Force photo.

A C-124 Globemaster. In March 1951 an American Globemaster disappeared north of the Triangle on a flight to Ireland. Official U.S. Air Force photo.

A Super Constellation. In October 1954 a U.S. Navy Super Constellation disappeared with 42 persons aboard. The Navy searched for several days but had to give up when the weather turned bad. Official U.S. Navy photo.

A Martin Marlin. A Navy patrol bomber which was lost north of Bermuda on November 9, 1956, is believed to be the one reported "overhead in flames" by a freighter. Courtesy of Martin Marietta Aerospace.

A KB-50. On January 8, 1962, an Air Force KB-50 disappeared between Langley Air Force Base, Virginia, and the Azores. Official U.S. Air Force photo.

The *Marine Sulphur Queen* vanished with a cargo of molten sulfur and a crew of 39 men sometime after sending a routine radio message on the morning of February 4, 1963. Official U.S. Coast Guard photo.

Debris from the *Marine Sulphur Queen*, including a shattered name board, a life ring with a shirt tied to it, and a ripped life jacket. Official U.S. Coast Guard photo.

A KC-135. Two Air Force KC-135 stratotankers were lost on August 28, 1963, while on a refueling mission near Bermuda. Official U.S. Air Force photo.

A C-119. An Air Force C-119 was lost between Miami and Grand Turk Island on June 5, 1965. Its last radio message was sent only 45 minutes before the estimated time of arrival. Official U.S. Air Force photo.

The *Scorpion* outside Claywall Harbor, Naples, Italy. This is believed to be one of the last photographs of *Scorpion* before it was lost with all hands in May 1968. U.S. Navy photo.

The hull of the *Scorpion* on the ocean floor, approximately 400 miles southwest of the Azores, under 10,000 feet of water. From the collection of Samuel L. Morison. Official U.S. Navy photo.

29

March 1950

〜〜〜〜〜〜〜〜〜〜〜〜〜〜〜〜〜〜〜〜〜〜〜〜〜〜〜〜〜〜〜〜

Globemaster

An American Globemaster disappeared north of the Triangle in March 1950 on a flight to Ireland.

New York Times, March 24, 1951, p. 1:

LONDON, Saturday, March 24 [AP]. A United States Air Force officer at Shannon Airport said early today that the pilot of a search plane had reported sighting flares and wreckage along the Atlantic route followed by a huge United States Air Force C-124, missing for twenty-four hours with fifty-three persons aboard.

The vast armada of search planes that had been sweeping the 800-mile stretch of ocean was sped to the area where the flares had been reported, some 450 miles due west of Ireland. . . .

The giant transport plane was last heard from early yesterday on its routine flight from the United States to Britain. . . .

The pilot of a B-29 Superfort radioed the hope-giving report of seeing flares and wreckage. . . . [He] also reported sighting what he believed to be a life-raft.

The R.A.F. officer said that seas were running high and that there were strong winds in the area. Gale warnings had been posted along the British coast.

Maj. Horace A. Stephenson, commanding the United States air-rescue mission at Ireland's Shannon airport, told reporters . . . "I am

The Globemaster

afraid it will take some time—possibly hours—for the weather ships to get there. . . ." He was awaiting the return of the B-29 "to find out from the airman that he definitely saw what he reported he saw."

He added that, in the darkness, the pilot may have been mistaken. The pilot reported he had made the sighting at 12:45 A.M., Saturday, London time . . . twenty-four hours after the big transport had last been heard from.

"Further wreckage and flares have been sighted sixty miles from the spot where the first wreckage was sighted," Major Stephenson said.

Major Stephenson said he meant that the second wreckage and flares were sixty miles closer to the coast of Ireland. . . .

The transport . . . took off Thursday from the Limestone, Me., air base and refueled at Gander, Nfld.

Reporters were told that any rescued survivors would be brought to Shannon. . . .

A routine radio message from the transport at 1 A.M. Friday . . . gave its position as 800 miles southwest of Ireland and said it expected to land at 6 A.M. at the United States air base at Mildenhall, England.

New York Times, March 30, 1951, p. 3:

LONDON, March 29 [UP]. The United States Air Force Globemaster missing over the Atlantic since Good Friday was blown to bits by a terrific explosion that almost certainly killed all fifty-three men aboard, an Air Force spokesman said today.

He announced that the aircraft carrier *Coral Sea,* one of the sixty ships and planes searching for the missing transport, had found the ocean littered with tiny pieces of debris near the spot where a gasoline tank platform from the plane was found. He said authorities had not yet determined whether the plane exploded in flight or when it hit the water.

"In any investigation of this kind, the possibility of sabotage must be taken into account," the spokesman said. "But it should be stressed that so far there is absolutely no evidence to indicate sabotage in the case of the Globemaster."

The Air Force called off the search at the end of the eighth day when it became obvious that there could no longer be any survivors. There was increasing evidence that the plane had apparently exploded about 600 miles southwest of Ireland.

The *New York Times Index,* the best source of information on incidents of this type, did not list any such incident in 1950. The disappearance described here, which occurred in 1951, is too similar to the one mentioned in the Legend of the Bermuda Triangle not to be the same. It was a Globemaster, the incident occurred in March, and search headquarters were in Ireland, although the plane was not on a flight there, but to Britain.

The loss occurred far away from the Bermuda Triangle, and it appeared to have been caused by an explosion.

30

June 1950

Sandra

The 350-foot freighter Sandra, *radio-equipped and loaded with 300 tons of insecticide, sailed from Savannah, Georgia, in June 1950, headed for Puerto Cabello, Venezuela. Thumping her way south in the heavily traveled coastal shipping lanes, she passed Jacksonville and St. Augustine, then vanished without a trace in the calm, tropic dusk.*

The air and sea search was futile. No trace of floating wreckage was ever found in the shipping lanes, and no debris or bodies ever floated in to shore.

Lloyd's List, April 24, 1950: Miami, April 19—The 185-foot Costa Rican *Sandra,* with 11 men on board, has been reported six days overdue.

Lloyd's List, May 2, 1950: Miami, April 27—Search is being made for . . . motor vessel *Sandra,* which left Savannah on April 5 for Puerto Cabello with a cargo of 340 tons of DDT in bags and has not since been reported.

Lloyd's List, June 3, 1950: Miami, May 29—The United States Coast Guard has given up the search for motor vessel *Sandra* and the vessel is considered lost.

Although the Legend and *Lloyd's List* disagree about the sailing date and the length of the vessel, the ship is obviously the same one.

The evolution of the *Sandra*'s story in the Legend of the Bermuda Triangle is one of the more interesting examples of what can happen when authors take their information from each other, rather than from original sources.

The *Sandra* was first reported as part of an area-wide mystery in a short newspaper article* in September 1950 along with the better-known Avenger incident, the *Star Tiger,* the DC-3, and the *Star Ariel.* The article, which was the beginning of the Legend of the Bermuda Triangle (although the area would not receive its name for another decade), erroneously reported that the *Sandra* was a 350-foot freighter, and that the search for it was abandoned on June 16. All later articles gave the 350-foot figure for the ship's length (almost double its true size) and stated that it had disappeared in June rather than April.

The *Sandra* next appeared in a *Fate* magazine article in 1952, in which the author displayed a fine creative talent. He "described" the rust spots along its 350-foot length and told how the ship leisurely thumped along, on course, through the heavily traveled steamer lanes off Jacksonville. He told how the "friendly, winking beacon of St. Augustine Light *must have been*† easily visible through the peaceful tropic dusk that shrouded the low Florida coastline off the starboard rail." And he told of the men, just up from mess, drifting around the deck, smoking, talking, and reflecting on the past day. A very peaceful scene.

Almost all versions of the story after the *Fate* article state that the ship passed Jacksonville and was last seen off St. Augustine in the calm, semitropical dusk.

---

* E. V. W. Jones, Associated Press article released September 16, 1950.
† Italics mine.

The actual date of the departure of the ship (April 5) provides an important clue:

Miami Herald, Saturday, April 8, 1950, p. 1:

A storm growing from the low pressure areas which caused thundershowers and strong winds in Florida during the past three days approached hurricane force and buffeted Atlantic shipping lanes Friday. . . . [Winds] reached a speed of 73 miles an hour off the Virginia Capes, two miles an hour under hurricane strength. . . .

The Florida winds left a 40-foot shrimp boat, the *St. Paul,* missing at sea . . . and the Coast Guard started a search Friday.

Although Florida was not hit with winds as strong as those that wracked the Virginia Capes, it did suffer thunderstorms and strong winds from the same storm system on April 5, the day the *Sandra* sailed, and the next few days.

All was not placid as the steamer "thumped" its way south in April.

31

February 1953

British York Transport

Thirty-nine persons vanished north of the Triangle on a flight to Jamaica on February 2, 1953. An SOS, which ended abruptly without explanation, was sent by the British York Transport just before it disappeared. No trace was ever found.

New York Times, Tuesday, February 3, 1953, p. 8:

HALIFAX, Nova Scotia, February 2 [AP]. A four-engine British troop transport plane with thirty-nine persons aboard was believed to have crashed in the icy, gale-whipped North Atlantic today. Strong winds and torrential rains restricted search operations and little hope was held for rescue.

The plane, operated by Skyways, Ltd., of London, was bound for Gander, Newfoundland, from the Azores. It radioed an SOS 359 miles east-southeast of Gander. At the time winds up to seventy-five miles an hour churned the ocean.

The British freighter *Woodward* reached the scene where the transport plane was believed to have crashed but found no trace of it.

The plane was used by Skyways, Ltd., to ferry British troops between London and the West Indies.

It's true, the plane did vanish north of the Triangle on a flight to Jamaica, but several sins of omission have been com-

The British York Transport

mitted in order to provide another mystery for the "Triangle of Death." Rather than reporting that the plane was only on the Azores-to-Newfoundland leg of its journey, the Legend merely says that the destination was Jamaica, which is, of course, deep in the heart of the Bermuda Triangle. The disappearance was said to have occurred "north of the Bermuda Triangle," which is true; it happened 900 miles north of it! The weather is not mentioned in the Legend, which is often the case when it was bad at the time an incident took place.

It is seldom that an explanation is given when an SOS is ended abruptly.

32

October 1954
~~~~~~

Navy Super Constellation

In October 1954 a U.S. Navy Super Constellation disappeared just north of the Triangle with forty-two persons aboard. Although it carried two powerful radio transmitters it did not send an emergency message. Hundreds of planes and ships searched the area but failed to find a trace. Commander Andrew Bright, director of the Navy's Aviation Section, admitted that there was no official explanation to account for the loss.

New York Times, Monday, November 1, 1954, p. 1:

A four-engined Navy Super-Constellation with forty-two persons aboard is missing and "presumed lost" on a trans-Atlantic flight, the Navy announced last night. All available ships and planes were engaged in a vast search and rescue operation covering a path 120 miles wide from the New Jersey coast to the Azores. . . .

The forty-two crewmen and passengers, including four women and five children, made their . . . takeoff at 9:39 P.M. The plane was headed for Lagens, the Azores, and then Port Lyautey, Africa, but it went down somewhere en route.

Last word from the triple-tailed transport plane was a routine position report at 11 P.M. Saturday from a point more than 350 miles off the Maryland coast. . . .

Search operations got underway at 1 A.M. yesterday after the plane had failed to make two of its scheduled hourly contacts with shore. Joining the operation were planes and ships from up and down the Eastern Seaboard, from Bermuda and the Azores, and from the Mediterranean. . . .

Search conditions yesterday were reported generally favorable. . . .

Planes and ships with special radar for night operations pressed on with the search after darkness fell. The Navy said the plane was equipped with five twenty-man life rafts, 102 life vests, ninety exposure suits, emergency radio and a signal pistol with twelve shells.

The Navy continued to search for several more days, refusing to give up hope that the large plane had made a successful forced landing on the water and that the survivors had been able to climb into the life rafts. The search was abandoned on November 4 because of "extreme weather conditions."

33

December 1954

Southern Districts

    The Southern Districts, *a converted Navy LST used for hauling sulfur, disappeared somewhere in the Straits of Florida in December 1954. No SOS was sent, and one life ring was the only trace ever found of the ship or its crew of twenty-two.*

New York Times, December 14, 1954, p. 26:
    PORTLAND, ME., Dec. 13 (AP). An aerial search of coastal waters failed to turn up a freighter overdue here three days with a crew of twenty-four and a cargo of sulphur.
    The ship is the 3,337-ton *Southern Districts,* out of Port Sulphur, La., for Bucksport [Maine], and Portland. Last word from her came from the Gulf of Mexico Dec. 3. She would have been off the South Carolina coast Dec. 7, the day after a storm struck that area.

New York Times, December 15, 1954, p. 63:
    The Coast Guard continued unsuccessfully yesterday its search for the . . . *Southern Districts* which . . . last was in radio contact with the Southern Steamship Company, the owner, on Dec. 4. Another vessel reported seeing the ship on Dec. 7 off Charleston, S.C., but she has not been heard of since.
    It is feared that the ship suffered the same fate as her sister-ship,

the *Southern Isles,* which went down off Cape Hatteras on October 5, 1951, with the loss of seventeen lives. Six survivors were pulled from the water.

Other ships following the *Southern Isles* said the vessel's lights simply disappeared and when they reached the scene only minutes later there was nothing but debris and the few survivors.

New York Times, December 18, 1954, p. 31:
The Coast Guard abandoned hope yesterday for the . . . *Southern Districts.* . . . The vessel is a sister ship of the *Southern Isles,* which . . . foundered so quickly that no distress signal could be transmitted.

New York Times, January 1, 1955, p. 25:
WASHINGTON, Dec. 31 (AP). A Navy vessel, the *Anacostia,* is believed to have had the last contact with the lost ship. . . . On Dec. 7 she sighted a vessel of the *Southern Districts'* description battling high seas and gale winds off Charleston, S.C.

New York Times, January 3, 1955, p. 39:
Hearings will begin today in New Orleans on the disappearance of a converted landing ship with her crew last month on one of the world's most heavily traveled sea routes. . . . The *Southern Districts* apparently met the same fate that befell a sister ship. . . . She had broken in half in a pounding sea.

In the light of the twin disasters, the Coast Guard last Friday ordered its officials to board all converted ships of the same type and cancel all certificates that would allow the vessels to engage in ocean and coastwise commerce. . . .

The *Tullahoma* picked up at 2:30 P.M. [January 2] off Sand Key, Fla., a life ring bearing the name of the *Southern Districts.*

New York Times, January 4, 1955, p. 91:
NEW ORLEANS, Jan. 3 (UP). A seaman said today at a Coast Guard hearing . . . that the vessel was "just one big bucket of rust," and "the first ship that I'd ever been afraid to ride on." . . . Mr. Collins, who sailed three times on the *Southern Districts* but left the ship a week before her ill-fated trip, said that on a prior voyage the

"cargo was always wet. A number of guys warned me in Houston not to get on. . . ."

"The vessel groaned and creaked whenever there were rough seas. . . ." Mr. Collins said the vessel was to go on to Nova Scotia after touching port in Maine. . . . "I would never go to Nova Scotia on that ship—I know how the seas are up there," he said.

The wife of a seaman who had intended to quit the vessel upon its arrival in Maine testified that he had considered it unseaworthy. He had told her that the engines were "all fouled up" and that the bottom was "full of holes." According to another witness, rusty plates on the bottom of the ship had been repaired rather than replaced.

After several months of deliberation the Coast Guard Commandant ruled that the *Southern Districts* had sunk for "cause or causes unknown," and that no punitive action would be taken against its owners or the inspectors who had certified it for its last voyage.

Although the master and officers apparently did not agree, several of the crewmen had expressed the opinion that the ship was not seaworthy, and at least three crew members had refused to go on the voyage that was to be her last.

The ship's final radio contact with its owner was on either December 4 or 5, when it sent an "all's well" message while off the South Carolina coast.* Although it had been instructed to communicate every 48 hours, it was not reported to the Coast Guard as overdue for another week. Because of bad weather, which not only slows down the progress of ships but interferes with radio communications, the owners did not become alarmed until the ship failed to arrive in Bucksport on December 11. They then informed the Coast Guard, which immediately launched a massive and thorough search.

The board of inquiry found that a north-northeast wind

---

* Two reliable sources disagree about the date, but it is not a crucial matter which one is correct.

had blown in the area at the time the ship was thought to have sunk. Such a wind has a notorious reputation in the Gulf Stream area, as it blows against the northbound current and causes the Stream to become choppy and violent, driving even the largest ships away from the strongest part of the current.

The board criticized the owners for the long delay in informing the Coast Guard of the overdue ship, and recommended that all ships be required to report their positions every 48 hours. It also required ships to furnish the Coast Guard with a crew list for each voyage, as the captain of the *Southern Districts* had not done so, and it was never known for certain exactly who was lost when the ship sank. The board also criticized the inspectors for failing to perform a more thorough inspection despite knowledge that there were small holes in the bottom plating. The Commandant did not uphold the board's criticisms, but said that although the exact cause of the disaster would never be known, it appeared that the condition of the ship may have been a contributing factor.

One remaining mystery related to the ship appears to have been solved. Although the ship was last seen off Charleston, South Carolina, one of its life belts was found near the southern tip of Florida, raising the question of how it could have moved south against the northbound Gulf Stream. The answer generally accepted is that since the cover of the life belt had been torn, a crew member had thrown it overboard some time before the accident, having considered it worn out.

34

September 1955

Connemara IV

In September 1955 the yacht Connemara IV *was found completely abandoned between Bermuda and the Bahamas.*

Ione, the fourth Atlantic hurricane of the month, was first reported 250 miles east of San Juan on September 14, moving westward. The southeastern United States was warned to prepare for the most severe storm in years.

Torrential rains and winds up to 125 mph struck the eastern seaboard as the storm moved inland. An Air Force reconnaissance crew reported that it was the worst storm of what had been a very busy hurricane season, with winds as high as 182 mph and waves up to 40 feet. Gale winds extended almost to Bermuda on the north and to the Bahamas on the south.

The storm took an unusual turn at Norfolk. It veered out to sea, paralleled the east coast, and struck Newfoundland on September 21.

Lloyd's Weekly Casualty Reports, October to December, 1955, Vol. 142, p. 5:

LONDON, Sept. 29. Agents of tank steamer *Olympic Cloud* have

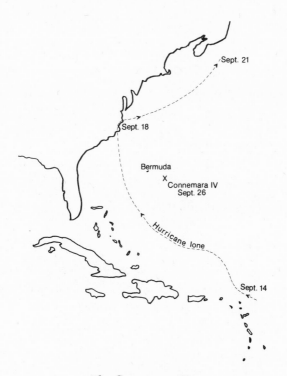

The *Connemara IV*

received the following message from the master, timed 11 35 P.M., G.M.T., Sept. 26: On my course, in position lat. 31 41 N., long. 60 19 W. [about 150 miles southeast of Bermuda], found motor yacht *Connemara IV,* of London, approximate length 22 metres, equipped with two diesels and radio, drifting abandoned high sea. Made fast and will tow her to Dakar.

LONDON, Sept. 30. From the master of the tank steamer *Olympic Cloud:* Towing rope broken, yacht *Connemara IV* sunk.

35

November 1956

Navy Patrol Bomber

A Navy patrol bomber vanished on Friday, November 9, 1956, near Bermuda, without sending a radio call to warn of any impending disaster. No debris was ever found.

New York Times, Sunday, November 11, 1956, p. 80:

A missing Navy patrol plane with ten men aboard was being hunted yesterday by Navy and Coast Guard units in waters north of Bermuda.

The plane is believed to be the one . . . spotted in flames on Friday night.

An SOS message from the freighter—the *Captain Lyras*—at 8:51 P.M. Friday reported "a plane overhead in flames" at a point about 400 miles east southeast of New York. . . .

The freighter at 9:15 o'clock report[ed] that an explosion had been heard and felt strongly aboard the vessel. Still another message from the freighter reported the sighting about four miles away of what appeared to be a life raft with a light on it. The freighter's report added, however, that the raft had become obscured by rain, heavy seas and darkness.

According to the Navy, weather conditions at the time of the SOS were scattered clouds at 1,500 feet, showers with good visibility and moderate seas. . . .

The Navy Patrol Bomber

Vice Admiral Frederick W. McMahon was quoted as declaring the Navy plane "may or may not" be the sighted craft. Other Naval authorities in Norfolk, Va., and in Bermuda, home base of the plane, apparently were presuming it was. There have been no other reports of a missing civilian or military craft.

The missing plane is a Martin "Marlin" P5M. . . . It had radioed its last position report at 8:30 P.M. Friday when "roughly" in the area of the freighter's report.

The United States Naval Station in Bermuda, where the airplane is assigned to Navy Squadron 49, reported the craft's last position report as 352 miles north of Bermuda. . . .

The search was begun Friday night by three Coast Guard aircraft and a cutter, . . . two Navy destroyers and six Navy planes.

New York Times, Monday, November 12, 1956, p. 36:
Naval aircraft and surface ships were dispatched last night to a point 300 miles northwest of Bermuda after the Spanish freighter A*stro* reported a white flare at 6 P.M. . . .

No trace of the airplane was ever found, and nothing was sighted in the area where the flare was reported. Several days later the search was terminated. The Navy summarized the incident briefly:

NAVSAFECEN ltr ser 395, 4426, NAS, Norfolk, Va.:
P-5M Flying Boat. 9 November 1956. Lost off Maryland coast. No debris or survivors, but crash observed by merchant ship.

The loss of the Martin Marlin was almost exactly like the loss of the Martin Mariner during the search for Flight 19 eleven years before. Both explosions occurred while the planes appeared to be in normal flight well above the ocean, and both were observed by a surface vessel. In each case heavy seas and darkness prevented the recovery of debris and possible survivors, and by the time daylight arrived the wind and waves had had many hours to disperse any traces of the accident.

36

January 1958

Revonoc

Harvey Conover, millionaire publisher of Yachting *and* Aviation Age, *was considered to be the outstanding yachts-man of his time. He and the sleek* Revonoc *had won the Miami to Nassau race three times, and the vessel had the reputation of being the best sailboat in ocean racing, as well as the last word in construction and the safest craft afloat. Nevertheless, the* Revonoc *vanished on the 150-mile trip from Key West to Miami in January 1958.*

Although the intended path would have always kept them within sight of land, Conover and his skilled crew of four completely disappeared. Those who knew the captain and his boat insisted that the storm that passed through the area could not possibly have done them in, as it had not been that severe. Despite an extensive search the Revonoc *and her crew were never found. It is yet another vessel to have vanished in the Bermuda Triangle during the Christmas season.*

New York Times, Tuesday, January 7, 1958, p. 24:
    MIAMI, Fla., Jan. 6 (UP). Harvey Conover . . . and four other persons were missing in wind-lashed seas off the southern coast of Florida today in a forty-five-foot racing yawl.

Two other boats were missing and another was in danger of capsizing in the stormy seas.

The Coast Guard reported tonight that a life raft from the missing yawl had been found near Jupiter Inlet, eighty miles north of here. It was the only trace found in the day-long search.

The Coast Guard said Mr. Conover's two-masted yawl, *Revonoc,** was sailing from Key West to Miami last Thursday when she apparently was caught in near hurricane winds from the worst mid-winter storm in the history of south Florida. . . .

Two fifty-five-foot shrimp boats with two crewmen each also were missing in the same area.

"Caught in near hurricane winds from the worst mid-winter storm in the history of south Florida."

---

* Some previous reports of this incident have the name incorrectly spelled *Renovac. Revonoc* is Conover spelled backward.

37

January 1962
～～～～～～～～～～～～～～～～～～～～～～～～～～～～～～～～

KB-50

An Air Force KB-50, commanded by Major Robert Taw-ney, disappeared shortly after leaving Langley Air Force Base, Virginia, for the Azores. Although a single distress call was too weak and garbled to be understood, the pilot did manage to convey the message that he was in some sort of trouble. The exact nature of the problem was not learned before the airplane faded into silence. No trace of it or its nine occupants was ever found despite a 1,700-hour, six-day search.

Virginian-Pilot, Wednesday, January 10, 1962, p. 1:

LANGLEY AIR FORCE BASE—By Ed Frede. A vast air and sea search of the Atlantic Tuesday failed to locate a missing Air Force aerial tanker with nine crewmen aboard.

The plane, a KB50, was on a flight from Langley Air Force Base to Lajes Field in the Azores.

The six-engine plane . . . left Langley Monday at 11:17 A.M., and was due in Lajes at 6:59 P.M. . . .

Maj. Tawney had logged almost 4,000 hours in the air and had been qualified as a KB50 commander for a year. . . .

The last transmission from the plane was shortly after noon Monday. The pilot gave his position as 250 miles east of Cape Charles. He gave no indication of trouble.

When the plane failed to land at Lajes on schedule, officials at the field started a check with other fields. An air search from Lajes was started immediately. An aerial tanker also searched near Cape Charles. With daylight Tuesday the Air Force pressed the search with sister tankers at Langley.

Virginian-Pilot, Thursday, January 11, 1962, p. 21:
NEW YORK [AP]. The Coast Guard said Wednesday an oil slick has been sighted in the area where an Air Force tanker plane vanished Tuesday* during a flight to the Azores.

The KB-50 . . . was last heard from about 240 miles due east of Norfolk early Tuesday.*

The oil slick, the Coast Guard said, was sighted by search planes about 300 miles east of Norfolk.

Taking part in Wednesday's search were 24 Air Force planes—18 from Bermuda and six from Langley—and several Coast Guard planes. Three Coast Guard cutters also searched. A Langley spokesman said weather conditions in the search area were good. . . .

More than 60 planes took part in the search Tuesday. Snow and reduced visibility grounded all but 26 search planes Wednesday.

Unfortunately there is not much information available on this incident, and the few articles that did appear leave many questions unanswered. According to the only article in the *New York Times,* Wednesday, January 10, the "search concentrated along a 130-mile-wide path running east from the missing plane's position toward its destination. Weather in the area was reported as 'windy but good, with visibility ten miles.'"

There are no clues as to why the plane might have gone down and only a few minor differences between the Legend and the incident as the newspapers reported it.

There apparently was not any "garbled" distress call that "faded into silence." On the contrary, the pilot's last trans-

---

* The newspaper is in error. Both sentences should say "Monday" rather than "Tuesday."

The KB-50. X, the last position report; Y, the oil slick.

mission was a position report in which he gave no indication of trouble.

An oil slick was found directly in the aircraft's path, about 60 miles beyond the last reported position, but it was not known if it came from the plane, as no debris was sighted in the area.

According to the papers, a search was not begun until the

tanker failed to arrive in the Azores at 6:59 P.M., even though the plane had last reported about noon. Normally, seven hours with no contact would not be permitted to pass without a search being initiated.

The two planes that began searching Monday night, one at each end of the route, would have been searching in the dark, and it was not reported if they carried radar scanners. If they did not, their only hope would have been to spot a light or a flare; they could not have seen debris. By the next morning, when the full-scale search began, the plane could have been down as many as eighteen hours.

The missing KB-50 is another case where a long delay in beginning the search may possibly have contributed to the lack of its success.

38

April 1962

Piper Apache

On a clear, sunny day in April 1962, the Nassau control tower received a call for guidance from a twin-engine Apache that was approaching from the north. Despite excellent weather the pilot was unable to determine his position and could not understand the instructions radioed to him. The tower operator later was quoted as saying that the pilot acted as if he were flying in a dense fog.

After several minutes of confusion, radio contact was suddenly lost. The wing of the plane was found later in the day approximately 20 miles from Nassau. The strangest part of the story is that the pilot was easily within sight of his destination when he reported being lost.

I searched every page of the *Nassau Daily Tribune* and the *Nassau Guardian* from January 1 through June 30, 1962, and found no mention of the incident. Suspecting that the date might be incorrect, I sent a letter to Nassau International Airport, giving the above account of the mishap and requesting that they inform me of any accident that was in any way similar. The answer came several weeks later.

D. A. F. Ingraham, Director of Civil Aviation, Nassau International Airport, Bahamas, 25th March 1974:

I refer to your letter, dated 11th March, 1974.

We have no record of the alleged disappearance of the aircraft that you describe. Some of my staff and I have been with the Department of Civil Aviation since 1946. We have no recollection of the alleged occurrence to which you refer.

I can only assume that [it] is a figment of someone's vivid imagination.

September

39

September

September

September

February 1963

Marine Sulphur Queen

The Marine Sulphur Queen *and her crew of thirty-nine began a voyage on February 2, 1963, from Beaumont, Texas, to Norfolk, Virginia, a trip that she was destined never to finish. Her cargo, a full load of molten sulfur kept at 275°F, was held in a huge tank in the hold of the converted World War II vessel and was said to be no more and no less dangerous than any other type of cargo.*

In the early morning hours of February 4 she sent a routine radio call from a position approximately 270 miles west of Key West. Several unsuccessful attempts were made to contact her after that, and she was reported missing three days later when she failed to arrive in Norfolk as scheduled. A vast search resulted in the recovery of a few life jackets and a little debris, but nothing more. The Coast Guard held a lengthy series of hearings, but admitted that it failed to find an explanation for the loss.

The following information is from two reports issued by the Coast Guard.*

---

* U.S. Coast Guard. Marine Board of Investigation. SS *Marine Sulphur Queen; Disappearance at sea on or about 4 February 1963* and U.S. Coast Guard. Commandant. *Commandant's Action on Marine Board of Investigation; Disappearance of the* SS *Marine Sulphur Queen.* . . .

September

September
185

Commandant, Item 2:

The SS *Marine Sulphur Queen,* a T2-SE-A1 type tank vessel of U.S. Registry, converted to carry molten sulfur, departed Beaumont, Texas, with a full cargo of 15,260 tons on the afternoon of 2 February 1963 enroute Norfolk, Va. The ship and crew of 39 men disappeared. The vessel was last heard from at 0125 EST on 4 February 1963.

Board of Investigation, Item 38:

At 0125 EST, 4 February 1963 a personal message from a crew member was transmitted by the vessel. . . . At this time the estimated position of the ship was 25°45′N, 86°W [position A on map below]. . . . At 1123, 4 February, RCA Radio commenced the first of two unsuccessful attempts to contact the vessel by radio. At this time the *Marine Sulphur Queen,* if she had continued on her voyage, would have been at an estimated position of 24°40′N, 83°19′W [position B]. . . . At noon on 3 February, the SS *Texaco California* was [at position C] estimated to be 40 miles from the *Marine Sulphur Queen.* . . . [It] experienced generally northerly winds from force 6 to 11, Beaufort Scale,* very rough northerly seas and her decks were awash. . . . The U.S. Navy Oceanographic Office . . . indicates that the vessel may have encountered seas with a maximum wave height of 16.5 feet. . . . Winds would have [had] a maximum force of 25 knots and gusting to 46. . . .

Board of Investigation, Item 39:

The first information that the *Marine Sulphur Queen* was overdue was received by the Commander, Fifth Coast Guard District, at 2100 EST, 7 February 1963.

Board of Investigation, Item 40:

At 0800 EST 8 February 1963 . . . the search was commenced. . . . During the period 8–13 February 1963, Coast Guard, Navy, Marine Corps and Air Force aircraft participated in 83 sorties, flying 499.6 hours and searched a total of 348,400 square miles† with

---

* Beaufort number 11 is just below hurricane strength. The wind is 64 to 71 mph and waves can be as high as 30 to 45 feet. Beaufort number 6 is a wind of 22 to 27 knots and the waves are 8 to 13 feet.

† Slightly larger than Arizona, New Mexico, and Colorado combined.

The *Marine Sulphur Queen*. A, the last position report; B, estimated position when first call to ship failed; C, position of the *Texaco California* when it gave its weather report.

negative results. . . . The Coast Guard Atlantic Merchant Vessel Reporting system . . . located 42 vessels that could possibly have sighted the *Marine Sulphur Queen* on 4 and 5 February. All of these vessels were checked out by Coast Guard personnel with negative results. Several telephone calls [reported] that the ship would be found in Cuba or in Puerto Rico. These leads were checked out by other Federal agencies with negative results.

Board of Investigation, Conclusion 27:

The operating company failed to give timely notice to the Coast Guard concerning the lack of communication from the vessel. . . . The company rationalized the failure to receive the 48 hour and 24 hour arrival message on the basis of bad weather conditions. . . . As a result of this delay, very valuable time was lost in instituting the search. . . .

Board of Investigation, Item 41:

On 20 February, a U.S. Navy torpedo retriever boat operating about 12 miles southwest of Key West, Florida, sighted and picked up a fog horn and life jacket stencilled with the vessel's name. The second phase of the search . . . was then instituted. . . . The probability of sighting during both search phases was computed to be 95% for a vessel, 70% for a metal lifeboat and 65% for a life raft. The U.S. Navy conducted an underwater search . . . with possibility of detection of 80% for the hulk. During this period, additional debris was recovered and identified as coming from the *Marine Sulphur Queen*. [On] 14 March 1963 . . . the search for the vessel was discontinued.

Board of Investigation, Item 42:

The material recovered and identified as from the *Marine Sulphur Queen* consisted of 8 life jackets, 5 life rings, 2 name boards, 1 shirt, 1 piece of an oar, 1 storm oil can, 1 gasoline can, 1 cone buoy, and 1 fog horn. . . . The consensus of opinion was that possibly two life jackets had been worn by persons and that the shirt tied to a life jacket had also been worn by a person. Numerous tears on the life jackets indicated attack by predatory fish. . . . No trace of sulphur particles was evident on any of the material [nor was there any] trace of either explosion or fire.

Board of Investigation, Conclusion 4:

. . . The failure to transmit a distress message would appear to justify the conclusion that the loss of the vessel occurred so rapidly as to preclude the transmission of such a message. . . .

Commandant, Remark 4:

The Marine Board of Investigation *considered many possibilities*

which may have caused the loss of the ship and rightly declined to
assign any order of probability to these causes. . . .

A. An explosion may have occurred in the cargo tanks.
B. A complete failure of the vessel's hull girder may have caused
   it to break in two.
C. The vessel may have capsized in synchronous rolling.
D. A steam explosion may have occurred as the result of a rapid
   filling of the void space with water.

The record contains ample evidence to support the Board's supposi-
tions.*

[Explosion in the Cargo Tanks]

Board of Investigation, Conclusion 7:

. . . Agitation of the mass of sulphur acts to increase the amount
of gases liberated from solution. It is concluded that the sulphur was
agitated as the vessel worked in the rough seas which she apparently
encountered on this voyage. . . . It, therefore, follows that this agitation . . . increased the volume of these gases liberated from the
molten sulphur.

Board of Investigation, Conclusion 8:

Although each tank had [three] vents . . . the fact that all tanks had
a full load of cargo . . . prevented a free flow of air. . . . It appears
that . . . the venting arrangement was not too effective in clearing
off these gases. . . . In rough weather, such as the vessel probably
encountered on this voyage, the molten sulphur would pour out of the
forward vents of the cargo tanks at least partially obstructing these
vents as the sulphur solidified.

Board of Investigation, Conclusion 9:

. . . It could be possible that an explosion of the gases in the
vapor space of one of the cargo tanks occurred. . . . Although a
close inspection of the debris fails to show any evidence of charring

---

* Italics mine. The Legend has it that the Coast Guard was not able to
suggest any reasons for the loss.

or of an explosion, this . . . does not completely discount the possibility that an explosion did occur.

[The Ship May Have Broken in Two]

Commandant, Item 3:
   The ship's conversion in 1960 to a molten sulphur carrier necessitated the *removal of all transverse bulkheads** in way of the original centerline tanks and modification of the internal structure to accommodate one continuous independent tank 306 ft. long. . . . A watertight bulkhead was installed . . . which divided the void [outside the cargo tank] into two spaces.

Board of Investigation, Conclusion 12:
   The Board has extensively considered the possibility that the casualty to this vessel was caused by a complete longitudinal failure of the vessel's hull girder causing it to break in two. . . . There have been ten known cases of complete fractures of T-2 type tank vessels. That this type of casualty has persisted after the problem has been thoroughly studied and measures taken to prevent the same, tends to support the view held by some that this type of vessel has basic design imperfections which cannot be feasibly corrected. . . . Additionally, it is now rather generally recognized . . . that the age of a vessel has some relationship to structural failure. This . . . vessel was about 17 years old at the time of the conversion [to a sulfur carrier] and about 19 years old at the time of her disappearance.

Board of Investigation, Conclusion 21:
   The sea conditions which the vessel in all likelihood encountered . . . have a definite bearing on another possible cause for the vessel's disappearance. As a result of the conversion, nine transverse bulkheads . . . were practically eliminated. . . . In short, at the nine frames where originally there had been a watertight bulkhead in the amidship section of the vessel, after conversion there was one watertight bulkhead, two [partial] bulkheads and six top connections.

---

   * Italics mine. A transverse bulkhead divides the interior of the ship into watertight compartments and also strengthens the hull.

However, it is apparent that the replacement members did not possess the strength of the original watertight bulkheads. . . . Therefore, the vessel after conversion did not possess the same transverse strength and stiffness as it had originally. Accordingly, it is considered possible that the [forces] induced by this racking [from the condition of the sea] may have [caused a] cracking of the bottom shell. . . . It cannot be discounted that the foundering of the vessel could have occurred quite suddenly.

[The Ship May Have Capsized]

Board of Investigation, Conclusion 20:

The concentration of the weight [close to] its centerline [caused the ship's] period of roll [to be] faster than [that of] another vessel of the same height. The hindcast prepared by the U.S. Naval Oceanographic Office indicates the possibility that . . . the period of encounter of the [waves] was within 10% of the vessel's period of roll, which was 8.5 seconds. Under these circumstances, heavy rolling of the vessel could be expected, accompanied by yawing, lurching and difficulty in steering. If such a situation developed, prompt appreciation of the danger by the watch officer and an immediate and drastic speed and/or course change would have been most vital. If complete resonance was approached, the vessel could have experienced several violent rolls in a minute's time. . . . The possibility that the vessel capsized without previous structural damage cannot be discounted. Finally, it is possible that the capsizing of the vessel might have been preceded and caused in part by the partial failure of and some lateral displacement of the cargo tank. . . .

[Steam Explosion]

Board of Investigation, Conclusion 22:

There originally was some support for the view that the contact of [sea water and molten sulfur] in a confined space would result in a steam explosion. . . . However, the more recent thinking appears to discount the possibility of this reaction [but it cannot be completely eliminated as a possible cause].

[Fumes Explosion]

Commandant, Remark 5:

Another possible cause for the loss of the vessel and one which the Board did not comment upon concerns the possibility of an explosion in the void space surrounding the cargo tanks. Hydrogen sulphide and carbon disulphide gases released by agitated molten sulphur as well as sulphur vapor could have . . . formed an explosive mixture. The recent history of fires in the insulation on No. 4 tank indicates that a source of ignition existed.

Commandant, Item 6:

Commencing in the late summer of 1962 and continuing until the vessel sailed on its last voyage, molten sulphur leaked from the insulation at the after end of No. 4 tank. . . . The amount of sulphur was so great that it was necessary for the crew to remove the solidified sulphur on each return voyage to keep it from plugging the bilge suctions. When the vessel sailed on its last voyage, an estimated 20 to 70 tons of solidified sulphur remained in the bilges. . . .

Commandant, Item 8:

Numerous fires had occurred in the sulphur-impregnated insulation in the void spaces. These fires were of a local nature seldom covering an area of more than a few square feet, and caused little or no apprehension on the part of the crew. They were extinguished with the steam smothering system and fresh water. Commencing in October of 1962, these fires occurred with increasing frequency. . . . During a voyage in the latter part of December, 1962, fires burned almost continuously in the insulation . . . of No. 4 tank. . . .

Board of Investigation, Recommendation 1:

In the future, the same conversion of another T-2 type tanker [into a sulfur carrier] should not be approved.

Board of Investigation, Recommendation 12:

In view of the complete structural failures of several T-2 type tank vessels, and in view of the fact that such type failure may have contributed to the [loss of the *Marine Sulphur Queen*], it is recommended

that . . . a portable emergency radio transmitter to be kept . . . in
the vicinity of the after lifeboats. . . . It is also recommended . . .
that all T-2 type tank vessels be equipped with two inflatable life
rafts, one . . . forward . . . the other [aft].

Although the Coast Guard report considered the structural
importance of bulkheads it did not mention another very important function that they perform.

Bulkheads are vertical partitions which divide the interior
of a ship into a number of watertight compartments. They
not only keep the hull from flexing in a heavy sea, but also

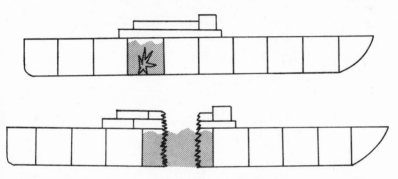

Fig. 1 Ship with nine bulkheads. *Above,* hole in side; *below,* broken
in half. The bulkheads prevent water from entering adjacent compartments, and in either case the ship would continue to float.

serve to prevent the foundering of the ship should the hull be
torn open by an explosion, a collision, or by running aground.

A 500-foot ship would normally have about nine bulkheads. If an explosion were to tear a hole through the hull,
only one or two compartments would be likely to be flooded,
since the bulkheads would prevent water from entering adjacent compartments. The ship would continue to float, per-
mitting its occupants to board a rescue ship or, depending on
the weather and the extent of the damages, to proceed to port.

Although ships have been known to break in half and remain afloat because of their bulkheads, most vessels of this size would be expected to remain afloat in moderate weather with, at most, two compartments flooded. Beyond that there would be grave danger of sinking, especially in a heavy sea.

The conversion of the *Marine Sulphur Queen* to a molten sulfur carrier necessitated the removal of all watertight bulkheads in the way of the 306-foot-long cargo tank. In their place one watertight bulkhead was installed near the midpoint of the ship and two partial bulkheads were constructed,

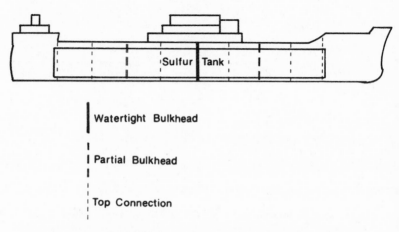

Fig. 2 *Marine Sulphur Queen,* with only one watertight bulkhead.

one forward and one aft of the main bulkhead. Top connections were placed at the six other locations. The partial bulkheads and the top connections were for structural purposes only, partially replacing the strength of the bulkheads that had been removed. They were not watertight.

If an explosion or structural failure did open a hole in the side of the *Marine Sulphur Queen,* one half of the ship would have quickly filled; if it had broken in half the entire ship would have taken on water. It would have sunk so rapidly that there would have been no time for an SOS.

Writers on the Bermuda Triangle have made much of the lack of debris when a ship sinks. Most of the floatable gear on a ship plowing through a stormy sea would be below in the various compartments. Gear on deck would be firmly attached to the ship to prevent its being blown or washed away; in either case it would go down with the sinking ship. A few items did manage to break away from the *Marine Sulphur Queen* and were subsequently recovered.

The Legend of the Bermuda Triangle has it that the Coast Guard failed to find an explanation for the loss of the *Marine*

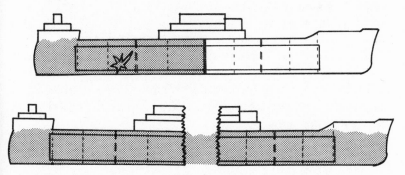

Fig. 3 *Marine Sulphur Queen. Above,* hole in side; *below,* broken in half. In either case, the ship would have sunk.

Sulphur Queen. In reality, the Board of Investigation listed four possible causes and the Commandant added a fifth. Any of the suggested causes, either by itself or in combination with any of the others, could have caused the accident. The Coast Guard merely declined to specify which one it felt was most likely to have occurred.

The discovery of a shattered name board* has led several researchers to conclude that the ship sank because of an explosion which occurred when seawater came into contact

---

* A name board, made of wood, bears the ship's name and is solid! tached to its side.

with the molten sulfur. This theory has several flaws, however. The first is that it does not explain how the water managed to reach the sulfur. The second is that the condition of the board could have been caused by something other than an explosion. It could have been "popped" off the side of the ship as it buckled after having suffered structural failure. Of the five suggested causes of the disaster, the Coast Guard felt that an explosion was the least likely to have occurred.

Widows and relatives of the men filed suit soon after the incident, asking damages from the owner of the ship. The legal battle has continued for more than ten years. On the tenth anniversary of the *Marine Sulphur Queen*'s disappearance it was announced that one of the first of the wrongful death claims had been settled, with court approval of an award of $115,000 to the widow of an ordinary seaman.

In 1972 the Supreme Court let stand a lower court ruling that the ship was unseaworthy. Claims reported to total over $7 million may now be pressed.

The rapid sinking of the ship prompted an investigation into the use of automatic emergency warning systems and position-indicating radio beacons.

Liquid sulfur carriers are now rare in world shipping. Only eleven are in regular service, and none of these has suffered a major accident in the last decade.

40

July 1963

Sno' Boy

Within a few months of the loss of the Marine Sulphur Queen, *a 63-foot charter fishing boat vanished in good weather on the 80-mile voyage from Kingston, Jamaica, to the Pedro Banks. The* Sno' Boy *and her forty occupants were never heard from again, although several bits of debris believed to be from the vessel were observed.*

Miami Herald, Friday, July 5, 1963, p. 1:

[UP]—The Coast Guard here said Thursday it is searching the Caribbean for a ship with 55 passengers aboard which is overdue on a voyage from Jamaica to a tiny island in the Pedro Banks, about eighty miles to the south. . . .

At least seven air-sea rescue planes are looking for the 63-foot *Sno' Boy* which was due in Northeast Cay, Pedro Banks, shortly after noon Tuesday. . . .

The search is being conducted out of the U.S. Naval Air Station at Guantanamo, Cuba.

Lloyd's Weekly Casualty Reports, July 9, 1963, p. 23:

Vessel *Sno' Boy* has been found safe south of Kingston, Jamaica, the United States Navy reported today. A Navy spokesman said that the vessel radioed her position to United States Atlantic Headquarters at Norfolk. The spokesman said that the ship apparently had been held up because of bad weather and that she had no problems. . . .

Miami Herald, Saturday, July 6, 1963, p. 1:

By Steve Trumbell. Search continued over a wide area of the Caribbean Sea Friday for a missing 63-foot Miami-owned motor vessel with 55 persons reported aboard. The craft, *Sno' Boy,* has been missing three days.

The search was intensified Friday when a tabletop identified as being from the craft was found south of Jamaica where the *Sno' Boy* planned to fish.

Through an error, it was reported for a time Friday that the craft had been found. The "find" turned out to be another vessel . . . held up by bad weather near Progresso, Mexico.

No one could explain the reported presence of 55 persons on a 63-foot boat.

"I don't know how that many could make a fishing trip on the boat," said Boyd Snow . . . former owner who still holds a mortgage on the boat. "When I converted it from a surplus aircraft rescue craft there were overnight accommodations for seven people, including the crew."

Miami Herald, Sunday, July 7, 1963, p. 1:

By Lee Winfrey. A body was found floating in the Caribbean Sea Saturday in the "same general area" where the . . . *Sno' Boy* is missing with 40 men aboard. . . .

The aircraft carrier *Wasp,* directing the search, found the body. There was no immediate identification.

Several pieces of debris, all believed to be from the *Sno' Boy,* were also sighted Saturday by the six Navy and Coast Guard planes taking part in the search.

The debris included a deck house, a life jacket, a white spar, a gasoline drum, and several bamboo poles.

The Coast Guard said the deck cargo of the *Sno' Boy* included 99 35-gallon drums of gasoline and 50 bundles of four-foot bamboo poles.

A tabletop identified as coming from the *Sno' Boy* was recovered

Friday by the fishing vessel *Marsutana*. The debris was scattered over an area several miles wide. . . .

Besides the men, the gasoline drums and the bamboo poles, the vessel was also reported to be carrying 68 35-gallon drums of water.

The Coast Guard expressed amazement at the volume of passengers and cargo, calling the vessel "tremendously overloaded."*

Miami Herald, Tuesday, July 9, 1963, p. 10:

By Kurt Luedtke. A task force of Navy and Coast Guard ships and planes will comb a 50-square mile area of the Caribbean for the last time today searching for the fishing vessel *Sno' Boy* which vanished a week ago with 40 persons aboard. . . .

In the seven-day search, rescuers found only scattered debris—a deckhouse, a dinghy, a life raft—that provides the only testimony to the ship's last voyage. A body was sighted but never recovered. . . .

The Navy said there was "virtually no hope" for the *Sno' Boy* passengers after a week in shark-infested waters, and said the search would be "reluctantly abandoned" Tuesday night.

A Navy spokesman said the vessel apparently swamped or struck a reef and sunk.

There were indications that the *Sno' Boy* may have been overloaded when it left Kingston harbor.

---

* It was also reported that 19 tons of ice were aboard.

41

August 1963

Two KC-135s

On Wednesday, August 28, 1963, two KC-135 stratotankers left Homestead Air Force Base, Florida, on a classified mission over the Atlantic Ocean. KC-135s, the military version of the 707, have a cruising speed of 600 mph and a range of 4,500 miles, and are used to refuel other aircraft on long-distance flights.

The two jets made a routine report about noon from a position 800 miles northeast of Miami and 300 miles west of Bermuda, and were never heard from again. Debris identified as coming from a KC-135 was soon found near the last reported position, and it was assumed that the planes had collided in midair. However, two days later more debris was found almost 200 miles from the scene of the first find, contradicting the theory that the jets had collided. Several days after that the Air Force gave up the search, announcing that the debris definitely had come from the two missing airplanes.

There are two explanations of how the planes could have vanished without one of them being able to send a distress message. The most obvious is that the "flying gas stations" collided and exploded at the cruising altitude of more than

30,000 feet. The speed of such a disaster would preclude any emergency calls. But, if the disappearance was caused by a midair collision, why was debris found in two separate areas, almost 200 miles apart?

If a midair is ruled out because of the distance between the debris, each plane must have had its own individual problem and gone down separately. This is extremely unlikely. The odds against separate disasters overcoming two multi-million-dollar planes at the same time are so infinitesimally small that the possibility is inconceivable. They would have had to occur so close together that neither crew would have been able to raise the alert that the other plane was in an emergency situation. Such a call was never received.

There are two possible ways, then, to explain the incident, but logic rules against accepting either one as the solution. Officials are still scratching their heads over the case and will say only that "something very strange is going on out there." Old-timers in the area rack up another two points for the jinx and ask each other, "Who knows what evil lurks in the heart of the Bermuda Triangle?"

Miami Herald, Thursday, August 29, 1963, p. 1:

By Kurt Luedtke and Larry Miller. Two giant Air Force tankers vanished over the Atlantic Wednesday with 11 Homestead airmen aboard.

A search plane from Bermuda reported sighting an oil slick Wednesday night and surface vessels recovered lifejackets. There was no positive identification that either came from the missing aircraft. . . .

Based at Homestead Air Force Base, the huge KC-135s were returning from a refueling mission. They were reported overdue at 3 P.M. and a search was launched immediately.

Planes . . . and Coast Guard surface vessels combed an area about 800 miles northeast of Miami. . . .

At least 24 planes joined the search by midnight and the number was to double by morning. Four Coast Guard ships were called out to help.

The first planes in the air followed the path the tankers would have taken to Homestead. Others flew in squares extending out from the route, flying low with lights over the water. . . .

There was hope that survival gear aboard the planes would allow the men to stay afloat until dawn, when visibility would speed the search.

Last radio contact with the twin tankers came at noon. They reported their position about 900 miles northeast of Miami and that they expected to arrive at Homestead at 2 P.M.

The 4-million-dollar tankers, carrying a payload of more than 25,-000 gallons of high octane jet fuel, had completed a rendezvous with two B47 jet bombers from Schilling Air Force Base, Kansas.

The next report, prescribed by Air Force routine, never came . . . and the planes were declared missing.

Miami Herald, Friday, August 30, 1963, p. 1:

By Leighton McLaughlin. Scattered debris pulled from the Atlantic Thursday by searchers led to fears that two missing KC135 Strato-tankers collided in the air. Hope for the 11 Homestead crewmen aboard waned as rescuers failed to turn up any sign of survivors.

Three empty life rafts and a flier's helmet bearing the name of one of the 11 missing crewmen were found bobbing in the ocean.

A freighter, the *Azalea City,* picked up the debris about midway between Nassau and Bermuda.

Found besides the helmet and life rafts were a yellow rubberized exposure suit and bits of aircraft paneling. The Air Force said 50 planes and 36 ships would press the search for the missing men throughout the night.

The flier's helmet pulled from the sea, had "Gardner" stenciled on it. One of the missing men was identified as Capt. Gerald Gardner.

Air Force officials at the Pentagon had "speculated" that the planes collided as they flew toward Homestead from a routine, but classified, refueling mission over the ocean. . . .

A collision would explain why contact was lost with the two huge "flying gas stations" after a routine radio check at about noon.

No distress call was heard, and the bomber crews reported "a normal, routine refueling mission in good weather," according to a base spokesman from Schilling. . . .

The bomber crews said they saw nothing amiss with the tankers when they parted company for their flights home. The refueling, said the spokesman, took place "in the same general area" the tankers were last heard from.

That was about 900 miles northeast of Miami. The sighted debris was about 780 miles in the same direction.

Miami Herald, Saturday, August 31, 1963, p. 2:

By Lee Winfrey. Planes searching for two jet tankers . . . sighted a second concentration of wreckage Friday, 160 miles away from a "floating junkyard" of debris found earlier.

Darkness fell before the second collection of debris could be recovered by ships. A Coast Guard cutter was expected at the scene soon after dawn today.

There was no sign at either scene of any survivors. . . .

The wide distance between the two patches of wreckage seemed to reduce speculation that the two planes collided in flight. The Air Force has declined comment so far on the probable cause of the planes' disappearances.

In the first concentration of wreckage found Friday were fliers' helmets, life jackets, navigation charts, plane paneling and equipment covers. A pilot said the 10-square-mile scene some 260 miles southwest of Bermuda looked like a "floating junkyard."

An Air Force spokesman said search directors were "pretty definite that the findings came from at least one of the aircraft."

Miami Herald, Sunday, September 1, 1963, p. 2:

Search for survivors from two missing jet tankers shifted Saturday to a single 10-square-mile area about 260 miles southwest of Bermuda.

Another patch of debris was sighted Friday about 160 miles away, but searchers said Saturday none of it came from either of the two planes.

"It appears to be just large patches of seaweed, driftwood and an old buoy," said Maj. Fred Brent, of the Air Rescue Service at Orlando Air Force Base.

The second reported area of debris, the one that gave rise to the mystery, was not from one of the planes, but was nothing more than seaweed, driftwood, and an old buoy!

A report of the Military Airlift Command provided additional information on the search.

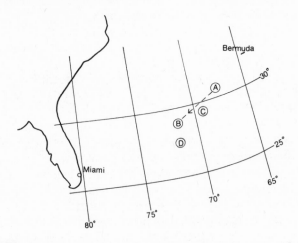

The two KC-135s. *A*, the 12:10 position report; *B*, proposed position at 12:37; *C*, first debris area; *D*, second debris area.

A Narrative Report on the Search for Two SAC KC-135 Aircraft, 55th Air Rescue Squadron Historical Data Report, 1 Aug 63–31 Aug 63. Military Airlift Command:

Two KC-135s, Pry 38 and Pry 41 . . . reported at [point A on map below] at [12:10 PM] with an estimate at [point B, 275 miles away] at [12:37 PM] and were unreported since that time. Headquarters ARS requested . . . a route search. . . .

Numerous sightings were made. . . . In the general area of [region C] . . . debris . . . was identified as coming from the KC-135 aircraft. Life preserver LPU-2/P local number 314 was identified as coming from KC-135, Pry 38, and a helmet with the name "Gardner"

. . . was identified as coming from KC-135, Pry 41. Two radar receiver transmitting units were picked up and later identified as one
each coming from the KC-135 type aircraft.

On Saturday, Sunday, and Monday many sightings were
made in the search area, but all those other than in the
vicinity of region C were found to be only the flotsam normally found in sea-lanes. There is no mention in the search
report of a second major concentration of debris, such as the
newspapers reported at "D," only numerous sightings of debris throughout the entire region, none of which was from
the planes. The search was discontinued late Monday afternoon.

The ARS report presents ample evidence that the planes
crashed close together, and that despite the Air Force statement that they were in radio contact with each other and
not flying close together, they apparently collided. At the
speed the airplanes were capable of, it is possible to close a
gap of a mile in just a few seconds. If they were on a collision
course it would have been too late to react by the time it was
seen, either visually or on the radar screens.

Richard F. Gerwig, Chief of the Reporting and Documents
Division at Norton Air Force Base, where all Air Force accident reports are housed, wrote in answer to a query from me
that "it was definitely established that a midair collision did
occur between the aircraft in question." Despite the Legend,
the Air Force does not appear to be "scratching its head" over
this incident.

Perhaps the only remaining mystery is why search planes
reported sighting a second possible area of aircraft debris
when it was nothing more than seaweed and trash. The sighting was made as the sun was about to set, a time when visibility is not at its best. It is difficult under even the most
favorable conditions for searchers in aircraft to be certain of
what it is that they spot bobbing around hundreds of feet

below in the ocean. A good example of the type of mistake that can be made occurred in this very search on Saturday morning, August 31, when a KB-50, en route to the search area, reported a raft with a body floating near it five miles south of Kindley Air Force Base, Bermuda. Within half an hour it was recovered and identified as an orange life raft discarded from a boat, a tree trunk, and an ammunition dump sign. Erroneous sightings are made in almost every search, and such false reports are not at all uncommon.

42

June 1965

C-119 Flying Boxcar

The Legend and the newspaper version of this incident agree, although the conclusions differ.

Miami Herald, Monday, June 7, 1965, p. 1:

A wide search was launched Sunday for an Air Force Flying Boxcar . . . with ten persons aboard. . . .

The Coast Guard said it presumed the C-119 to be lost in South Bahamian waters, about 280 miles from Miami.

The bulky, twin-engine plane took off from Homestead Air Force Base at 7:47 P.M. Saturday. . . .

The plane, based at Milwaukee's Billy Mitchell Air Force Base, flew to Homestead early Saturday with a cargo of plane parts for the Grand Turk installation. . . .

A Homestead spokesman said ''. . . there has not been one sign of the craft since early last evening.''

The C-119 was due to touch down on Grand Turk at 11:23 P.M. Saturday.

A search of over 2,000 square miles of the Atlantic began at dawn.

Miami Herald, Tuesday, June 8, 1965, p. 12:

A missing Air Force plane with 10 airmen aboard was only 45 minutes from its Bahamas destination when it mysteriously disappeared. . . .

Flying near Crooked Island in the southern Bahamas, the bulky twin-engine plane was only about 100 miles from the Grand Turk Air Force landing strip when the last radio contact was made. This was at 11 P.M.

"There was no indication of trouble, and nothing has been heard from them since," a Miami Coast Guard spokesman said.

"Possibly the plane had steering trouble and veered off course or overflew the destination." . . .

By Monday [searchers] were combing the 100,000 square-mile area known to veteran pilots as the "Bermuda Triangle." . . .

It is in this huge swath of water that hundreds of planes, ships, and submarines went down during World War II. . . . Since then . . . a number of other planes have vanished mysteriously there.

"It's strange," said an old-timer at Homestead who has flown in peace and war, "that the planes that go down in the south Bahamas never leave a trace."

And so it has been with the C-119—not a piece of wreckage or evidence of life. Not a flare at night, though seven planes scoured the area Sunday night.

The search was called off at dark on Thursday, June 10. Many similar incidents have already been examined, and there is no reason to repeat the same analysis here. Unless the plane was off course, it appears to have gone down between Crooked Island and Grand Turk, possibly because of structural failure, an explosion, or engine failure. It was a twin-engine plane, so failure of one engine would have immediately created a critical situation, and the pilots may have been too busy handling the emergency to take time to make a distress call.

If the plane ditched, the pilot would have been faced with a night landing at sea in a disabled craft. The sky was overcast, waves were two to three feet high, and the wind was 15 knots. Although the weather would be called fair, the waves and the breeze could have caused a problem for a disabled land plane ditching in the dark.

In late 1973 the International UFO Bureau published a series of articles* in which it "could not help but wonder if the C-119 had not been captured by a UFO." It seems that Gemini IV was in flight at the time of the plane's loss, and astronaut James McDivitt spotted a UFO with arms. Several minutes later both McDivitt and Ed White observed another (the same?) object over the Caribbean. Since it was realized that the C-119 may have been captured by the UFO, according to the bureau, a full-scale investigation was initiated. (The articles were not clear about whether the Air Force or the bureau held these fears and launched the investigation.) An examination of the films taken by the astronauts showed nothing that looked like a satellite, and to this day, says the bureau, the UFO has never been explained.

According to news accounts at the time, on June 4 Mc-Divitt reported an object that appeared to have big arms sticking out. Analysts and computers spent several days trying to discover what it was that had flashed by at an estimated distance of 10 to 20 miles. The first guess was that it was Pegasus 2, a gigantic satellite with 96-foot-long armlike antennae, but it was later calculated to have been more than a thousand miles away at the time. McDivitt described the object as white, cylindrical, and appearing to have an arm sticking out, but that the "arm" could have been a reflection. According to news accounts, McDivitt said he believed it was a rocket booster, one of the 1,390 satellites, burned-out boosters, and assorted pieces of space junk then in orbit.

The North American Air Defense Command, which had ruled out Pegasus 2 as a possibility, estimated that ten pieces of space junk were in the area at the time. For a while it was also thought that it might have been a new Russian spacecraft.

The object showed up on film as a large white spot on a

---

* *Midnight*, 15 October 1973, p. 11; 22nd p. 11; 29th p. 7.

black background, but it could not be positively identified. The astronauts reported sighting two other satellites during the flight, but they were merely points of light and did not show up on the photographs. Pegasus 2 came by one time, but they missed sighting it.

I contacted James McDivitt and asked for his reaction to the story.

In reply to your letter of January 22, I would like to say that during my flight of Gemini 4 I did indeed see what some people would call a UFO. I think it is important to realize that the letters U F O stand for Unidentified Flying Object.

The object which I saw remains unidentified. This does not mean that it is, therefore, a spacecraft from some remote planet in the universe. It also doesn't mean that it isn't such a spacecraft. It only means that I saw something in flight which neither I nor anyone else was ever able to identify.

43

January 1967

Black Week

Chase YC-122, Fort Lauderdale to Bimini
Beechcraft Bonanza, Florida Keys
Piper Apache, San Juan to St. Thomas

In one "black week" in January 1967, three planes with experienced, safety-conscious pilots and a total of eight passengers vanished on short flights during good weather.

The first victim was a Chase YC-122 cargo plane which disappeared on the 60-mile flight from Fort Lauderdale to Bimini. The twin-engine plane had been chartered for use in the filming of a Lloyd Bridges movie, The Unkillables. *Debris and an oil slick were found miles apart northwest of Bimini, but it was not determined if either came from the missing plane.*

Three days later two couples took off in a Beechcraft Bonanza from Miami International Airport for a short pleasure flight to the Florida Keys and back. They were not seen again.

Three days after that, a couple in a chartered Piper Apache disappeared on the one-hour flight from San Juan, Puerto Rico, to St. Thomas, Virgin Islands.

In all three cases the weather had been good, no distress message was sent, and no debris was identified.

Chase YC-122

Miami Herald, Thursday, January 12, 1967, p. B1:

By Jon Nordheimer. A converted World War II troop glider used in the filming of a new Ivan Tors adventure picture disappeared on route to Bimini Wednesday and the four men aboard were missing . . . The twin engine plane took off from Fort Lauderdale-Hollywood International Airport at 9:25 A.M. and wasn't heard from again. A search plane . . . spotted debris in the Gulf Stream about one hour later, floating about 30 miles northwest of Bimini.

"We could see oil drums, unopened parachutes, and pieces of the plane, but no sign of survivors," said Joe Maugeri, pilot of the search plane.

A large oil slick was later seen about 12 miles south of the floating debris, the spot where the plane apparently crashed. . . . By midafternoon, a Coast Guard helicopter returned to the Opalocka base with what debris it could find from the crash scene: a 55-gallon red and yellow drum, part of a landing gear, and a safety motion picture film can.

The separate oil slick is no cause for mystery, as there are many slicks on the ocean's surface, from many sources. Although the crash site was found and debris from the plane was recovered, the reason for the crash was not determined.

Beechcraft Bonanza

Miami Herald, Wednesday, January 18, 1967, p. B2:

By Robert Reno. A $3000 reward was posted Tuesday for the discovery of a single engine plane missing with four Miamians aboard. Hope . . . waned as the Coast Guard failed to find a trace of the plane after three days of search. . . .

[The Beechcraft Bonanza] vanished after takeoff from Miami International Airport Saturday afternoon. [The Miamians] were bound for

North Key Largo and possibly Marathon, and had planned to return via Flamingo and the southern Everglades.

Three Coast Guard planes criss-crossed an 8000 square mile area between Miami and Key West all day Tuesday despite limited visibility and rain. The weather cancelled plans for 12 planes of the Civil Air Patrol to join the search. . . . Most of the area being searched is either open water or swamp where the wreckage of the plane could easily be concealed from air searchers.

Miami Herald, Saturday, January 21, 1967, p. B2:
The Coast Guard continued its extensive air search for two Miami couples. . . . There were reports Friday that the couples had lunched at the Ocean Reef Yacht Club on Key Largo. Upon taking off again, the plane developed engine trouble, reports say. . . .

Miami Herald, Sunday, January 22, 1967, p. B1, col. 4:
By Miller Davis. John Rawson, an investigator for the Civil Aeronautics Board, was asking . . . guests at North Key Largo's Ocean Reef Club . . . if they remembered seeing [the Beechcraft Bonanza]. . . . A man and his wife, out fishing, remember a small blue and white plane. . . . It soared off the runway and the couple reported a sputtering noise as it headed out to sea. . . . If it went down at sea, "it wouldn't stay up very long," Rawson said. The plane is not designed to float. When the waters near the key clear up the area will be searched again. For now, however, the Coast Guard has officially suspended its search.

Piper Apache

Miami Herald, Saturday, January 21, 1967, p. B2:
A large contingent of aircraft and ships converged on waters around Puerto Rico to help in the search for the daughter of the American ambassador to Britain, her husband, and the couple's pilot. . . .

[The Ambassador said] the search for the plane and survivors seemed "pretty hopeless." There are some indications the plane may have run into bad weather on the 70-mile flight that usually takes one hour.

Miami Herald, Sunday, January 22, 1967, p. B1, col. 2:

By James Buchanan. How, within a week, could [two] safety-conscious pilots, their airplanes, and their [five] passengers, virtually disappear in thin air? The question uppermost in the minds of aviation officials today is: "Could these [seven] persons have been saved by additional precautions prior to the crashes, or could they have been saved after the crash?"

The answers to their disappearance may never be known. But they could lie in part with the . . . Flight Plan. . . . A flight plan, filed with the FAA, is a simple document that has saved more pilots than can be counted. It tells, briefly, when the airplane will leave, where it is going and over what route, and more importantly, when it will get there. Should an airplane be as much as 15 minutes late in reaching its destination the FAA then begins tracking it down. . . .

"[The Bonanza pilot]," the FAA said Saturday, "was one of our staunchest advocates of flight safety. He attended safety meetings regularly. He urged fellow pilots to file flight plans wherever they went." Yet [he] took off for a two to three hour flight without telling anyone where he was going or when to expect him back. . . . The . . . plane was not reported missing until 12:35 A.M. last Sunday morning, more than 12 hours after its takeoff and some six hours after the foursome had planned to return to Miami.

"[The Apache pilot] always filed a flight plan," FAA officials at San Juan said. "Always except this time." [The plane] wasn't reported missing until nine hours had elapsed after [the] scheduled landing time.

In each case, had they filed flight plans the search would have begun almost immediately after their scheduled landing time. In each case, the possibility exists the aircraft could have been spotted before it sank in the water or the occupants could have been rescued as they clung to the wreckage. . . .

[The searchers'] batting average for finding the missing plane is abnormally high. Providing the pilot filed a free Flight Plan.

Like many other disappearances, such as the *Star Tiger,* the *Star Ariel,* and the *Marine Sulphur Queen,* a long delay in starting the search may have contributed to the failure to find any trace of the missing planes. Of the three planes that disappeared in the "black week" of January 1967, the crash scene was found only in the case of the Chase YC-122, in which a search was initiated minutes after it became overdue.

44

December 1967
~~~~~~

Witchcraft

Christmas week claimed more victims for the Bermuda Triangle in 1967 when two Florida men disappeared while only a mile out to sea, off Miami Beach. They had gone for an evening jaunt in a 23-foot cabin cruiser, the Witchcraft, *to view the Christmas lights of the city from the ocean. At 9:00 PM on December 22 the Seventh District Coast Guard Office in Miami received a call from the men that the boat's propeller had struck a submerged object and the engine could not be run without excessive vibration. The hull was undamaged, and the boat was virtually unsinkable in any case because of the built-in flotation chambers. The Coast Guard was told that there was no immediate danger, but that a tow back to port would be necessary. Within minutes a crew was on the way, and the two men at Number Seven life buoy had nothing to do but relax and watch the scenery.*

The Coast Guard reached the location in nineteen minutes, but found nothing—no boat, no men, no life jackets. The men had somehow vanished while still within the glow of the lights they had gone to watch.

The Coast Guard gave up a vast search several days later, announcing that the men were "presumed missing, but not lost at sea."

Miami Herald, Friday, December 22, 1967, p. 2:

SMALL BOAT FORECAST . . . winds 10 to 20 knots. Seas four to six feet and inland waters choppy.

Miami Herald, Sunday, December 24, 1967, p. B1:

By Arnold Markowitz and Pat Sealey. A retired hotelman and a priest friend who took a boat ride to look at Miami's holiday lights Friday night still are missing in spite of a massive search by the Coast Guard, the Civil Air Patrol and private boats and aircraft.

Dan Burack . . . and the Rev. Father Padraig (Patrick) Horgan of . . . Fort Lauderdale were missing with Burack's 23-foot boat, *Witchcraft.**

Burack radioed the Coast Guard Friday night that the boat had become disabled about a mile off Miami Beach. . . .

The Coast Guard said a radio-telephone distress message was received Friday night, and that Burack was told to fire off a flare in about 20 minutes, in order to guide a rescue boat to his location.

The rescue crew never saw the flare, and there was no further radio contact with the *Witchcraft.*

Stiff winds blowing from the north and northeast whipped the surface of the Atlantic into a carpet of foam against which a white boat like *Witchcraft* would have been well camouflaged.

The search Friday covered 1,200 square miles, reaching from Miami to Delray Beach and Bimini. . . .

"Dan's an expert sailor and a good navigator," said [a friend]. "I don't know if Father Horgan can swim, but Dan can, and neither of them is the type to panic in an emergency.

"They were carrying all the safety devices on the boat, too."

Miami Herald, Thursday, December 29, 1967, p. B2:

The Coast Guard Wednesday called off a five day air-sea search. . . . The men . . . and the *Witchcraft* were never spotted.

The search covered an area from Islamorada north to St. Augustine, and out to sea as far as 120 miles—about 24,500 square miles, the Coast Guard said.

After reading the version of the *Witchcraft* incident as it appears in the Legend of the Bermuda Triangle it would be

---

* Burack's name has often been incorrectly spelled "Burrack."

easy to picture the two friends sitting on the deck of the boat, feet up on the side rails, enjoying the still, silent beauty of the lights of the city.

In reality the weather was rather rough and continued so for several days. The wind was strong enough to form white-caps a mile out at sea, and the waves were forecast to be as much as six feet high. Without the use of its engine the boat would have had no power for maintaining the proper heading into the waves, and could easily have been swamped.

The boat was not at a specified location, as the Legend goes, but was supposed to fire a flare to show the Coast Guard where it was. Without the flare the Coast Guard would have had to search an enormous area. On a dark night with the sea "whipped into a carpet of white foam," the chances of finding a white boat in an unknown location would be almost nil. The noise of the wind and the waves would have drowned out any cries for help, and survival time in the ocean in winter, even in Florida, is very limited.

It is not likely that the Coast Guard would announce that the boat was "presumed missing, but not lost at sea," after having searched in vain for it for five days. Many of the statements attributed to the Coast Guard and the Navy in accounts of the Bermuda Triangle mystery have proved to be untrue in the cases where accident reports are available. Unfortunately, no such report is available for this incident, so the statement can be neither proved nor disproved. For the same reason the nature of the distress message and the purported location of the boat at a specific buoy also can be neither proved nor disproved, but the newspaper version differs considerably from the version told in the Legend.

45

May 1968

Scorpion

The Scorpion, *a nuclear-powered submarine with ninety-nine crewmen aboard, broke radio silence about midnight, May 21, 1968, to make a routine position report to her Norfolk base. She was then near the Azores on a run home from the Mediterranean where she had been on duty with the U.S. Sixth Fleet. When she failed to arrive on schedule a massive search was begun, but no sign of her was found. She was officially listed as "presumed lost."*

Five months later the research ship Mizar *located and photographed a shattered wreck 400 miles southwest of the Azores that was believed to be the* Scorpion. *It was in water more than 10,000 feet deep. The Navy was unable to find the reason for the loss, but old-time seamen in the area knew that the path of the doomed sub led through the infamous Bermuda Triangle.*

It was first hoped that Commander Slattery of the *Scorpion* had delayed his approach over the shallow waters of the continental shelf because of the storms and waves up to 20 feet that were lashing the area. As these hopes faded a search for survivors and debris began, and a court of inquiry was appointed to investigate the incident.

On May 29 a U.S. Navy plane off Norfolk picked up a radio message that included the *Scorpion*'s code name, but it was labeled a hoax. A submarine hull found 100 miles off Norfolk proved to be a casualty of World War II. In June the Navy notified the families of the crewmen that the submarine was presumed lost, but that the search would continue.

The depth to which the *Scorpion* could submerge had been restricted because safety improvements recommended after the loss of the *Thresher* in April 1963 had been only partially completed. The submarine had been considered safe even though the adequacy of the regular surfacing system was debated, and the emergency surfacing system was known to be defective and inoperative. The sub had collided with a barge in Naples, but a survey had found no damage.

As the number of search vessels was being reduced in June, *Newsweek* reported that the Navy had tapes from underwater sound-detecting devices that had recorded the implosion of the hull on May 21 about 450 miles southwest of the Azores. The Department of Defense remained silent as *Newsweek* further reported that the Navy was searching the area with photographic equipment. In October Admiral Moorer disclosed that the oceanographic research ship *Mizar* had photographed part of the hull 400 miles southwest of the Azores, but that it was unlikely that debris would be recovered. The court of inquiry reconvened to give the matter further study.

Arizona Republic, February 1, 1969, p. 1:

WASHINGTON [Washington Post Service] . . . The Navy disclosed that a seven-member court of inquiry was unable to explain the sinking of the *Scorpion,* which went down last May. . . .

So far, the only evidence of the *Scorpion* comes from pictures taken by underwater cameras from the research vessel *Mizar.*

In the unclassified portion of the findings released yesterday, the Navy said it had eliminated two possible causes of the sinking:

Running into a seamount or ridge rising from the ocean floor, or a mishap with the submarine's nuclear power plant.

It said there were no seamounts in the area where the submarine sank and it concluded after hearing expert testimony that a nuclear mishap could be "dismissed" as a possible cause.

The court was also satisfied that "the loss of *Scorpion* is not attributable to the delayed completion of her full subsafe (submarine safety) program." . . .

"No evidence of any kind to suggest foul play or sabotage was found by the court," the report said.

It also found no evidence to support a possible collision with another sub or a surface vessel because "no U.S. ships have reported such a collision, nor have those of any other nation."

Throughout the report, the Navy stressed that the crew was highly experienced and stable, and that it would have responded quickly to any emergency.

"A flooding accident would normally be brought quickly under control by a crew as well-trained and experienced as *Scorpion*'s," the report said.

"Although the photographs gave no indication that loss of the submarine was due to an explosion of one of her own torpedoes," the report said, "the court probed this possibility."

Photographs taken by the *Mizar* showed the sub's "sail" or superstructure intact but lying on its side more than 100 feet away from the *Scorpion*'s bow.

Although the loss of the *Scorpion* is often considered to be a part of the mystery of the Bermuda Triangle, the incident occurred much closer to Africa and Portugal. The *Thresher*, which is occasionally mentioned in relation to the Triangle, sank 220 miles east of Cape Cod on April 10, 1963. Its shattered hull was found a few months later by the bathyscaph *Trieste*. A Congressional investigation revealed that a water pipe failure in the engine room was probably the cause of the accident.

Several other submarines have vanished well outside the Triangle. A few months before the loss of the *Scorpion* two

The *Scorpion* and the *Thresher*

subs, the French *Minerve* and the Israeli *Dakar*, disappeared in the Mediterranean. No trace of either was ever found.

Two years later the French submarine *Eurydice* vanished within a few miles of where the *Minerve* had disappeared. Although a geophysical laboratory recorded a violent explosion and the *Mizar* later located a major section of the submarine, the cause of the accident could not be found.

Like other expensive machines, a nuclear submarine could be lost because of the failure of a relatively inexpensive part. In March 1973 the USS *Greenling*, operating near Bermuda, dived far beyond its normal depth but was able to return safely to port when the error was discovered in time. A crewman alleged that the submarine was within 200 feet of being crushed in water more than three miles deep. The near-tragedy, which almost gave the *Greenling* a place in naval history alongside the *Thresher* and the *Scorpion,* was caused by a sticky depth gauge. It would also have given it a place in the Legend of the Bermuda Triangle.

46

July 1969

Five Abandoned Vessels

On July 10, 1969, the Teignmouth Electron, a 41-foot three-hulled yacht, was found abandoned between Bermuda and the Azores. A number of planes and ships searched unsuccessfully for the vessel's only crewman, Donald Crowhurst, the leading yachtsman in a round-the-world race.

The boat was the fifth* abandoned vessel to be found in that area in eleven days, prompting a spokesman for Lloyd's to exclaim, "It's rare to get reports like this in such a close area in such a vast ocean. It is rather odd."

There had been no bad weather for some time in the area, which incidentally was very near where the Mary Celeste had been found almost a century before. One expert who had been studying the Bermuda Triangle for many years said he would not be surprised if all the crews had been saucer-napped, as there would be no better place in the world to find a specimen than on a small boat in the middle of the vast, lonely ocean.

Several weeks later it was announced that there was overwhelming proof that Crowhurst had committed suicide by

---

* Some of the previous writers have stated that four boats were found in the area, others have reported five. The latter figure is correct.

jumping overboard, but the four other derelicts, including* the Vagabond, *sailed by Peter Wallin of Sweden, were never explained.*

The *Teignmouth Electron*

London *Times,* July 11, 1969, p. 1:

By Jonas Smith. Donald Crowhurst, the lone round-the-world yachtsman, was feared lost last night only a few days from completion of the voyage.

His trimaran *Teignmouth Electron*† in which he was expected to win the £5,000 for the fastest circumnavigation of the world in the *Sunday Times* Golden Globe race, was found abandoned 700 miles south-west of the Azores.

There was no sign of the yachtsman nor anything to suggest what had happened to him. Books, papers, films and tapes, and Mr. Crowhurst's log were found intact. . . .

The yachtsman's dinghy and emergency liferaft were still on the trimaran. . . .

He was [the] favourite to collect the £5,000 prize for the fastest non-stop circumnavigation. . . .

Last night Teignmouth, which was preparing a "Welcome Home Donald" banner, a civic reception, champagne party and a general hero's welcome, was grief-stricken. The carnival gaiety had already given way to mourning.

London *Times,* July 12, 1969, p. 4:

The search for Mr. Donald Crowhurst . . . was called off late last night. . . .

New York Times, July 27, 1969, p. 21:

LONDON, July 26—Donald Crowhurst, the missing British yachtsman who had been thought to be on the last stage of a solo voyage

---

* At least one writer who told of the Crowhurst incident neglected to mention his suicide.

† Some writers have erroneously spelled it *Teignmouth Electronic.*

Azores

X
Teignmouth Electron

Bermuda

The *Teignmouth Electron*

around the world, never left the Atlantic during the 243 days he was at sea, it was disclosed tonight.

The *Sunday Times* of London, sponsor of the round-the-world yacht race, said . . . that examination of the entries in his log showed that he had sent "misleading" radio messages on his position and was "under considerable mental strain toward the end of his voyage." . . .

Until July 10, when the trimaran . . . was found . . . Mr. Crowhurst was the favorite to win the prize of £5,000 ($12,000) offered by the *Sunday Times* for the fastest time.

Had he returned, said the paper, he would not have qualified for any prize.

In fact, he had sailed all together 4,500 miles in the Atlantic on an erratic course to South America. He also put into land for two days somewhere . . . whereas the yachtsmen in the race had to sail around the world without touching land.

An investigation* of the logbooks, tape recorder, and movie camera found on the yacht proved beyond a doubt that Crowhurst had not sailed around the world as he had been claiming, but had spent eight months cruising about the South Atlantic Ocean putting false entries in one set of logbooks and sending phony position reports by radio. Sir Francis Chichester, one of the judges of the race, had begun to suspect Crowhurst even before his abandoned boat was found.

According to investigations, Crowhurst grew increasingly anxious as he approached England, and vacillated between wanting to win the race and allowing someone else to have the prize so that his logbook and its false entries would not be checked. The irony is that Crowhurst's false reports had him gaining so rapidly on Nigel Tetley, the one man ahead of Crowhurst, that Tetley pushed his boat too hard and it broke apart and sank near the Azores, making Crowhurst a sure winner.

The thought of a fraudulent victory and the subsequent embarrassment apparently overwhelmed Crowhurst. His last entry in the logbook, written on July 1, was that at 20 minutes and 40 seconds past 11 o'clock in the morning he would "resign the game." Since the chronometer was missing it appeared that he had carried it with him to the edge of the deck and stepped into the sea at the appointed time.

---

* The investigation was performed by Nicholas Tomalin, editor of the *Sunday Times* (sponsor of the race), and Ron Hall. The details were reported in their book, *The Strange Last Voyage of Donald Crowhurst*.

■■■

The Four Other Derelicts

June 30. The British ship Maplebank *discovered an abandoned 60-foot vessel a few hundred miles northeast of Bermuda. No survivors could be found.*

London *Times*, July 12, 1969, p. 4:

On July 1 the British motor vessel *Maplebank* reported seeing a 60 ft. vessel floating bottom-up off northwest Africa.

■■■

July 4. The Cotopaxi *encountered a 35-foot yacht sailing along in fine weather with no sign of anyone aboard.*

London *Times*, July 12, 1969, p. 4:

On July 4 a yacht set on automatic steering was seen heading easterly in mid-Atlantic. No one was in the cockpit of the 35 ft. yacht. But Lloyd's say it was not necessarily abandoned.

■■■

July 6. The Swedish ship Golar Frost *found the yacht* Vagabond *on July 6, sails set and in perfect order except that she lacked a crew. No solution was ever found for the disappearance.*

London *Times*, July 12, 1969, p. 4:

A Swedish sailing yacht, the *Vagabond,* was picked up by a motor vessel after being found abandoned on July 2 some 200 miles from where the *Teignmouth Electron* was found.

New York *Times*, July 13, 1969, p. 11:

[It] was the 20-foot *Vagabond*, in which Peter Wallin* of Stockholm was sailing alone to Australia.

------

* Wallin's first name is sometimes given as William. I was not able to establish which one is correct.

••

July 8. The British tanker Helisoma *found a crewless 36-foot yacht between Bermuda and the Azores. There was nothing to indicate why the crew had left her.*

New York Times, *July 13, 1969, p. 11:*
   [The drifting boat was] an overturned 36-footer.

The INFO Journal, *Fall, 1969, p. 5:*
   July 8, 1969—The British tanker *Helsona* passed an upturned yacht, size unstated, whose bottom was encrusted with barnacles.

••

Extensive research shows that the weather was good when the boats were found. There were no accounts of storms in the area, nor of any ships that reported problems. The first hurricane of the season, Anna, was not reported until July 31. The Tomalin and Hall book on Crowhurst also confirms the weather situation.

Previous accounts of this incident, however, have failed to mention that the vessel found on June 30 was bottom-up and that it was found near Africa, not Bermuda.

The July 4 vessel was apparently on "automatic pilot" and had no problems.

The abandonment of the *Vagabond*, the 20-foot sloop, was never explained. It has not been verified that the last entry in the log was made on July 2, and there is no way to know how many days or miles it might have drifted.

Previous accounts do not point out that the July 8 yacht was overturned and covered with barnacles. It had apparently been floating around for some time.

The *Teignmouth Electron* was found by the *Picardy* at $33°11'N, 40°28'W$, or about 700 miles southwest of the Azores and 1,300 miles northeast of Bermuda. The locations of the other derelicts were not precisely given, although all indications are that they were in the same general area as Crowhurst's boat, which was far from the Bermuda Triangle.

47

August 1969

~~~~~~

Bill Verity

*In August 1969 ocean voyager Bill Verity of Fort Lauder-
dale, Florida, vanished north of Puerto Rico in the 20-foot
sailboat,* Brendan the Bold. *He had previously crossed the
ocean alone in a 12-foot boat, and was an experienced sailor.*

In 1969 Bill Verity set out from Ireland in a boat styled
after the craft he thinks may have been used by Brendan
the Bold, an Irish monk, to sail to Florida in A.D. 550.

On August 21, 1969, the Coast Guard issued a request for
all ships to be on the lookout for Verity, who was known to
be dangerously near the path of hurricane Debbie. Nothing
was heard until he arrived safely on San Salvador Island on
September 14, saying that he had thought he was "a
goner."

On November 30, 1973, I spoke by telephone with Verity,
who was then in his Bounty Launch, Inc. headquarters at
the South Street Seaport in New York City, building a boat
in which he intended to duplicate the voyage of Captain
Bligh.

He told me of his experience with hurricane Debbie and
how he had been witness to five days of the finest display of

wind, waves, and lightning that anyone could ever wish to see, but that he had, indeed, completed the voyage.

He was amused to learn that he was being reported as a victim of the Bermuda Triangle, but said that it was nothing new as he had previously been reported missing in several other places.

48

November 1970
~~~~~~

Jillie Bean and the Piper Comanche

The Bermuda Triangle took two more victims in November 1970. The cabin cruiser Jillie Bean *disappeared near the Bahamas and a Piper Comanche vanished on a flight from West Palm Beach to Jamaica. Neither sent a distress call.*

Miami Herald, Thursday, November 26, 1970, p. 22D:

"TRIANGLE" CLAIMS PLANE, BOAT

The infamous Bermuda Triangle of the Atlantic Ocean has apparently claimed two more victims, a single engine airplane and a 42-foot cabin cruiser, off the Bahama Islands.

Coast Guard and Air Force search planes are looking for the missing craft, which have not been heard from since leaving South Florida. . . . The cabin cruiser left Miami on Nov. 15, bound for Andros Island and the airplane left West Palm Beach Airport Monday afternoon en route to Jamaica.

Aboard the cruiser were its owner . . . his wife, and possibly another passenger and a pet dog. The Coast Guard said . . . a cargo of 5 tons of soda pop [was] aboard.

The airplane, a Piper Comanche owned by an Orlando flying service, left West Palm Beach Airport at 3:45 Monday on a four-hour flight, with enough gas to stay airborne for six hours. Along with the pilot . . . were two other Atlantans.

Miami Herald, Saturday, November 28, 1970, p. 28:

BERMUDA TRIANGLE RELEASES CRUISER

By Richard Wallace. The *Jillie Bean* casually cruised into Miami as darkness fell Friday, with three persons aboard the 42-foot boat unaware that they were providing a happy but anti-climactic ending for an intensive Coast Guard air-sea search.

"One of our helicopters spotted them leisurely cruising toward Government Cut just before sundown," a Miami Coast Guard spokesman said.

Six reconnaissance aircraft . . . two cutters and three smaller boats had been scouring a 30,000 square mile patch of the Atlantic off the Bahamas in a combined search for the *Jillie Bean* and a missing small plane.

No trace of the aircraft, carrying three men from Atlanta, had been found . . . as of Friday night. The search for the plane was suspended and will not be resumed unless the Coast Guard receives new clues to its location. . . .

The three aboard the *Jillie Bean* . . . were in no trouble and had no idea they were being sought. . . .

"It was reported missing by the owner's son," the Coast Guard spokesman said. "He was a little over-anxious."

It had been thought that both the *Jillie Bean* and the missing aircraft . . . had become victims of the infamous zone of the Atlantic known as the Bermuda Triangle.

The *Jillie Bean* episode demonstrates how readily the Bermuda Triangle is blamed for any incident in the area. The news that the boat returned safely has not received as much publicity as the initial report of the "disappearance." The incident also shows that searchers can fail to find a target even though it is within the search area. The *Jillie Bean* hunt had been in progress for at least three days, but the boat was not seen until it sailed back into its home port.

The Piper Comanche was never found. This is apparently another case of a search's being delayed by darkness. The weather was, from all available accounts, good at the time of the disappearance. The plane took off at 3:45 PM on the four-hour flight and was last heard from 31 minutes later. Although specific details are not given in either the FAA or the Military Airlift Command report, there would not have been any concern for the plane until at least 5:30 PM, when its position report would have been overdue (provided the pilot had filed a flight plan), and possibly not until as late as 8:00 PM, when it would have been overdue at Jamaica. All accounts of the incident are sketchy, but it appears that the search was not initiated until the following morning, by which time the ocean had at least 12 hours to dispose of debris.

The time of the day is important for several other reasons. First, according to the FAA accident report, the pilot held only a private pilot's certificate with no instrument rating. The pilot who flies away from lighted areas at night needs an instrument rating almost as much as the pilot who flies during bad weather, as the conditions are very similar. In either case he is deprived of all outside visual references and must keep his plane under control and headed in the right direction entirely by the use of instruments. The noninstrument pilot who encounters anything less than good conditions at night is immediately in a critical situation.

The second factor related to the time of day is that if the Comanche's trouble developed after 5:00 the pilot would have had to ditch in the dark, greatly increasing the chances for a disastrous crash.

49

April 1971

Elizabeth

The Elizabeth, *a 191-foot converted LST, left Fort Lauderdale early in April 1971, bound for Venezuela with a cargo of scrap paper. The Orinoco Shipping Company, owners of the New Jersey-based 2,000-ton ship, received a message on April 5 that she was passing the Bahamas. She never reported again. No trace of the ship was ever found despite a large search along the entire route.*

Since she was an old tub, the rumor was that she broke apart and sank. But if she had, the search area would have been covered with hundreds of bales of floating scrap paper that surely could not have been missed. What could possibly have happened to the Elizabeth?

Well, for one thing, it might have sunk without breaking apart—then the area would not have been covered with paper.

I was unsuccessful in my search for information on the *Elizabeth*. Lloyd's could find nothing in its records. There were no references to it in the *New York Times*, and there was nothing in the *Miami Herald* as late as April 15. The Casualty Review Branch of the Coast Guard reported that although there were many vessels by that name, none had a gross tonnage of approximately 2,000, none were converted LSTs, and none were listed as casualties. The American Bureau of Shipping could find no record of the vessel or of the Orinoco Shipping Company.

I searched the ship owners section of *Merchant Vessels of the United States* and did not find the company, nor was it listed in several other shipping directories.

It could be that both the company and the ship, even though New Jersey-based, were foreign owned. In that case neither would have been listed in the Coast Guard and American Bureau of Shipping publications. It is possible that the name of the ship was given incorrectly in the Legend.

There were no reports of storms at the time. On the contrary, in April Florida was in the midst of its worst drought in fifteen years. Fires were raging in the Everglades and water rationing was necessary in the cities.

50

October 1971

El Caribe

On the night of October 15, 1971, the Caribe, *bound from Colombia to the Dominican Republic, radioed that she would enter port at 7:00 the next morning. The 338-foot freighter, the largest vessel in the Dominican merchant marine, was never seen or heard from again.*

San Juan Star, Saturday, October 16, 1971, p. 1:

By Yvonne Beltzer. The owner of the freighter *El Caribe,* four days overdue on a run from Barranquilla, Colombia to Santo Domingo, said Friday he believes the ship may have been hijacked to Cuba.

Diego Bordas, owner of Bordas Lines, the Dominican shipping firm that operates the 339-foot vessel, said . . . he has been trying to telephone Havana to inquire about the missing ship.

Meanwhile, the vessel has been the object of an intensive search . . . [of] a 36,000 square-mile area of the Caribbean since Thursday.

The vessel, with a crew of 28 Dominicans and two Colombians on board, was last heard from at noon [Sunday] Oct. 10, the day after it sailed from Barranquilla with a cargo of cement clinkers.

Ship Capt. Celso Esquea radioed Santo Domingo Sunday he was 240 miles out of Barranquilla and expected to arrive in the Dominican port at 5 A.M. Tuesday.

Bordas said Esquea always called the company every 24 hours

and this is one of the reasons he believes the vessel may have been pirated.

If the ship had foundered or sunk, he said, its radio auto-alarm system would automatically send out a distress signal. The ship's two inflatable life rafts are also equipped with radio beacons. . . .

"My impression is that the *El Caribe* was hijacked the day after it left Barranquilla," he said. "When a vessel is hijacked there is no radio communications."

Bordas theorized that several Colombian guerrillas may have hidden on his ship because "it is very difficult to hijack an airplane in Colombia, but very easy to get on board a vessel."

Meanwhile, the Coast Guard said it planned to continue hunting for *El Caribe*. . . .

There has not been too much sea traffic along the *El Caribe*'s 580-mile route because of the East Coast dock strike.

San Juan Star, October 19, 1971, p. 3:

By Margot Preece. The whereabouts of the cargo vessel *El Caribe* . . . may remain a mystery since the Coast Guard called off its search Monday and Havana sources say it is not in Cuba. . . .

Bordas has made repeated attempts to telephone Cuban Prime Minister Fidel Castro . . . but he has not been able to get through to him.

San Juan Star, October 23, 1971, p. 14:

By Yvonne Beltzer. A ship aground on the Quitasueno Bank of Nicaragua believed to be the missing Dominican freighter *El Caribe,* was identified . . . as the SS *Nicodemos,* a Liberian freighter. . . .

Now, according to the Coast Guard, the fate of the ship "is a mystery."

Lloyd's List, November 23, 1971:

CARIBE. London, Nov. 22. In reply to inquiry, Lloyd's Agents at Barranquilla write under date of Nov. 16: There is no further news of motor vessel *Caribe.*

Rumors have spread, but the fate of the ship has not been learned. A retired Dominican sailor was quoted as saying it sank, since it would not have been possible for enough hijackers to sneak aboard to hijack such a large ship. The February 1974 hijacking of an 11,000-ton freighter in Pakistan, however, showed that it would not have been too difficult to overtake the *El Caribe,* a much smaller vessel.

In January 1974 I received a letter from the Administrator General of a newspaper in Santo Domingo, named, by coincidence, *El Caribe.* He stated that friends of Captain Esquea reported that the ship had suffered serious damages on its last journey and that they also felt it had sunk. The damages were not specified.

On November 18, 1971, friends of the crewmen asked President Balaquer to take the necessary steps to learn if the ship had been hijacked to Cuba, but as of January 1974 neither an affirmation nor a denial had been received.

According to the Legend the ship sent a message on the night of October 15 saying that it would arrive in port early the next morning. The newspapers, however, report that the last radio message was sent at noon, October 10, telling that the ship would be in port early on the morning of October 12. The ship was not close to port at the time of the radio message, but somewhere in the open Caribbean between Venezuela and Santo Domingo.

I have not been able to find any reports of storms in the area at the time *El Caribe* disappeared, but this is not positive proof of good weather.

February 1972

V. A. Fogg

The 572-foot V. A. Fogg *disappeared somewhere south of Galveston on or shortly after February 1, 1972. The tanker was scheduled to journey into the Gulf of Mexico, flush out her tanks, and return. A search began shortly after she failed to arrive on schedule. Although some debris was found almost every day, the ship itself was not discovered until February 14, when a team of divers located the wreck south of Freeport in 90 feet of water.*

The Coast Guard could not say what had happened to the crewmen, as all thirty-eight had disappeared. The blood-chilling part of the story is that the thirty-ninth man, the captain, was found sitting in his cabin, a coffee cup still in his hand.

What caused the ship to sink so quickly that the automatic SOS was not sent, the crewmen were unable to use their lifesaving gear, and the captain's life was ended with no warning? The mystery, it seems, has no earthly explanation.

Galveston Daily News, Monday, February 14, 1972, p. 1:
    By David Lyons. The mystery of the *V. A. Fogg* was at least par-

The V. A. *Fogg*

tially solved Sunday when a team of divers made positive identification of wreckage found earlier on the floor of the Gulf of Mexico.

The underwater wreckage is located in 90 feet of water approximately 50 miles southeast of here.

Divers from the *Miss Freeport* . . . which located the tanker Saturday with its sonar searching equipment, found the name of the ill-fated ship on the side of the wreckage. . . .

The *V. A. Fogg* left Freeport Feb. 1 to sail 50 miles offshore and clean out empty tanks that had contained benzene, an explosive hydrocarbon. The ship also carried a load of xylene. After cleaning the tanks, the ship was to proceed to Galveston, but the ship and those aboard were never heard from after its departure from Freeport.

Galveston Daily News, February 15, 1972, p. 1:

By Joel Kirkpatrick. Divers Monday spotted bodies aboard the blast-shattered tanker *V. A. Fogg.* . . .

One source in Freeport said divers, who brought up some of the wreckage, . . . spotted one fully clothed body floating in the tanker's chartroom, and the arm of another protruding from debris.

Neither body appeared blast-damaged . . . but no identification attempt was made at the time.

"It must have been one hell of an explosion," the source said.

"The forward deck is bent to the right at a 45-degree angle. A big chunk of the bow was blown to one side." . . .

It appeared . . . that the *V. A. Fogg* had been blasted open from midship forward and was not salvageable. . . .

What had been a 572-foot jumboized T-2 tanker . . . now shows up on the side-scanning sonar as being debris 450 feet in length.

Galveston Daily News, February 16, 1972, p. 1:

By Joel Kirkpatrick. A two-mile tall mushroom of smoke with a luminescent top grew up through a cloud layer before a NASA flight instructor's jet on the afternoon the tanker *V. A. Fogg* disappeared. . . .

He testified he first thought there had been an underwater volcanic eruption. The top of the mushroom was more than a mile across, and growing. . . .

[The] first report of the mushrooming smoke came at 4:04 P.M. on Feb. 1. . . . "It looks like an explosion in the water. . . . It was the biggest thing I had ever seen." . . .

[One witness] told of . . . hearing a tremendous boom coming from out of the Gulf southeast somewhere.

"There was a boom and then rumbling continued for about five rumbles," he said, "and there was not a second in between them."

Galveston Daily News, February 19, 1972, p. 1:

Scuba divers . . . recovered one body and . . . were bringing it in. . . .

At Friday's hearings . . . another former crewman of the shattered and sunken tanker told of seeing sparks and smoke belching from the stack of the vessel while it carried highly flammable chemicals.

Galveston Daily News, February 20, 1972, p. 1:
The body recovered from the sunken *V. A. Fogg* has been tentatively identified as that of [the] captain, Lt. Toney Solano of the Sheriff's Department said. . . .
Identification probably was made from dental records.

The incident occurred so far from the Bermuda Triangle that most writers have not mentioned it. Of the two who did, one reported it without any suggestion of mystery, while the other presented it as I have shown. It is the latter version that I investigated, since it is the one most likely to be repeated in future articles on the Triangle.

Although the final results of the Coast Guard inquiry and many lawsuits are still pending, there is no doubt that the loss of the ship was due to an explosion of its volatile cargo. Although the exact cause is not known, a number of possible ignition sources on the ship have been suggested.

The remaining question is whether the captain was found sitting in his cabin still clutching a coffee cup. The newspapers did not go into detail on the circumstances surrounding the discovery of the bodies. The February 15 *Galveston Daily News* said "one fully clothed body was found floating in the tanker's chartroom," and the February 20 *Houston Post* said the captain's body "had been in the ship's chartroom." Adding these together it would seem that the captain's body was found floating in the chartroom.

To be certain that this deduction was correct I contacted several individuals who were involved in the case, explained the story of the captain, and asked if it were true.

Lieutenant Solano, the investigator for the Galveston County Medical Examiner, replied that he was at the dock when the three bodies were brought in. All had been recovered from the chartroom, and fingerprints later proved that one was the captain. Solano said that the statement about the captain was ridiculous.

Joel Kirkpatrick, City Editor of the *Galveston Daily News,* replied:

From the beginning, I did all the writing here about the loss of the SS *V. A. Fogg.*

That's from the first "ship overdue" story to the initial report of an explosion; Coast Guard hearings; the lawsuits; the battle by scuba divers to preserve the superstructure of the ship for a tourist attraction—the whole thing.

In all that time, I have never heard of anyone who said [the captain] was still "clutching his coffee cup" when found.

The body was not found in his cabin, but in the wheelhouse [next to the chartroom], floating against the ceiling. U.S. Coast Guard divers brought him up. There was no report of anything clutched in his hand.

I can only conclude that business about the coffee was a pure work of fiction. . . .

The cold facts in the continuing story of the SS *V. A. Fogg* were dramatic enough without [someone] having to fictionalize them.

On January 16, 1974, I received a telephone call from Lt. Arthur Whiting of the Coast Guard's Casualty Review Branch in Washington, D.C. Although the final report of the investigation had not yet been issued, Whiting checked into the situation at my request. He learned that the captain had been found floating in the chartroom up against the ceiling in a corner, his arms and legs hanging down. Part of a wooden chart table was floating near him but there was no mention of a coffee cup. Two other bodies were found, one of which was identified.

On March 4, 1974, Commander F. A. Rice, Chief of the Casualty Review Branch, wrote me that Commander W. E. Whaley, Jr., the Recorder for the Marine Board of Investigation on the *V. A. Fogg*, verified this account of the discovery of the body which was later identified as being that of the captain.

One of the most difficult problems there is is to show that something did not occur when someone else says it did. In this case it was relatively easy because the event occurred recently and many of the individuals involved were still available to comment. Had the incident happened a number of years ago it might have been impossible to discover that what was reported as fact was really only fiction.

52

March 1973

Norse Variant and Anita

Had it not been for the "one in a million" rescue of a crewman, the Bermuda Triangle would have claimed its biggest prize of all time in March 1973. As it was, one man lived to tell the tale.

On Wednesday, March 21, the *Norse Variant* sailed from Norfolk, bound for Hamburg, with a load of coal from the Appalachian mountains. Two days later, just after noon, the 541-foot, 13,000-ton freighter radioed that it was foundering 150 miles southeast of Cape May, New Jersey, and the crew was taking to the lifeboats. The winds were 85 miles an hour at the time, and the sea was running 35 to 45 feet high.

Rescue ships and aircraft sped to the stormy scene, but the *Kittiwake*, the first ship to arrive, reported no trace of the freighter or any debris or survivors. To allow for possible error in the ship's reported position, the Coast Guard began a methodical search of an area of 6,400 square miles, a square 80 miles on a side, centered on the vessel's reported position.

On Sunday a twenty-three-year-old Norwegian seaman was sighted "waving and jumping" on a large orange raft amid the towering waves, 300 miles due east of Cape Henry,

Virginia. Although he was exhausted and dehydrated from his three-day ordeal in the cold winds and high seas, Stein Gabrielsen was in excellent condition. An observer in another Air Force rescue plane working 40 miles farther down the drift line of debris thought he saw another survivor clinging to a floating door, but repeated crossings of the area failed to confirm the sighting.

Gabrielsen told that a 40- by 40-foot hatch cover had been ripped off by the storm and the towering seas had quickly flooded two cargo holds. The ship sank within five minutes after the order had been given to abandon it.

As Gabrielsen was resting in the hospital in the aircraft carrier *Independence* the search continued for other survivors of the *Norse Variant,* and for survivors of a second Norwegian ship that had been reported missing just as Gabrielsen was being rescued.

The other ship, the *Anita,* was not only a sister of the *Norse Variant,* it was an identical twin. It, too, was carrying coal to Hamburg; it had left Norfolk two hours after the *Norse Variant* and had met disaster in the same storm. Unlike the first ship, no SOS was heard from the *Anita.* The ship's representative in Norfolk notified the Coast Guard that he had not been able to establish contact with the ship since it had left port.

A life ring with the name M/S *Anita* turned up later, but this was the only debris recovered from either vessel, said to be the largest cargo ships ever to disappear.

The *Anita* has been given a start toward becoming a part of the Legend of the Bermuda Triangle. One recent account included the loss of the ship as an unexplained mystery while neglecting to mention the storm or the *Norse Variant* and its survivor.

53

October 1973

Linda

In the fall of 1973 I heard from several sources that the Coast Guard had just issued orders that all traffic through the Bermuda Triangle was to cease because of the dangers in that area. One of my informants had heard the news on the radio while traveling through Canada, and another had supposedly read it in "the newspaper."

According to the *Arizona Republic*, the *Miami Herald,* and the Public Information Office of the Coast Guard's Seventh District in Miami, however, the true story was quite different.

The sequence of events began early in the month when two Cuban fishing boats were found crewless and afire north of Cuba. Shortly thereafter an American fishing boat, the *Linda,* disappeared from the same area. This prompted the State Department to issue a warning through the Coast Guard that the Old Bahama Channel, north of Cuba, "may be hazardous." The warning went to all American-flag vessels operating in the channel, recommending that they use alternate routes around Cuba until the reasons for the incidents were learned.

A Coast Guard spokesman stated that the unusual warning had been issued because there had been "two incidents with not too many answers."

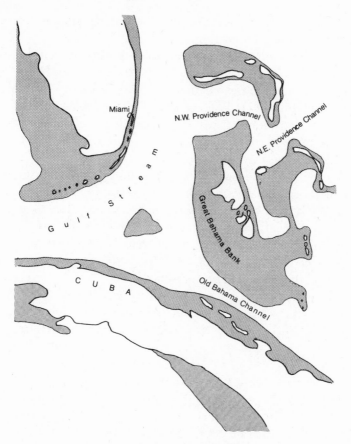

The Old Bahama Channel

A typical map of the Florida-Cuba-Bahamas area is deceiving; it does not show water depths, and thus gives the impression that a vessel could cruise just south of the Bahamas while on its way from Miami to the islands of the West Indies and remain a safe distance from Cuba. Although small boats might be able to travel that route during good weather, most vessels could not because of the Great Bahama Bank. The bank, south of the Bahamas and approximately the size of Florida, is a shallow-water region of cays, rocks, shoals, and sandbars that poke out of the water or are just barely hidden beneath its surface.

The only deep-water routes leading southeast from Miami are the Providence channels, north of Nassau, and the Old Bahama Channel, near Cuba. The Old Bahama Channel is approximately 100 miles long, varies from 12 to 20 miles wide, and is immediately adjacent to the north side of Cuba. Large vessels must use the channel and are unable to give Cuba a wide berth as they pass.

Shortly after the Coast Guard warning was issued the National Liberation Front, a Cuban exile group, took credit for the attack on the Cuban fishing boats, saying that they had been destroyed because they carried electronic monitoring equipment. One of the crewmen had been killed and the other eleven had been set adrift in lifeboats. Havana radio reported that they had been rescued.

The Swiss embassy in Havana later notified the Coast Guard that the *Linda* had been taken into Cuba, where it was being detained along with its three-man crew. Three weeks later the *Linda* and the men were released unharmed, along with the *Gracia a Dios*, another U.S. vessel that had been apprehended at the same time.

The State Department lifted the warning on October 23.

Although the temporary disappearance of the *Linda* was apparently a case of detention in retaliation for the loss of the two Cuban fishing boats, the episode demonstrated how quickly any incident in the region is credited to the Bermuda Triangle. For those who had heard of the Triangle and had no concept of the geography of the area, it was a simple step to assume that a warning issued to ships traveling north of Cuba was an order to shut down the Bermuda Triangle.

54

The Devil's Sea

The Bermuda Triangle is not the only area where ships and airplanes disappear at a rate well beyond the laws of chance. Southeast of Japan is the treacherous *Devil's Sea*, which has long been feared by the Japanese because of the many strange disappearances that have occurred there.

Japanese authorities previously paid little attention to the stories, assuming that most of the lost vessels were small fishing craft, easily upset by storms of any strength. But they began to listen when nine ships, an incredible number for any area, vanished between 1950 and 1954. These were not tiny fishing boats, but large freighters equipped with good engines and radios—and they all vanished during perfect weather. Only one is known to have made a distress call. Alarmed, the Japanese government began a survey of the region. The result? One of the investigating ships, the Kaiyo Maru, was blown up by an underwater volcano. Recognizing that volcanic activity could not account for all the losses, especially those of the airplanes, the Japanese government declared the Devil's Sea to be a danger zone.

Experts frequently point out the similarity between the Devil's Sea and the Bermuda Triangle, both of which are off

*the southeast coast of the nearest land, and both of which
have an insatiable appetite for unwary vessels.*

The original source of the information on the Devil's Sea
appears to be four articles that appeared in the *New York
Times* in the early 1950s.

New York Times, Saturday, September 27, 1952, p. 35:
TOKYO, Sept. 26 (AP). Japanese authorities said tonight either a
tidal wave or suction from an underground volcano must have sunk a
Japanese observation ship that vanished Tuesday with thirty-one
aboard.

Japanese Coast Guard boats and United States Air Force planes
found no trace of the 210-ton *No. 5 Kaiyo Maru,* which vanished
Tuesday 200 miles southeast of Tokyo. She was on an inspection
tour of the Myojin Reefs, which rose from the ocean floor two weeks
ago in a violent submarine explosion. The missing vessel carried
nine scientists and a crew of twenty-two toward the seething caul-
dron.

A spokesman for the Central Meteorological Observatory said the
Kaiyo Maru "must have been sucked into the submarine volcano
crater."

Yonekichi Yagisawa, director of the Maritime Safety Board (Coast
Guard), said: "It is highly probable that a tidal wave washed the
vessel to the bottom." He recalled that a tidal wave was seen north
of the reef Wednesday. The volcano erupted Tuesday and again
today.

New York Times, Sunday, September 28, 1952, p. 30:
TOKYO, Sept. 27 (AP). The Japanese Coast Guard said tonight
it had definitely decided that a scientific observation ship . . . had
been blown to bits near the scene of a boiling underseas volcano. . . .

Far East Air Force planes and Japanese ships combed the area in
vain. One ship spotted bits of wreckage, and today a Japanese patrol
boat picked up a buoy off the ill-fated craft.

New York Times, Tuesday, September 30, 1952, p. 2:
TOKYO, Sept. 29 (Reuters). A second Japanese vessel may have

been swallowed up by the volcanic explosion and tidal wave last week on Myojin Reef, 200 miles south of here, maritime authorities said today. They reported the sixty-ton *Toshi Maru*, with an undisclosed number of persons aboard, had been missing in the area since the explosion . . . and [the] tidal wave that followed.

No further accounts of the incident, the fate of the *Toshi Maru*, or the area appeared for more than two years, until:

New York Times, January 16, 1955, V, p. 8:
TOKYO, Jan. 15 (Reuters). A faint radio signal heard here today told fear-stricken Japanese fishermen that the "devil's sea," mystery graveyard of nine ships in the last five years, had at last been cheated of a victim.

The signal came from the Japanese Coast Guard survey ship *Shinyo Maru*,* for which a full-scale search was ordered yesterday, ten days after it was reported missing with its crew of fourteen. The ship vanished in the same perfect weather that had marked previous disappearances.

Contact was lost with the ship as it reached an area, about seventy miles off Japan's east coast, where nine other ships and 215 men have been lost. Only one of the ships—a fishery patrol vessel that was the third to disappear—left any trace of wreckage or bodies.

Fear struck through every nearby Japanese fishing village when it was known that the 144-ton *Shinyo Maru* was missing. Fishermen spoke of a "devil" lurking off the shore. Coast Guard authorities have designated the area a "special danger zone."

Today's unexpected radio signal from the survey ship told the anxious searchers that radio trouble alone had prevented her from making contact before. The crew were well and the ship, undamaged, was making for Uraga, about thirty miles from here, under her own steam, the message said.

Several parts of the Legend of the Devil's Sea seemed curious to me.

First, there did not seem to be any particular mystery about the *Kaiyo Maru*, as some writers have suggested. Although

---

* The correct name of the boat is *Shihyo Maru*.

the destruction of a ship by an underwater volcano was unusual, it could hardly be considered mysterious.

Second, a comparison of many accounts of the Devil's Sea showed them to be very much alike. The basic information in all of them seems to have come from the *New York Times* articles or from writings based on the articles. Apparently no additional research had ever been done.

Third, the only time period ever mentioned is 1950 to 1954. If the region was so dangerous, mysterious, and well known, why had nothing new been written about it for twenty years?

Fourth, the time sequence in the disappearance of the *Kaiyo Maru* had been changed in the Legend. According to the Legend, the Japanese government became alarmed after a number of ships had disappeared in the Devil's Sea and sent the *Kaiyo Maru*, a scientifically equipped vessel, to investigate. It was then blown up! Actually, the *Kaiyo Maru* was dispatched to investigate the new volcano several years before the other boats were supposedly lost.

Fifth, although it was said that nine ships and many planes had vanished, nothing specific was ever told about them, except for the *Kaiyo Maru*.

With the intention of updating the twenty-year-old information I sent many letters to Japan and to nearby islands, and received a number of replies.

Embassy of the United States of America, Tokyo, Japan, October 31, 1973:
We have not heard of the Devil's Sea. The Japanese Government Maritime Safety Agency [Coast Guard] informed us they have no knowledge of such a place and that no danger zone appears on their chart of Iwojima and Marcus Island. . . .

Similar answers came from Guam, Wake Island, the Bonin Islands, the Consulate General of Japan in Los Angeles, the Commander in Chief of the United States Pacific Fleet, and the *Honolulu Star-Bulletin*—they knew nothing about, nor could they find any information on the Devil's Sea, danger areas near Japan, or disappearing ships or planes in the region.

Mr. Shigeru Kimura, Associate Editor, Science Department, *Asahi Shimbun* (Japan's largest newspaper), October 30, 1973:
I inform you that there is no such an area called the Devil's Sea near Iwo Jima. But, in September, 1952, there was a big eruption of an undersea volcano called Myojinsho. . . . A research ship *Daigo Kaiyo-maru,* which was dispatched by the Japanese government to the sea, was sunk by a blast of the eruption and the lives of 31 persons on board were lost. Up till now the Myojinsho becomes active intermittently. Recently . . . another undersea volcano erupted near Myojinsho. . . . It is still active.
Generally speaking, the neighborhood of these volcanoes is thought dangerous, but after the tragedy of the *Daigo Kaiyo-maru* there has been no ship wrecked near the volcanoes. So we do not think the area the Devil's Sea.

On November 18, 1973, Mr. Kimura wrote again:
I surveyed all the articles of the *Asahi Shimbun* on the accidents of ships from 1954 to 1955, but I could not find any articles which had used the words "Devil's Sea." So I think the article of the *New York Times* on the Devil's Sea was written on a kind of misunderstanding. In 1954 to 1955, Japan was not a rich country, so there were many fishing ships which had no radio transmitter or had only a very poor one. Then if such ships were wrecked or sunk, they appeared as if they had suddenly vanished. Such vanishment of ships occurred in every district of sea around Japan. In fact we cannot point out any particular district that was specially dangerous or specially feared by fishermen. . . .
There was a ship named *No. 2 Tosui-Maru* [reported missing in the September 30, 1952, *New York Times* article] that was missing just after the disaster of the *Kaiyo-Maru.* But the ship was only in a trouble of the engine, and was found and saved on September 30. . . . In this case also the ship had no radio transmitter, so the crew could not send SOS.

Yasuchika Ohno, Foreign Liaison Officer, Maritime Safety Agency, Tokyo, January 10, 1974:

As for the newspaper clipping [the 1955 *New York Times* article] enclosed in your letter, we are afraid that [it] includes several mis-understandings and confusion. First of all, it is stated in the article that nine ships were mysteriously lost during the five years in the Myojin Sho Reef area. However, as far as our records are concerned, the *Kaiyo Maru No. 5* was the only survey vessel lost in the same area.

As for your question: [Is] the area . . . still considered danger-ous? we might say that ever since the declaration of "Dangerous zone" was made in 1953 in our *Notice to Mariners* at the time, the area has remained dangerous to date. Mariners have been strictly cautioned not to be within ten miles of the Myojin Sho Reef due to possible submarine volcanic activity.

Feeling that the Legend of the Devil's Sea had to some-how have been based on fact, I pursued the matter further and finally found someone who had heard the term "Devil's Sea."

Unsigned letter from "Action Line," *Mainichi Daily News* (Tokyo), December 26, 1973:

"Devil Sea" . . . is a pseudonym of the area about 70 miles off Japan's east coast [named] by fishermen. The number of the missing or wrecked ships in the other areas such as the Inland Sea (Seto Naikai) . . . is much more than that of the "Devil Sea." Namely "Devil Sea" is not the only dangerous area for ships in Japan.

Also, staffers of the Guard and Rescue Department of the Mari-time Safety Agency in Tokyo and Yokohama branch said they don't call the area a "Devil Sea" nor designate [it] as a "special danger zone."

The area is not specially dangerous in comparison with the other areas. In summer it's rather safe except typhoons and in winter the sea is rough, if any.

Although Reuters, the news agency that supplied the 1955 article to the *New York Times*, had no record of the source of information, "Action Line" of the *Mainichi Daily News* sent the following article from another newspaper that did provide specific facts about the nine vessels that were lost. It appears that the basis for the entire story of the Devil's Sea may have been several articles that appeared in Japanese newspapers in January 1955.

Yomiuri Shimbun, January 14, 1955:*

THE DEVIL'S SEA, WHERE "SHIHYO MARU" IS LOST
NINE BOATS LOST DURING FIVE YEARS
REASONS REMAIN UNKNOWN

Since January 4, 1955, when radio contact with the fishing inspection boat *Shihyo Maru* failed, a search has continued. For more than ten days the fate of the 14 crewmen has remained unknown. The approximate location of the disappearance was about 30 miles southeast of Mikura Island. In the last five years about nine fishing boats disappeared and the area became called the Devil's Sea.†

It was assumed that these fishing boats disappeared because of wind, rough seas, or engine trouble. . . .

In September, 1952, an inspection boat, the *Kaiyo Maru,* disappeared. Since then it has been indicated that this area is dangerous. Since no bodies of the crewmen were found and only a little debris was seen, it was assumed that these missing boats were sunk in deep water by rough seas. Because it was not the monsoon season the reasons for the missing boats are completely unknown, but there is a rumor that it may be because of some unknown power connected with the "Atomic Age." The loss of the *Shihyo Maru* was completely unexpected because it was well-equipped to survive any possible difficulties.‡

---

* The same information appeared in the January 11 through 16 *Asahi Shimbun.*

† The Japanese character for "devil" could also be translated as "ghost" or "magic."

‡ The next day the *Shihyo Maru* sailed into Uraga. The crew had not been able to report because of a radio failure, and they were surprised to learn that they were the object of so much attention.

The list of boats missing in the area in the last five years is shown next:

1. April 4, 1949. *No. 1 Guro Sio Maru,* 145 tons, 23 crewmen, missing in the vicinity of the Ogasawara [Bonin] Islands.

2. April 21, 1949. *No. 2 Guro Sio Maru,* 24 crewmen, missing after leaving the seaport of Miyake.

3. June, 1952. *Chyo Huku Maru,* 66 tons, 29 crewmen, missing 120 miles east of Mikura Island after sending SOS.

4. September 24, 1952. *Kaiyo Maru,* missing near Mikura Island. Some debris was found.*

5. January 6, 1953. *Shin Shei Maru,* 62 tons, 17 crewmen, missing near Sumisu Island.

6. February, 1953. *No. 3 Guro Shio Maru,* an inspection boat, 145 tons, 18 crewmen, was missing east of Nishino Island.

7. September 25, 1953. The *Fu Ya Maru,* 189 tons, 26 crewmen, was missing near Miyake Island.

8. October 10, 1953. The *Shei Shyo Maru,* 190 tons, 25 crewmen, was missing 20 miles east of Mikura Island.

9. December, 1953. The *Ko Zi Maru,* 150 tons, 22 crewmen, was missing east of Iwo Jima.

Several conclusions may be drawn from the information sent from Japan:

Two of the nine vessels are accounted for. The *Kaiyo Maru* was demolished by a volcano or tidal wave, and the *Chyo Huku Maru* sank after sending an SOS.

The other seven boats were lost in the four and a half years between April 1949 and October 1953. They were not lost in a small, restricted area, but in a 750-mile stretch of sea between Miyake Island and Iwo Jima.

The lost vessels were not "large freighters with good engines and radios" as the Legend has it, but small fishing boats ranging from 62 to 190 tons. According to Mr. Kimura of the *Asahi Shimbun,* it is doubtful that they all had radios. The

---

* This is an error, as the boat was lost 150 miles south of Mikura. This account also fails to mention that it was destroyed by a volcano.

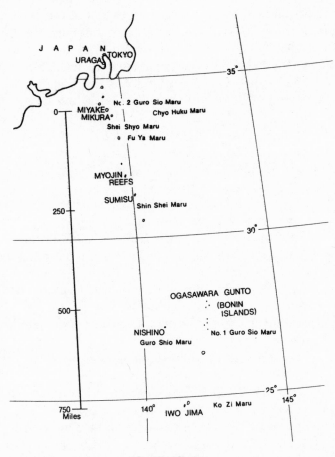

The Devil's Sea

weather was not perfect, as in the Legend, but on the contrary those who wrote the Japanese articles felt that wind and rough seas were to blame for the losses.

The writers of the Legend do not know the size of the Devil's Sea or even where it is located. Some say it is 70 miles off Japan's east coast (which part of the coast?). Others place it near the Myojin Reefs, which are about 300 miles from the

coast. Still others place it near Iwo Jima and the Bonin Islands, or about 750 miles from the coast. Although the *Yomiuri Shimbun* lists boats that disappeared in all three locations,
it appears that the area known, at least in the 1950s, as the
Devil's Sea, is between Japan and Miyake Island. Four of
the nine boats that supposedly vanished in the Devil's Sea
were within several hundred miles of Miyake.

The Maritime Safety Agency has issued periodic *Notices
to Mariners* warning boatmen to approach no closer than
ten miles to the Myojin Reefs. The agency denies having ever
issued any warning about the Devil's Sea.

The disappearance of a few fishing boats is not viewed
with awe by those who are familiar with the ocean. A Maritime Safety Agency white paper issued in 1973 (sent to me
by the *Mainichi Daily News*) showed that 471 fishing boats
went missing around Japan in 1972, 435 in 1970, and 521 in
1968. The Japanese do not blame magnetic anomalies, UFOs,
and mysterious forces, however, but realize that the losses are
due to nothing more than the normal hazards of the sea.

Although a part of the Legend is that planes regularly disappear between Guam and Japan, no specific information has
ever been presented to support that claim.

It appears that the Devil's Sea, known in the United States
as a counterpart of the Bermuda Triangle, is virtually unknown in Japan. The story is based on nothing more than the
loss of a few fishing boats twenty years ago in a 750-mile
stretch of ocean over a period of five years. The tale has been
reported so many times that it has come to be accepted as
fact.

No one, until now, ever took the trouble to ask the Japanese
about their Devil's Sea. It was hard to find anyone who could
remember ever having heard of it.

55

Vile Vortices

Armed with the knowledge of the existence of the Bermuda Triangle and the Devil's Sea, researchers began a systematic investigation to ascertain if there might be other anomalic regions in which the number of disappearing vessels is all out of proportion to that in other areas. In spite of their skeptical approach to the problem they found that there were three other such areas in the northern hemisphere, areas in which disappearance rates were far and away above what could be accounted for by the regular hazards such as weather and faulty equipment. These areas were near the Mediterranean Sea, Afghanistan, and northeast of Hawaii, in the Pacific Ocean. To their amazement, the scientists found that by plotting all these anomalic areas on a globe, not only were they all the same distance above the equator, but they were evenly distributed around the globe, precisely 72 degrees apart. As the positions of more lost vessels were plotted, each area began to take on an oval, or lozenge, shape, and each one was tilted up on the eastern end by exactly the same amount.

Further investigation revealed five similar lozenge-shaped areas in the southern hemisphere, evenly spaced around the *globe, all tilted upward at the eastern end, and all the same distance south of the equator as the others were north of it!*

The only correlation that could be found between the ten zones (that is, eight, since the Mediterranean and Afghanistan areas are obvious exceptions) is that they all are located near well-defined warm ocean currents. These same areas are also famous, incidentally, for other strange phenomena, most notably a high incidence of poltergeist manifestations and UFO sightings.

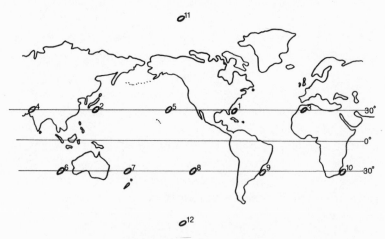

The twelve "Vile Vortices"

It would seem that the atmospheric and maritime disturbances caused by the ocean currents in these regions, which also fall near heavily populated land masses and hence are well traveled, might account for the especially high rate of disappearances. But Lloyd's, the U.S. Navy, and other maritime agencies continue to be baffled by the losses. Even the special geographical situations do not explain the large number of complete disappearances in the ten areas, as compared to regular founderings and ditchings.

Mathematicians and engineers have found evidence that the two polar areas should also be considered as anomalic regions. If all twelve areas were to be marked on a globe, and lines drawn from one to another, it can be seen that the globe is divided into a number of equilateral triangles.

Surely, there must be some scientific explanation for nature working in such a manner.

The winds, ocean currents, rough water, and temperature differentials in these areas might explain a large number of accidents and founderings, even UFO sightings, but they do not account for the many complete disappearances. Nor do they explain spinning compasses, loss of radio and radar contact, and aeromagnetic and gravitational anomalies.

Until it can be explained where all those lost airplanes, ships, submarines, and people have gone, such theories as UFO kidnappings, reverse gravity fields, and time warps must be considered as possible explanations.

The Vile Vortices concept was first introduced by Ivan T. Sanderson and his Society for the Investigation of the Unexplained (SITU) in 1968.* Five articles or book chapters have now been written on the subject by Sanderson, one each year since the initial article, except for 1972 when there was none. Each succeeding article appears to have been based on its predecessor but contains updated and revised material.

An examination of all evidence presented in the five articles in support of the Vile Vortices concept shows that the Bermuda Triangle was accepted as the first vortex because it was known to be the scene of many unusual disappearances. The Devil's Sea was the second vortex because "we knew already that there was such an area alleged to exist" off Japan, and because "plane after plane vanished en route to Guam." No further substantiation was ever given, nor have any specific examples of disappearing ships or planes been presented for the Devil's Sea.

The loss of two submarines in the Mediterranean and four

---

* See Bibliography, Section I.

small boats in the Atlantic near Portugal was the only proof given to show the existence of a third anomalic area.

The loss of "a number" of military planes in the mountains of Afghanistan during World War II proved another, and the disappearance of one plane between Hawaii and the United States proved that region to be anomalic.

The five southern vortices were presented with no proof, merely the statement that correspondence and research showed that they existed, and were all 72 degrees apart.

The north and south poles were added because "several space and time anomalies have been alleged" to have occurred at the north pole. No reason was given for including the south pole.

The writings that tell of the Vile Vortices show that the researchers first "suspected" where the areas were and that evidence that any kind of "incident" had ever occurred in the area was proof that it was "anomalic." There is, according to SITU, a "good deal of evidence" for some of the areas, a "fair amount" for others, and "almost nothing" for a few. Because the supposed arrangement of the vortices "seemed so regular" it was assumed that the other parts existed. All the parts, assumed or "proven," were then joined to form the corners of equilateral triangles, and the creators marveled at the "orderliness of Nature."

Computer people use the acronym GIGO—Garbage In, Garbage Out—which means that if bad information is given to the computer, the output will be equally, or even more, unreliable. There is no possible way that vague, estimated input can lead to precise, accurate answers. How, by plotting the estimated positions of a number of vessels that disappeared in unknown locations, would it be possible to compute lozenge-shaped areas, all tilted up at the same angle and evenly spaced around the world? How, for instance, would the position of the *Atalanta* be plotted?—it might have sunk anywhere on the 3,000-mile voyage to England. Was it assumed that it sank in the Bermuda Triangle?

Were the *Connemara IV* and the *Rubicon* included as part of the data to show that the Bermuda Triangle is a Vile Vortex? Research shows that these vessels, formerly considered to be victims of some unknown mystery, were found shortly after the passage of hurricanes. Was the loss of Al Snider in a 16-foot plywood skiff during a 50-mile-an-hour wind part of the evidence?

Several other efforts to account mathematically or geometrically for the losses of vessels are under way, but the results cannot be anything but erroneous if they are based on the same faulty data that was used to "prove" the "anomalic properties" of the Bermuda Triangle, the Devil's Sea, and the other Vile Vortices.

56

Magnetism, Mystery, and the Bermuda Triangle

Many types of magnetic aberrations have been reported in the Bermuda Triangle, and it is thought that they may play a part in the mystery. Pilots have told of compasses that pointed in the wrong direction or spun wildly. Veterans of the area have witnessed magnetic storms that could lead navigators astray.

One of the most logical of all the theories that have attempted to account for the many disappearing vessels in the Triangle is that magnetic variation may be responsible. As most high school physics students know, the compass does not point to the true north pole, but to the magnetic north pole, which is some distance away. The difference in direction from any point to the two poles is called magnetic variation. The amount of variation differs from place to place, and is as much as 20 degrees in some localities. Should a navigator neglect to account for the variation in his area he could very well end up hundreds of miles from where his calculations show him to be.

The Bermuda Triangle is unusual in that it is one of the few places on the earth where the compass points to true *north instead of to magnetic north. Another area where this occurs is the Devil's Sea, off Japan, where an inordinate number of vessels have also disappeared. The Coast Guard has stated that this is only a coincidence.*

Many attempts have been made to determine the nature of the magnetic aberrations in the Bermuda Triangle. One of these is the Navy's Project Magnet, which is using Super Constellations equipped with highly sensitive magnetometers to study the disturbances.

A number of "magnetic aberration" theories have been suggested to account for the losses, but they all are faulty, as anyone with a basic knowledge of the compass could attest. The various "aberrations" ascribed to the Bermuda Triangle that supposedly show it is an unusual region are nothing more than the normal properties of magnetism and the compass that can be observed throughout the world. They are so fundamental that they are discussed as a part of the most elementary course in navigation.

Even if there were some substance to any of the magnetic aberration theories they would explain only how a vessel might deviate from its course. They would not account for the disappearances. In addition, the statement that the variation in the Bermuda Triangle is zero has only a grain of truth. Although it is zero close to Florida it gradually increases toward the east and is 15 degrees at Bermuda.

Magnetic Variation

The belief that magnetic variation may be "the most logical of all the theories" put forth to explain the disappearances has no basis whatsoever. Ironically, magnetic variation would have to be considered as a possible reason for vessels becoming lost in almost every part of the world *except* near Florida and the Devil's Sea.

Compasses do not point to the north pole, but to the magnetic north pole, which is near Prince of Wales Island in northern Canada, 1,300 miles from the north pole. The difference between the direction to the magnetic north pole and the direction to the true north pole varies from place to place on the earth's surface. The difference at any given point is known to pilots as magnetic variation.*

For example, magnetic variation at the Azores is 20 degrees, since, in pointing to the magnetic north pole, the compass points 20 degrees away from the true north pole. The variation for Phoenix, Arizona, is 14 degrees, since from Phoenix, the north pole and the magnetic north pole are 14 degrees apart. From the part of the Bermuda Triangle near Florida, however, the variation is close to zero. There is no difference in the direction to the two poles from Florida, since Florida, the magnetic pole, and the north pole are in a straight line.

There are other locations that are also in line with the two poles. The line connecting all these points is called the Agonic Line, and although it is affected somewhat by irregularities in the earth's magnetic field, it is essentially a straight line running from the magnetic pole across Canada and Lake Michigan, across the eastern United States, Florida, Cuba, and South America.† Navigators near the Agonic Line need not be concerned with magnetic variation because there is none in the area.

The farther a vessel is from the Agonic Line, however, the larger the magnetic variation which must be reckoned with. The variation for each area is prominently shown on navigation charts, and it is a simple matter to apply the appropriate correction. Pilots must adjust their headings accordingly or they will head off course.

---

* Geologists and geographers refer to it as magnetic declination.

† Since the earth's magnetic field is continually changing, the magnetic variation in any given area changes over a period of several years. Navigation charts made at different times show the Agonic Line in slightly different locations.

Near Phoenix, for example, a pilot wishing to fly a course of true west (270°) must correct for the 14-degree variation in that area by steering a magnetic course of 256°. If he were to forget to compensate and were not paying attention to landmarks, he would fly 14 degrees to the right of his intended course, and after 500 miles would be about 124 miles north of where his calculations told him he was. A pilot near the Azores who forgot to make the necessary 20-degree cor-

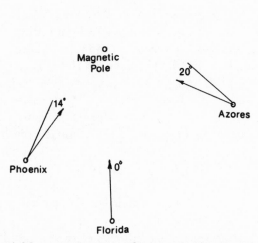

Fig. 4 Magnetic variation: Phoenix, Florida, the Azores.

rection for that area would end up 173 miles off course after a 500-mile flight.

Although correcting for magnetic variation is a basic procedure that not even the rankest beginner would be likely to overlook, there is no denying that neglecting to perform this simple correction would lead the navigator astray. However, a pilot near Florida or the Bahamas would not fly off course by forgetting to compensate for magnetic variation, since there is none in that area for which to compensate.

Although a compass near Florida does point toward the north pole, it is actually attracted to the magnetic north pole. The north pole just happens to be in a straight line with Florida and the magnetic pole. Using the same logic as in the Legend, it could be claimed that compasses near Florida all point to Kalamazoo, since Kalamazoo is also on the Agonic Line and all compasses near Florida point toward it.

Magnetic Disturbances, Anomalies, and Storms

The earth's magnetic field is produced by strong forces emanating from its magnetic core. Although these forces are fairly regular across the surface of the globe, there are certain places where local magnetic forces interfere. These places are usually areas with high iron ore deposits, such as in northern Minnesota and over Lake Superior, or extensive lava beds, such as those near Grants, New Mexico. Because of the disturbances near local magnetic fields, compasses in the region cannot be relied on, and notices on aeronautical charts warn pilots of the situation. Such areas are not considered strange or mysterious.

According to the Navy, which has conducted tests in the area (not while investigating the mystery of the Bermuda Triangle, as is often stated, but as a part of a regular world-wide program for updating navigation charts), there are no local magnetic disturbances in the Bermuda Triangle.

In contrast to a local magnetic disturbance which can cause an appreciable irregularity in the earth's magnetic field, a magnetic anomaly is a very small force caused by a submarine or other ferromagnetic objects. It is too slight to have an effect on the compass of a passing boat or plane.

Magnetic storms are caused by streams of charged particles from the sun which interfere with the earth's magnetic field. The storms, which occur irregularly, are intense for several hours, during which time a compass might be in error a maximum of one or two degrees. An error of this magnitude would have no appreciable effect on navigation.

Spinning Compasses

One characteristic of the compass that is well known by the navigator is its instability in unsmooth air or water.

The compass needle is mounted on a small pivot, which allows it to rotate almost friction-free as it seeks the magnetic pole. Although the needle is housed in a bowl containing a light oil which dampens down its sensitive movements, gravity will cause it to rotate if the compass is not perfectly level. As long as the airplane or boat lists from side to side, as in rough weather, the needle will swing back and forth. The stronger the turbulence becomes, the more the needle swings. The weather need not be extremely rough for the needle to swing too widely to give a usable reading, and it may spin completely around in violent weather.

Much of the time a navigator steers by interpolating the extreme readings of the compass. For example, if the needle swings regularly from 30 degrees to 50 degrees and back, the vessel is heading on a course of 40 degrees. This flaw in the compass's character is the reason why electric or air-driven gyroscopic compasses are used. Although they have a few problems of their own, they remain relatively steady during turbulent weather.

Any pilot who has ever rocked his wings or any sailor who has ever ridden the waves knows how easy it is to spin the compass needle. It requires almost no more effort than that necessary to rotate an ice cube in a glass.

Project Magnet

Project Magnet was supposedly a secret until 1963, when a reporter for the *UFO Investigator* "revealed" its existence.[*]

---

[*] "U.S. Special Project Linked to UFOs." *U.F.O. Investigator.* June–September 1963, p. 1–2.

According to the reporter, who "discovered" one of the project's planes "on an auxiliary runway" at the San Francisco airport, the "carefully unpublicized program" was "significantly linked" with a Canadian Government UFO investigation. The project was using specially equipped Super Constellations and nonuniformed pilots (to help keep the project secret?).

The article included a picture of the tail of the plane, on which appeared in huge block letters the words PROJECT MAGNET. A strange way to "unpublicize" the project!

According to the reporter, who "managed to enter into a discussion" with the men, the "one important result" of the project at that time had been the discovery of "peculiar magnetic forces" coming from above the Caribbean area, where, although "no connection has been proved," five Navy airplanes once vanished just after reporting unexplained interference with their compasses. The reporter noted that it was obvious that the civilian scientist and pilot realized that their project was merely a cover for its true purpose, which was to search for information on UFOs. He strongly suspected that the Navy, which was financing the entire operation, was attempting to launch its own program for discovering how UFOs were powered and controlled, since the Air Force was not willing to share what it had already learned. The reporter ended by assuring his readers that although he had managed to take several photographs in addition to the one of the tail of the plane, he was not printing any that might be of value to an enemy power.

The Navy, upon being questioned about the project, denied that it was secret, or that unusual forces had been discovered in the Caribbean area. According to a pamphlet distributed by the Oceanographic Office, Project Magnet is an airborne geomagnetic survey of *all* the accessible ocean areas of the world. The data is being used to construct improved navigational and magnetic maps, many of which are thirty years old, for ships and aircraft of all nations. Cosmic rays emanating from outer space are also being measured.

It is not unusual for a study being conducted in the Caribbean to be reported as another secret attempt to solve the mystery of the Bermuda Triangle. Such studies always have a cover story, according to the reporter, and officials always deny, of course, the true purpose of their work.

Epilogue

Many theories have been proposed to solve the mystery of the Bermuda Triangle. Time warps, reverse gravity fields, even witchcraft have been suggested as possible causes of the disappearances. Atmospheric aberrations. Magnetic and gravitational anomalies. Strange forces that silence radios, block radar, and affect compasses.

Seaquakes. Waterspouts. Tidal waves. Freak seas. Death rays from Atlantis. Black holes in space. Underwater signaling devices to guide invaders from other planets. UFOs collecting earthlings and their vehicles for study in other galaxies, or to save them from an approaching holocaust.

The area has been described as a "Vile Vortex," or an anomaly, a place where events and objects do not behave as they normally would. It has been said that a murky mantle of death, or a jinx, lurks about the Triangle.

Some theorists have attempted to find a connection between all the lost vessels or their passengers. Perhaps an analysis of the cargos or a vast computerized genealogical survey of all the victims would provide a clue.

Did the incidents occur at the same time of day, or during eclipses or solar flareups? Might there be a relationship between the disappearances and earthquakes? Could the cause be astrological—a certain arrangement of the planets?

No theory so far proposed has been able to account satisfactorily for all or even most of the incidents. It has been suggested that to solve the mystery once and for all the area should be closed for a time to allow the government to send in remote-controlled vessels with monitoring equipment that would detect unusual phenomena. It has also been suggested that clairvoyants be called in to give their impressions of forces at work.

Such measures are not necessary.

My research, which began as an attempt to find as much information as possible about the Bermuda Triangle, had an unexpected result. After examining all the evidence I have reached the following conclusion: *There is no theory that solves the mystery.* It is no more logical to try to find a common cause for all the disappearances in the Triangle than, for example, to try to find one cause for all automobile accidents in Arizona. By abandoning the search for an overall theory and investigating each incident independently, the mystery began to unravel.

The findings of my research were consistent.

1. Once sufficient information was found, logical explanations appeared for most of the incidents. It is difficult, for example, to consider the *Rubicon* a mystery when it is known that a hurricane struck the harbor where it had been moored. It is similarly difficult to be baffled by the loss of the *Marine Sulphur Queen* after learning of the ship's weakened structure and the weather conditions as described in the report of the Coast Guard investigation.

2. With only a few exceptions, the mishaps that remain unsolved are those for which no information can be found. In several cases important details of the incident, and in other cases, entire incidents, are fictional.

3. Disappearances occur in all parts of the ocean and even

over land. During my research I found nearly two hundred vessels that disappeared or were found abandoned between the New England states and northern Europe since 1850.

Although the disappearances that took place in the Bermuda Triangle are the ones that have been widely publicized, some losses that occurred elsewhere have been "credited" to the Triangle. The most notable of these are the *Freya*, which was found abandoned in the Pacific Ocean in 1902, and the Globemaster that crashed near Ireland in 1951. If all the locations of "Bermuda Triangle incidents" were plotted on a globe it would be found that they had taken place in an area that included the Caribbean Sea, the Gulf of Mexico, and most of the North Atlantic Ocean. The Bermuda Triangle is hardly unique.

4. Some of the lost vessels passed through the Bermuda Triangle but it is not known that they vanished there. The *Atalanta*, for example, may have sunk anywhere between Bermuda and England.

5. In many cases the place where a vessel met its end was almost completely unknown and searchers were required to spread themselves thinly over vast areas. The only information known about the *Star Ariel* is that it went down somewhere between Bermuda and Jamaica.

6. Many incidents were not considered mysterious when they occurred, but became so many years later when writers, seeking reports of additional incidents in the Bermuda Triangle, found references to them. It is often difficult to find complete information (even when one wants it) on an event that occurred many years before.

7. Contrary to the Legend, the weather was bad when many of the incidents occurred. In several cases highly publicized hurricanes were responsible.

8. Many of the mishaps occurred late in the afternoon or at night, making it impossible for searchers to attempt visual sightings until the next morning and thus giving the sea

many additional hours to disperse whatever debris there might have been.

9. Many of the writers who publicized the events did no original research but merely rephrased the articles of previous writers, thereby perpetuating the errors and embellishments in earlier accounts.

10. In a number of incidents writers withheld information that provided an obvious solution to the disappearance.

With the exception of point 9, the above statements also apply to the region known as the Limbo of the Lost. Moreover, the fact that the Limbo of the Lost encompasses an area at least half as large as the North Atlantic Ocean (see map, page 15) makes it difficult to sustain the point that it, like the Bermuda Triangle, is somehow unique.

The Legend of the Bermuda Triangle is a manufactured mystery. It began because of careless research and was elaborated upon and perpetuated by writers who either purposely or unknowingly made use of misconceptions, faulty reasoning, and sensationalism. It was repeated so many times that it began to take on the aura of truth.

I, like everyone else, like a good mystery, an enigma that stretches the mind. We all seem to have an innate desire to remain in awe of those phenomena for which there appears to be no logical, scientific explanation. Yet we also exult in seeking and in finding legitimate answers to these same puzzles.

Perhaps we are beginning to grow a bit weary of being constantly bombarded by spectacular unsolved mysteries. It is satisfying to know that we need not remain forever baffled by all phenomena that seem to be beyond explanation.

Bibliography

Section I is a chronological list of the sources of information that have been influential in creating the Legend of the Bermuda Triangle.

Section II includes the sources I have used or consulted and, in some cases, additional material that is easier to obtain. Although I may have used an account from a local newspaper in the book, I have attempted also to list references from the *New York Times*, since it is the newspaper that is most widely available.

Section I
Chronological Bibliography of the Main Sources of
the Legend of the Bermuda Triangle

Jones, E. V. W. Associated Press feature roundup of disappearances, released September 16, 1950. In various newspapers within the next few days, including: *Miami Herald,* September 17, p. 6F; *Tampa Tribune,* September 17, p. 8.

Sand, George X. "Sea Mystery at Our Back Door." *Fate,* October 1952, pp. 11–17.

Jessup, Morris K. *The Case for the UFO.* New York: Citadel, 1955, pp. 119–134, 162–167.

Keyhoe, Donald E. *The Flying Saucer Conspiracy.* Chapter 19, "The Vanishing Planes." London: Hutchinson, 1957.

Edwards, Frank. *Stranger Than Science.* Chapter 19, "Sky Traps." New York: Lyle Stuart, 1959. Paperback: Bantam, 1973.

Eckert, Allen W. "The Mystery of the Lost Patrol." *American Legion Magazine,* April 1962, p. 12.

"U.S. Special Project Linked to UFOs." *U.F.O. Investigator.* June-September 1963, pp. 1–2.

Gaddis, Vincent H. "The Deadly Bermuda Triangle." *Argosy,* February 1964, p. 29. Also in *Flying Saucer Review,* July/Aug. 1964.

Gaddis, Vincent H. *Invisible Horizons.* Chapter 13, "The Triangle of Death." Philadelphia: Chilton, 1965. Paperback: Ace, 1972. Based on his *Argosy* article.

Titler, Dale. *Wings of Mystery.* Chapter 14, "The Mystery of Flight 19." New York: Dodd, 1966. Paperback: Tower, 1971.

"Bermuda Triangle Adds to Baffling Sea Lore." *National Geographic News Bulletin,* 22 December 1967. Widely reprinted in newspapers.

Godwin, John. *This Baffling World.* Chapter titled "The Hoodoo Sea." New York: Hart, 1968. Paperback: Bantam, 1971.

*Sanderson, Ivan T. "The Spreading Mystery of the Bermuda Triangle." *Argosy,* August 1968, p. 36.

Lieber, Leslie. "Limbo of Lost Ships." *This Week,* 4 August 1968, p. 7.

Maggio, Joe. "Mystery Lurks in the Bermuda Triangle." *Miami Beach Sun,* 25 June 1969, p. 3.

Boyd, Ellsworth. "Where *Scorpion* Lies." *Our Navy,* July 1969, p. 2.

Spencer, John Wallace. *Limbo of the Lost.* Westfield, Mass.: Phillips, 1969. Paperback: Bantam, 1973.

*Sanderson, Ivan T. *More "Things."* Chapter 9, "Vile Vortices." New York: Pyramid, 1969.

*Sanderson, Ivan T. *Invisible Residents.* Chapter 8, "The Bermuda Triangle"; Chapter 10, "The Disposition of Anomalies." New York: World, 1970. Paperback: Avon, 1973.

Winer, Richard. "The Devil's Triangle." *Tropic* (*Miami Herald* Sunday magazine), 15 November 1970, p. 12.

Winer, Richard. *The Devil's Triangle* (film narrated by Vincent Price). 1970.

Burgess, Robert F. *Sinkings, Salvages and Shipwrecks.* Chapter 13, "The Mystery of the Deadly Bermuda Triangle." New York: American Heritage Press, 1970. Also in *Catholic Digest,* May 1971, pp. 44–49.

*"Time Anomalies." *Pursuit,* April 1971, pp. 48–49.

---

* Primarily concerned with the Vile Vortices.

Winer, Richard. "Bermuda Triangle-UFO Twilight Zone." *Saga,* August, September, 1972.

Smith, Marshall. "The Devil's Triangle." *Cosmopolitan,* September 1973, pp. 198–202.

Cusack, Michael. "The Deadly Mystery of the 'Devil's Triangle.'" *Science World,* 20 September 1973, pp. 3–6.

Chance, Paul. "Parapsychology Is an Idea Whose Time Has Come." *Psychology Today,* October 1973, pp. 105–120.

*Sanderson, Ivan T. "The 12 Devil's Graveyards Around the World." *Saga,* October 1973, p. 14.

Watson, William W. "Are U.S. Ships and Planes Being Caught in UFO Traps?" *Male,* October 1973, p. 36.

Charroux, Robert. *Forgotten Worlds.* Chapter 2, "The Mystery of the Thirty-Fifth Parallel"; Chapter 3, "The Bermuda Triangle." New York: Walker, 1973. Paperback: Popular Library, 1974.

Jeffrey, Adi-Kent Thomas. *The Bermuda Triangle.* New Hope, Pa.: New Hope Pub. Co., 1973.

Landsburg, Alan and Sally. *In Search of Ancient Mysteries.* Chapter 8, "Voyages into Limbo." New York: Bantam, 1974.

In Search of Ancient Mysteries (on NBC-TV, January 1974, narrated by Rod Serling). Included several minutes on the Bermuda Triangle.

"Bermuda Triangle." *Encyclopaedia Britannica,* 1974. Micropedia, I, p. 1007.

Winer, Richard. *The Devil's Triangle.* New York: Bantam, 1974.

Berlitz, Charles, with J. Manson Valentine. *The Bermuda Triangle.* Garden City, New York: Doubleday, 1974.

Spencer, John Wallace. *No Earthly Explanation.* Westfield, Mass.: Phillips, 1974.

U.S. Coast Guard. "The Bermuda Triangle," n.d. Standard handout on the subject.

Section II
Sources Used or Consulted,
Listed by Incident

1492: Christopher Columbus

Gould, Rupert T. *Enigmas.* New York: University Books, 1965, pp. 82–91.

---

* Primarily concerned with the Vile Vortices.

Irving, Washington. *History of the Life and Voyages of Christopher Columbus.* Philadelphia: Carey, Lea, and Blanchard, 1835, Vol. 2, pp. 85–101.

August 1840: *Rosalie*

Cras, Hervé (Musée de la Marine, Paris). Letter to Kusche, 3 October 1973.

Fort, Charles. *Lo!* New York: C. Kendall, 1931. Paperback: Ace, 1941, p. 94.

Lane, J. F. (Lloyd's). Letter to Kusche, 15 August 1973.

Lloyd's List, 25 September, 17 October 1840.

Times (London), 6 November 1840, p. 6, col. 3.

Vice Admiralty Court (Nassau). *Minutes.* 1837–1842. SC 4/8.

April 1854: *Bella*

Wilkins, Harold T. *Strange Mysteries of Time and Space.* New York: Citadel Press, 1959, pp. 12–14.

December 1872: *Mary Celeste*

Baldwin, Hanson W. *Sea Fights and Shipwrecks.* New York: Curtis, 1938, pp. 243–272.

Doyle, Arthur Conan. "J. Habakuk Jephson's Statement." *Cornhill Magazine,* January 1884, pp. 1–32.

Fay, Charles Edey. *Mary Celeste.* Salem: Peabody Museum, 1942.

Freuchen, Peter. *Peter Freuchen's Book of the Seven Seas.* New York: Julian Messner, 1957, pp. 49–51.

Gould, Rupert T. *The Stargazer Talks.* London: Geoffrey Bles, 1944, pp. 22–30.

Hocking, Charles. *Dictionary of Disasters at Sea During the Age of Steam.* London: Lloyd's Register of Shipping, 1969, p. 459.

New York Times, 25 March 1873, p. 1.

Times (London), 14 February 1873, p. 9.

Villiers, Alan. *Posted Missing.* New York: Scribner's, 1956, pp. 267–269. Rev. ed. 1974.

Villiers, Alan. *Wild Ocean.* New York: McGraw-Hill, 1957, pp. 249–264.

Winter 1880: *Atalanta*

Hocking, Charles. *Dictionary of Disasters at Sea During the Age of Steam.* London: Lloyd's Register of Shipping, 1969, p. 55.

Hoehling, Adolph A. *They Sailed Into Oblivion*. New York: Yoseloff, 1959, pp. 82–92.

New York Times, 26 May 1880, p. 4.

O'Donnell, Elliott. *Strange Sea Mysteries*. London: John Lane, 1926, pp. 30–39.

Snow, Edward Rowe. *Mysteries and Adventures Along the Atlantic Coast*. New York: Dodd, Mead, 1948, pp. 272–275.

Times (London): 13 April 1881, p. 6 col. 5; 14th 8–2; 15th 10–4; 16th 5–5; 17th 11–6; 19th 6–5; 20th 12–1; 21st 8–3; 22nd 12–4; 23rd 5–6; 26th 8–5; 27th 10–3; 28th 7–6; 29th 7–5; 1 May 12–3; 3rd 8–2; 4th 5–5; 10th 8–6; 12th 7–5; 18th 10–5; 21st 8–4; 27th 10–6; 29th 11–6; 9 June 11–6; 10th 5–6; 12th 12–1; 14th 8–4; 29th 9–5; 6 January 1881, 11–1.

1881: *Ellen Austin*

Gould, Rupert T. *The Stargazer Talks*. London: Geoffrey Bles, 1944, p. 30.

1866: *Lotta*. 1868: *Viego*. 1884: *Miramon*

No sources were found.

October 1902: *Freya*

Fort, Charles. *The Books of Charles Fort*. New York: Holt, 1941, p. 642; or his *Lo!* New York, C. Kendall, 1931. Paperback: Ace, 1941, p. 101.

Lloyd's Register. Wreck Returns. 1900–1904. Abandoned at sea, number 446.

"The Mexican Earthquake." *Nature*, 25 April 1907, p. 610.

November 1909: *Joshua Slocum*

Dictionary of American Biography. New York: Scribner's, 1928– Vol. 17, p. 217.

Freuchen, Peter. *Peter Freuchen's Book of the Seven Seas*. New York: Julian Messner, 1957, pp. 240–246.

Slocum, Joshua. *Sailing Alone Around the World*. New York: Century, 1900.

Slocum, Victor. *Captain Joshua Slocum*. New York: Sheridan House, 1950.

Snow, Edward Rowe. *Mysterious Tales of the New England Coast*. New York: Dodd, Mead, 1961, pp. 174–185.

Teller, Walter. *Joshua Slocum*. New Brunswick: Rutgers University Press, 1971.

March 1918: *Cyclops*

THE INCIDENT

"Blaming the Giant Octopus for the 'Cyclops' Mystery." *Literary Digest*, 8 March 1919, p. 92.

"Collier Cyclops Mystery Still Causes Speculation." U.S. Naval Institute. *Proceedings*, September 1923, pp. 1569–1570.

Dictionary of American Naval Fighting Ships. Washington, D.C.: U.S. Navy, 1963–   . Vol. II, p. 226.

"Disappearance of the Cyclops Another Mystery of the Deep." *Literary Digest*, 8 June 1918, p. 47.

Fact Sheet for U.S.S. Cyclops. One-page sheet sent by most government agencies in response to queries.

Hoehling, Adolph A. *They Sailed Into Oblivion*. New York: Yoseloff, 1959, pp. 209–219.

Livingston, Brockholst. "Old Navy Auxiliary Service." U.S. Naval Institute. *Proceedings*, January 1929, pp. 50–51.

Miller, J. Earle. "Mysteries of the Sea." *Popular Mechanics*, July 1926, pp. 7–10.

Momsen, R. P. "Concerning the U.S.S. Cyclops . . ." 27 April 1918.°

"The Mystery of the *Cyclops*." *Scientific American*, May 1934, pp. 272–273.

Nervig, Conrad A. "The *Cyclops* Mystery." U.S. Naval Institute. *Proceedings*, July 1969, pp. 148–151.

New York Times: 15 April 1918, p. 1; 16th p. 3; 17th p. 3; 18th pp. 4, 7; 19th p. 5; 1 May p. 3; 23rd p. 13; 4 June p. 2; 13 Jan. 1919, p. 10; 25 June p. 21; 12 July p. 9; 9 May 1923, p. 22; 4 Dec. 1925, p. 1; 18 Feb. 1926, p. 5; 1 Sept. p. 3; 3 July 1930, p. 1; 4th p. 4; 5th p. 6; 8th p. 5; 10th p. 24.

Tisdale, Mahlon S. "Did the *Cyclops* Turn Turtle?" U.S. Naval Institute. *Proceedings*, January 1920, pp. 55–59.

U.S. Navy. Bureau of Construction and Repair. "*Cyclops*-Stability." 7 June 1918.°

U.S. Navy. Office of Naval Intelligence. "U.S.S. *Cyclops* Six Theories . . ." 29 June 1918.°

Villiers, Alan. *Wild Ocean*. New York: McGraw-Hill, 1957, pp. 248–249.

° Obtained From the Modern Military Branch, Military Archives Division, National Archives and Records Service, Washington, D.C.

Virginian-Pilot: 15 April 1918, p. 1; 16th p. 8; 18th p. 1; 19th p. 18; 28th p. 8.

Yates, I. I. "Discussion." U.S. Naval Institute. *Proceedings,* April 1920, pp. 603–607.

THE WEATHER

New York Times: 10 March 1918, p. 21; 11th pp. 1, 17; 12th p. 8.

"Storm Warnings." *Monthly Weather Review,* March 1918, p. 42.

U.S. National Climatic Center. *Original Monthly Record of Observations. Hourly Wind Velocity, Norfolk, Virginia.* March 1918.

U.S. National Climatic Center. *Original Monthly Record of Observations. Prevailing Hourly Wind Direction, Norfolk, Virginia.* March 1918.

Virginian-Pilot, 10 March 1918, pp. 1–2.

RECENT DEVELOPMENTS

Hawes, Dean D. Letter to Kusche. 21 November 1973.

Hawes, Dean D. Telephone conversation with Kusche. 3 December 1973, 17 August 1974.

"The Old Explorer." *National Geographic School Bulletin.* 9 October 1973, p. 126.

Virginian-Pilot, 22 June 1973, n. p.

January 1921: *Carroll A. Deering*

New York Times: 21 June 1921, p. 1; 22nd pp. 1, 10, 14; 23rd pp. 1, 2, 16; 24th p. 2; 25th p. 2; 27th p. 12; 4 July p. 8; 8th p. 2; 9th p. 7; 11th p. 10; 26 August p. 2.

Snow, Edward Rowe. *Mysteries and Adventures Along the Atlantic Coast.* New York: Dodd, Mead, 1948, pp. 288–304.

Virginian-Pilot: 1 February 1921, p. 3; 2nd p. 3; 3rd p. 3; 4th p. 2; 5th p. 4; 6th p. 1.

April 1925: *Raifuku Maru*

Hocking, Charles. *Dictionary of Disasters at Sea During the Age of Steam.* London: Lloyd's Register of Shipping, 1969, p. 577.

December 1925: *Cotopaxi*

Lloyd's Register. Wreck Returns. 1925–1929. October to December 1925, Steamers and motorships missing, p. 6. Number 17411.

Lloyd's Weekly Casualty Reports. 11 December 1925, p. 355; 18th p. 396; 24th p. 432.

New York Times: 2 December 1925, p. 17; 4 December p. 1.

March 1926: *Suduffco*

Lloyd's Register. Wreck Returns. 1925–1929. April to June 1926, Steamers and motorships missing, p. 5. Number 83955.

New York Times: 19 March 1926, p. 23; 8 April p. 2; 11th p. 3; 28th p. 27; 14 May p. 17.

October 1931: *Stavenger*

Nassau Guardian: 14 October 1931, p. 4; 21st p. 4.

Thorstvedt, Else May (Norwegian Maritime Museum, Oslo). Letter to Kusche. 28 December 1973.

Vinje, H. (Office of the Directorate General of Shipping and Navigation, Oslo, Norway). Letter to Kusche. 8 January 1974.

April 1932: *John and Mary*

Merchant Vessels of the United States (Including Yachts), p. 380, 1932; p. 939, 1933. Washington, D.C.: Bureau of Customs.

New York Maritime Register: 9 March 1932, p. 15; 27 April, p. 9.

August 1935: *La Dahama*

New York Times: 28 August 1935, p. 1; 30th p. 19.

Times (London), 10 September 1935, p. 9.

February 1940: *Gloria Colita*

New York Times, 5 February 1940, p. 63.

Times-Picayune (New Orleans): 5 February 1940, p. 1; 6th p. 1; 7th p. 1; 8th p. 1; 11th p. 20.

November, December 1941: *Proteus, Nereus*

Dictionary of American Naval Fighting Ships. Washington, D.C.: U.S. Navy, 1963–   . Vol. V, pp. 45, 394.

Hocking, Charles. *Dictionary of Disasters at Sea During the Age of Steam.* London: Lloyd's Register of Shipping, 1969, pp. 499, 569.

October 1944: *Rubicon*

New York Times: 17 October 1944, p. 25; 18th p. 1; 19th p. 36; 20th p. 1; 21st p. 19; 23rd p. 21.

U.S. Geological Survey. *The National Atlas of the United States.* "Devastating North Atlantic Hurricanes, 1938–1965." Washington, D.C., 1970, p. 116.

December 1945: Flight 19

Board of Investigation into five missing TBM airplanes and one PBM airplane convened by Naval Air Advanced Training Command, NAS Jacksonville, Florida, 7 December 1945, and related correspondence. Washington, D.C.: U.S. Navy, 1946.
McDonell, Michael. "Lost Patrol." *Naval Aviation News,* June 1973, p. 8.
Miami Herald: 6 December 1945, p. 1; 7th p. 1; 8th p. 1; 9th p. 1; 10th p. 1.
New York Times: 6 December 1945, p. 11; 7th p. 1; 8th p. 10; 10th p. 11; 11th p. 14; 9 March 1946, p. 9.

December 1946: *City Belle*

Miami Herald, 6 December 1946, p. 1.
Nassau Guardian: 5 December 1945, p. 2; 6th p. 2; 7th p. 4.

1947: Superfortress

No sources were found.

January 1948: *Star Tiger*

Barker, Ralph. *Great Mysteries of the Air.* London: Chatto and Windus, 1966, pp. 80–93.
Great Britain. Ministry of Civil Aviation. *Report of the Court investigation of the accident to the Tudor IV. Aircraft "Star Tiger" G-AHNP, on the 30th January, 1948.* (Cmd. 7517). London: His Majesty's Stationery Office, 1948.
New York Times: 1 February p. 5; 2nd p. 37; 3rd p. 51; 5th p. 45.
Times (London): 31 January 1948, p. 4; 2 February p. 4; 4th p. 4; 29 September, p. 2.

March 1948: Al Snider

Miami Herald: 7 March 1948, p. 1; 8th p. B1; 9th p. 1; 10th p. 1; 11th p. 9; 12th p. 13; 13th p. 1; 14th p. 1; 15th p. 1; 16th p. 1; 19th p. 19; 20th p. 4.
New York Times: 7 March 1948, p. 21; 8th p. 37; 9th p. 20.

December 1948: DC-3

Civil Aeronautics Board. Accident Investigation Report. *Airborne Transport, Inc.—Miami, Florida, December 28, 1948.*

Miami Herald: 29 December 1948, p. 1; 30th p. 1; 31st p. 1; 1 January 1949, p. 2; 19 July p. 7.

New York Times: 29 December 1948, p. 1; 30th p. 28; 31st p. 13; 19 July 1949, p. 44.

January 1949: *Star Ariel*

Great Britain. Ministry of Civil Aviation. Civil Aircraft Accident. *Report on the Loss of Tudor IVb Star Ariel G-AGRE Which Disappeared on a Flight Between Bermuda and Kingston (Jamaica) on 17th January, 1949.* (M.C.A.P. 78) London: His Majesty's Stationery Office, 1949.

New York Times: 18 January 1949, p. 1; 19th p. 55; 21st p. 14; 23rd p. 29.

Stewart, Oliver. *Danger in the Air.* New York: Philosophical Library, 1958, pp. 121–130.

Times (London): 18 January 1949, p. 4; 19th p. 4; 24th p. 3; 21 December p. 4.

March 1950: Globemaster

New York Times: 24 March 1951, p. 1; 30th p. 3; 31st p. 3.

June 1950: *Sandra*

Lloyd's List: April 24, 29; May 2, 3, 6, 10, 11, 15, 16, 18, 20; June 3, 1950, n. p.

Lloyd's Register. Wreck Returns. Supplement. 1950. Steamers and motorships lost, p. 46.

Miami Herald, 8 April 1950, p. 1.

Savannah Morning News, 20 April 1950, p. 20.

February 1953: British York Transport

New York Times: 3 February p. 8; 4th p. 15.

October 1954: Navy Super Constellation

New York Times: 1 November 1954, p. 1; 2nd p. 9; 3rd p. 10; 4th p. 34.

December 1954: *Southern Districts*

Hocking, Charles. *Dictionary of Disasters at Sea During the Age of Steam.* London: Lloyd's Register of Shipping, 1969, p. 656.
Lloyd's Weekly Casualty Reports: 4 January 1955, p. 35; 11th pp. 68, 72.
New York Times: 14 December 1954, p. 26; 15th p. 63; 18th p. 31; 21st p. 53; 25th p. 21; 1 January 1955, p. 25; 3rd p. 39; 4th p. 91; 5th p. 43; 6th p. 26; 8th p. 29; 9th V p. 9; 11th p. 51; 20th p. 55; 23 August p. 48.
Villiers, Alan. *Posted Missing.* New York: Scribner's, 1956, pp. 286–295. Rev. ed. 1974.

September 1955: *Connemara IV*

Lloyd's Weekly Casualty Reports. October–December, 1955, Vol. 142, p. 5.
Miami Herald: 18 September 1955, p. 1; 19th p. 1; 27th pp. 1, 12; 1 October p. 1.
New York Times: 15 September 1955, p. 46; 16th p. 47; 18th p. 1; 19th p. 1; 20th p. 25; 22nd p. 23; 23rd p. 27; 24th p. 36; 25th IV p. 11; 1 October p. 38.
U.S. Geological Survey. *The National Atlas of the United States of America.* "Devastating North Atlantic Hurricanes, 1938–1965." Washington, D.C.. 1970, p. 116.

November 1956: Navy Patrol Bomber

New York Times: 11 November 1956, p. 80; 12th p. 36; 13th p. 27.
U.S. Navy. Naval Safety Center. *NAVSAFECEN ltr ser* 395, 4426. Norfolk, Virginia, 1971.

January 1958: *Revonoc*

Merchant Vessels of the United States (Including Yachts). 1959. Washington, D.C.: U.S. Bureau of Customs, p. 802.
New York Times: 7 January 1958, p. 24; 8th p. 6; 9th p. 66; 10th p. 14; 11th p. 36; 15th p. 14; 19th p. 73; 21st p. 58.
Snow, Edward Rowe. *Unsolved Mysteries of Sea and Shore.* New York: Dodd, Mead, 1963, pp. 219–223.

January 1962: KB-50

New York Times, 10 January 1962, p. 9.
Virginian-Pilot: 10 January 1962, p. 1; 11th p. 21; 12th p. 43.

April 1962: Piper Apache

Ingraham, D. A. F. (Director of Civil Aviation, Nassau International Airport, Bahamas). Letter to Kusche. 25 March 1974.

February 1963: *Marine Sulphur Queen*

Lloyd's Weekly Casualty Reports. 26 March 1963, Vol. 171, p. 576.
New York Times: 11 February 1963, p. 1; 12th p. 3; 3 April p. 93; 6th p. 46; 23 May p. 74; 28th p. 74; 4 February 1973, p. 52.
U.S. Coast Guard. Commandant. *Commandant's Action on Marine Board of Investigation; Disappearance of the SS Marine Sulphur Queen at sea on or about 4 February 1963 with the presumed loss of all persons on board.* March 1964.
U.S. Coast Guard. Marine Board of Investigation. SS *Marine Sulphur Queen; Disappearance at sea on or about 4 February 1963.* August 1963.

July 1963: *Sno' Boy*

Lloyd's Weekly Casualty Reports: 9 July 1963, p. 22; 16th p. 54.
Miami Herald: 5 July 1963, p. 1; 6th p. 1; 7th p. 1; 8th p. 14; 9th p. 10.

August 1963: Two KC-135s

Gerwig, Richard F. (Chief of the Reporting and Documents Division, Directorate of Aerospace Safety, Norton Air Force Base, California). Letter to Kusche. 6 July 1973.
Miami Herald: 29 August 1963, p. 1; 30th p. 1; 31st p. 2; 1 September p. 2.
A *Narrative Report on the Search for Two SAC KC-135 Aircraft,* 55th Air Rescue Squadron Historical Data Report, 1 August–31 August 63, Military Airlift Command.
New York Times: 30 August 1963, p. 16; 31st p. 63; 3 September p. 16.

June 1965: C-119 Flying Boxcar

Arizona Republic, 5 June 1965, p. 1; 6th p. 1.
McDivitt, James A. Letter to Kusche. 7 February 1974.
Miami Herald: 7 June 1965, p. 1; 8th p. 12; 9th p. 2; 10th p. 1; 11th p. 1.
New York Times, 7 June 1965, p. 44.
United Press International. *Gemini; America's walk in space.* Englewood Cliffs, N.J.: Prentice-Hall, 1965, Chapter 4.
Articles on Gemini IV may be found in any newspaper of the time.

January 1967: Black Week

Miami Herald: 12 January 1967, p. B1; 13th p. 15; 14th p. B2; 18th p. B2; 19th p. 1; 20th p. 28; 21st p. B2; 22nd p. B1; 24th p. B2.

December 1967: *Witchcraft*

Miami Herald: 22 December 1967, p. 2; 24th p. B1; 25th p. B2; 26th p. B1; 27th p. B2; 29th p. B2.

May 1968: *Scorpion*

Arizona Republic, 1 February 1969, p. 1.
New York Times: 28 May 1968, pp. 1, 3; 29th pp. 1, 12, 16; 30th p. 1; 31st pp. 1, 5; 1 June, pp. 13, 26; 2nd pp. 15, IV 12; 3rd p. 12; 4th p. 93; 5th p. 9; 6th p. 13; 7th p. 78; 8th p. 63; 9th p. 17; 11th p. 19; 12th p. 93; 13th p. 13; 18th p. 5; 21st p. 24; 22nd p. 20; 4 July, p. 22; 26th p. 30; 5 August, p. 37; 26 October, p. 7; 1 November, p. 1; 2nd p. 30; 5th p. 43; 16th p. 27; 22nd p. 24; 23rd p. 33; 3 January 1969, p. 5; 1 February, p. 1; 12 July, p. 52.
Articles on the *Scorpion* may be found in any newspaper of the time.

GREENLING

New York Times, 5 May 1973, p. 4.

July 1969: Five Abandoned Vessels

TEIGNMOUTH ELECTRON

New York Times: 12 July 1969, p. 2; 13th p. 11; 27th p. 21.
Times (London): 11 July 1969, p. 1; 12th p. 4; 14th p. 3; 16th p. 2; 18th p. 6; 28th pp. 1, 2; 29th p. 1; 6 August p. 2; 13th p. 2; 26th p. 4.
Tomalin, Nicholas, and Hall, Ron. *The Strange Last Voyage of Donald Crowhurst.* New York: Stein and Day, 1970.

THE OTHERS

New York Times, 13 July 1969, p. 11.
Times (London), 12 July 1969, p. 4.
Willis, Ronald J. "Lost: Ships and Crews." *The INFO Journal,* Fall 1969, pp. 4–6.

August 1969: Bill Verity

Fort Lauderdale News-Sentinel: 28 March 1973, n. p.; 29th n. p.
New York Times: 22 August 1969, p. 70; 15 September p. 3; 21st p. 44; 27 June 1971, p. 55; 5 August 1973, V p. 11.
Verity, Bill. Telephone conversation with Kusche. 20 November 1973.

November 1970: *Jillie Bean* and the Piper Comanche

Miami Herald: 26 November 1970, p. 22D; 28th p. B2.

April 1971: *Elizabeth*

Dinan, T. M. (Head of Casualty Records and Historical Research, Lloyd's). Letter to Kusche. 29 November 1973.
Rice, Commander F. A. (Chief, Casualty Review Branch, U.S. Coast Guard, Washington, D.C.). Letter to Kusche. 6 November 1973.
Troy, Lawrence H. (Manager-Record, American Bureau of Shipping). Letter to Kusche. 19 March 1974.

October 1971: *El Caribe*

El Caribe (Santo Domingo): October 15, 16, 20, 21, 22, 23, 25, 26, 1971, n. p.
Lloyd's List: October 16, 18, 19, 20, November 23, 1971.
Mella Villanueva, Federico A. (Administrator General, *El Caribe*). Letter to Kusche. 9 January 1974.
Miami Herald: 16 October 1971, p. 2.
San Juan Star: 16 October 1971, p. 1; 17th p. 22; 18th p. 16; 19th p. 3; 20th p. 6; 22nd p. 1; 23rd p. 14.
El Tiempo (Bogotá, Colombia), October 16, 21, 1971, n. p.

February 1972: *V. A. Fogg*

Galveston Daily News: 3 February 1972, p. 1; 4th p. 1; 5th p. 1; 6th p. 1; 7th p. 1; 8th p. 1; 9th p. 1; 10th p. 1; 11th p. 1; 13th p. 1; 14th p. 1; 15th p. 1; 16th p. 1; 17th p. 1; 18th p. 1; 19th p. 1; 20th p. 1.
Houston Post: 3 February 1972, p. 1; 4th p. 1; 5th p. 1; 6th p. 1; 7th p. 1; 8th p. 2; 9th p. 1; 10th p. 1; 11th p. 6; 12th p. 13; 13th p. 1; 14th p. 1; 15th p. 1; 16th p. 4; 17th p. 3; 18th p. 1; 19th p. 1; 20th p. 6B; 22nd p. 5; 29th p. 3.
Kirkpatrick, Joel (City Editor, *Galveston Daily News*). Letter to Kusche. 20 December 1973.
New York Times: 3 February 1972, p. 30; 6th p. 62; 7th p. 63; 14th p. 57; 15th p. 36.

Rice, Commander F. A. (Chief, Casualty Review Branch, U.S. Coast Guard, Washington, D.C.). Letter to Kusche. 4 March 1974.

Solano, A. (Chief of Identification, Sheriff's Department, County of Galveston). Letter to Kusche. 20 December 1973.

Whiting, Lt. Arthur (Casualty Review Board, U.S. Coast Guard, Washington, D.C.). Telephone conversation with Kusche. 16 January 1974.

March 1973: *Norse Variant* and *Anita*

New York Times: 23 March 1973, p. 1; 24th p. 66; 25th p. 47; 26th p. 1; 27th p. 32; 28th p. 1; 29th p. 93.

October 1973: *Linda*

Arizona Republic: 8 October 1973, p. 14; 25 November p. 21; 28th p. 3.

Miami Herald: 8 October 1973, p. 1; 9th p. 3B.

U.S. Coast Guard. Public Information Office. Miami, Florida.

Johnson, Lt. (jg) G. F. (Public Information Officer). Letter to Kusche. 24 October 1973.

Press release, 10 October 1973.

Johnson, Lt. (jg) G. F. Letter to Kusche. 13 November 1973.

The Devil's Sea

"Action Line." *Mainichi Daily News* (Tokyo). Letter to Kusche. 26 December 1973.

Asahi Shimbun (Tokyo), 15 January 1955, n. p.

Charvet, Michael (Editor General News, North America, Reuters). Letter to Kusche. 27 November 1973.

Hataya, H. (Director of Government, Bonin Islands). Letter to Kusche. 11 January 1974.

Kimura, Shigeru (Associate Editor, Science Department, *Asahi Shimbun*, Tokyo). Letters to Kusche. 30 October, 18 November, 1973.

Kinkaid, Karol (Consulate General of Japan, Los Angeles). Letter to Kusche. 11 December 1973.

Neal, Alfred H., Jr. (American Vice Consul, United States Embassy, Tokyo). Letter to Kusche. 31 October 1973.

New York Times: 27 September 1952, p. 35; 28th p. 30; 30th p. 2; 16 January 1955, V p. 8.

Ohno, Yasuchika (Foreign Liaison Officer, Maritime Safety Agency, Tokyo). Letter to Kusche. 10 January 1974.

Project Magnet. Washington, D.C.: U.S. Naval Oceanographic Office, n. d.

Prone, Leo J. (Safety Supervisor, Wake Island Air Force Base). Letter to Kusche. 19 December 1973.

Stierman, J. W. (Fleet Public Affairs Officer, United States Pacific Fleet, Makalapa, Hawaii). Letter to Kusche. 17 December 1973.

Smyser, A. A. (Editor, *Honolulu Star-Bulletin*). Letter to Kusche. 25 November 1973.

Taitano, Magdalena (Librarian, Nieves M. Flores Memorial Library, Agana, Guam). Letter to Kusche. 30 November 1973.

"White Paper." Maritime Safety Agency, 1973, pp. 58–59.

Yomiuri Shimbun (Tokyo), 14 January 1955, n. p.

Magnetism, Mystery, and the Bermuda Triangle

The deductions are based on my own knowledge and experience as an instrument flight instructor and from the FAA's *Instrument Flying Handbook*. Accuracy of the aeronautical statements has also been verified by Larry Young, Chief Pilot and Flight Instructor, Sawyer School of Aviation, Sky Harbor Airport, Phoenix. Accuracy of the geological statements was verified by Dr. William A. Sauck, Assistant Professor of Geology, Arizona State University.

Index